"Textbooks are forged in the often-fiery cauldron of the classroom. Simply put, the best teachers write the best textbooks. Kirk MacGregor is one of the best undergraduate teachers I've had the pleasure of knowing in my more than thirty years teaching undergraduate courses. He inspires his students to 'learn to learn,' an important learning objective when teaching courses in logic. His students apply what they've learned in a manner that enhances their life experience. Assign *Exploring Modern Logic: Theory and Applications* in your undergraduate classes; you won't be disappointed. Let the learning begin."

—**John K. Simmons**, Professor Emeritus of Religious Studies, Western Illinois University

"Kirk MacGregor's *Exploring Modern Logic* is a superb introduction and guide to understanding symbolic logic. It takes students who have no background in logic step by step to making manageable advances as they proceed through each chapter. This well-crafted book is clear, engaging, and enjoyable, and it reflects the author's mastery of the subject as well as his seasoned pedagogy in the classroom."

—**Paul Copan**, Professor of Philosophy and Ethics, Palm Beach Atlantic University

"Written by a prolific philosopher and scholar of religion with more than twenty years of acclaimed teaching experience, *Exploring Modern Logic: Theory and Applications* offers a compelling introduction to logic at a time when lucid, critical thinking is urgently needed. In a conversational, student-friendly style, it guides learners from symbolizing statements and mastering proofs to spotting fallacies and analyzing arguments in daily life. Perfect for pre-law students, the book equips instructors with all they need for general education courses—including syllabus design, course pacing, illustrative examples, pre-homework practice, assignments with solutions, as well as built-in reviews and exams. With clarity and humor, MacGregor makes logic both accessible and enjoyable!"

—**Bin Song**, Associate Professor of Philosophy and Religion, Washington College

"Dr. MacGregor is a prolific and gifted scholar and writer. In *Exploring Modern Logic: Theory and Applications*, he expands his repertoire to demonstrate he is also an extraordinary teacher. Dr. MacGregor is drawing on years of teaching experience to create a text that matches the needs of contemporary students. His writing style is accessible and conversational. The chapters are broken into short readings with practice and homework and move from the most difficult theoretical work to application. I find this particularly useful not only because it develops the foundational skills in logic early but also because it demonstrates an excellent understanding of student abilities. The most difficult elements are early in the semester when the students are most fresh and have the mental bandwidth to focus. They learn they can do hard things. Dr. MacGregor has also thought carefully about teaching this book as a sole logic class in a curriculum, providing students the logic skills they need while structuring the text to match a standard semester with space for quizzes and practice sessions. This is a thoughtfully written and constructed textbook that takes into consideration the dynamics of the modern classroom."

—**Verna Marina Ehret**, Professor of Religious Studies, Mercyhurst University

"Accomplished historian-philosopher and outstanding classroom instructor Kirk MacGregor has achieved what few deem possible: the creation of a college-level textbook in symbolic logic that is simultaneously clear, rigorous, and genuinely enjoyable to study. In *Exploring Modern Logic: Theory and Applications*, MacGregor expertly draws out students' natural reasoning intuition and cultivates it into a robust analytical skill set indispensable in law, philosophy, theology, and in virtually every sphere of life where careful reasoning matters. Across thirty-two artfully scaffolded chapters—complete with accessible problem sets, assignments, and fully worked solutions—the text guides readers from ordinary English sentences to their symbolic representations, through proofs and common fallacies, and concludes with an introduction to modal logic designed to inspire further study. *Exploring Modern Logic* is as intellectually stimulating to learn from as it is rewarding to use in classroom or seminar teaching."

—**Romwald Maczka**, Professor Emeritus of Religious Studies, Carthage College

Exploring Modern Logic

Exploring Modern Logic

Theory and Applications

Kirk R. MacGregor

PICKWICK *Publications* • Eugene, Oregon

EXPLORING MODERN LOGIC
Theory and Applications

Pickwick Publications
An Imprint of Wipf and Stock Publishers
199 W. 8th Ave., Suite 3
Eugene, OR 97401

www.wipfandstock.com

PAPERBACK ISBN: 979-8-3852-6345-5
HARDCOVER ISBN: 979-8-3852-6346-2
EBOOK ISBN: 979-8-3852-6347-9

Cataloguing-in-Publication data:

Names: MacGregor, Kirk R. [author].

Title: Exploring modern logic : theory and applications / by Kirk R. MacGregor.

Description: Eugene, OR: Pickwick Publications, 2026 | Includes bibliographical references and index.

Identifiers: ISBN 979-8-3852-6345-5 (paperback) | ISBN 979-8-3852-6346-2 (hardcover) | ISBN 979-8-3852-6347-9 (ebook)

Subjects: LCSH: Logic, Symbolic and mathematical. | Logic. | Logic—Textbooks. | Reasoning. | Logic—Philosophy. | Logic—Problems, exercises, etc. | Logic—Study and teaching.

Classification: BC108 M33 2026 (paperback) | BC108 (ebook)

VERSION NUMBER 03/17/26

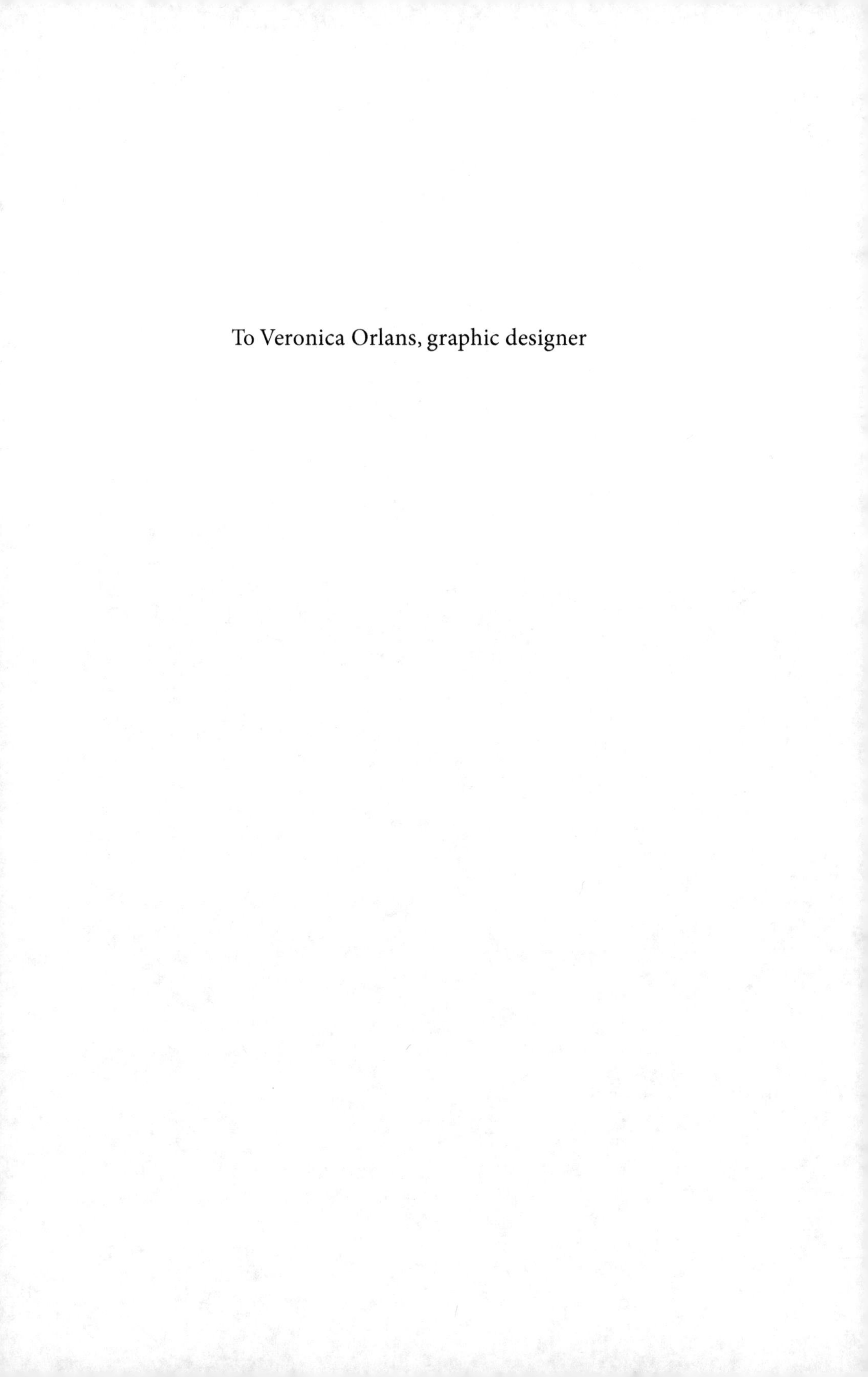

To Veronica Orlans, graphic designer

Contents

Acknowledgments

I WOULD LIKE TO thank the administration of McPherson College for firmly supporting my scholarship. Dr. Michael Schneider (president), Dr. Matthew G. Skillen (vice president for academic affairs and chief academic officer), Tricia Hartshorn (assistant academic dean and registrar), and Dr. Aaron Meis (executive vice president) deserve special gratitude for recognizing how my teaching and my research mutually enhance one another and celebrating both. My departmental colleague, Dr. Tom Hurst, is a wonderful friend and conversation partner. All of my institutional colleagues have made McPherson College an ideal place to be a teacher-scholar.

I am exceptionally grateful to Veronica Orlans, graphic designer, for designing all the graphics in this book. She took my less than aesthetically pleasing drawings and turned them into graphics that are simultaneously beautiful and precise. This book is rightfully dedicated to her.

Finally, I would like to thank two people whom I love with every fiber of my being: Rev. Lara MacGregor (my wife) and Dwiane MacGregor (my son). Lara and Dwiane frequently appear as characters in examples and homework problems throughout the book. Many of these—especially the more entertaining ones—spring out of my conversations with Lara or Dwiane.

Introduction

Exploring Modern Logic: Theory and Applications is an introductory undergraduate textbook in elementary modern logic—by which I mean symbolic logic—and the applications thereof that will prove most helpful to students in their other classes and throughout their lives. The skills learned in this book will be particularly useful for undergraduates preparing for law school, to whom I have taught modern logic throughout my career of over two decades in higher education. The book assumes no prior knowledge of logic in particular or philosophy in general. It is written in a very student-friendly way and therefore often takes a conversational tone. It is designed for use in a one-semester general education course in modern logic that meets the general education curriculum's critical thinking requirement. I recommend that such a course be taught in a MWF (as opposed to TR) format with three fifty-minute sessions per week. Such a course will contain approximately forty sessions during the semester. The thirty-two chapters should be covered in one session each, leaving eight sessions for quizzes, review sessions, and exams at the instructor's discretion. In my experience, four review sessions and four exams works best, with a review session and exam after chapters 8, 16, 24, and 32.

The pedagogical strategy of this book is to start with what students historically perceive as the hard skills (but which in reality are easy to grasp) and then, upon reaching the peak of perceived difficulty, descend into perceptibly easier material until the book's end. Not surprisingly, the material students initially regard as most intimidating is what "looks like math." As I tell my students, "No, it's philosophy, and in the history of thought, math borrowed it from philosophy." Unlike many logic textbooks which wait until the midpoint to begin teaching students how to symbolize English statements, this book teaches students how to symbolize English statements from the outset, starting in the first chapter. Student confidence grows in chapter 4, when students see that their knowledge of synonyms of logical connectors gained in chapters 2 and 3 enables them to symbolize even the most complicated and crazy-sounding English statements. My students have told me, "If I can symbolize these, I can symbolize anything!" By chapter 8 (one-quarter through the semester), students should be able to symbolize most indicative English sentences, whether a simple statement, a compound statement, or a quantified statement. With these symbolization skills under their belt, students then learn the laws of logic, simultaneously discovering how to analyze and annotate arguments. By chapter 16 (the midpoint of the semester), students will have all the skills in place necessary for learning how to write proofs.

Accordingly, chapter 17 teaches students how to write short direct proofs, and chapter 18 teaches students how to write longer direct proofs. Regarding indirect proof methods, conditional proof and *reductio ad absurdum* are respectively covered in chapters 19 and 20. To make sure students put all the pieces of the proof-writing puzzle together, chapter 21 reviews all methods of proof. When a proof can be written in multiple straightforward ways, I show students each of these ways. At this point the book's peak of perceived difficulty has been reached, which strategically corresponds with the point in the semester (the five-eighths mark) when student learning bandwidth begins to decline. Chapter 22 teaches students how to quickly check an argument's validity with a diagram. Perhaps the three chapters that students will find most immediately relevant to their daily lives are chapters 23 through 25 on formal and informal logical fallacies. My students have been amazed at how frequently they encounter these fallacies, especially on television and social media.

Chapters 26 through 32 focus on logical skills that pre-law students need most in rounding out their skill set. These skills include how to find the sufficient assumption of an invalid argument, find a necessary assumption of an invalid argument, strengthen an invalid argument, weaken an invalid argument, find the point of contention in a dispute, resolve a seemingly paradoxical situation, diagram an argument (and so determine the role each statement in an argument plays), draw the conclusion from various premises, and find a principle governing a situation that can be applied to any similar situation. I close out chapter 32—and the book—with just enough modal logic to apprise students of the most frequent modal logical fallacies.

Each of the book's chapters ends with a homework assignment of reasonable length which is short enough for students to finish. Each homework assignment is preceded by multiple worked examples and a pre-homework practice to maximize the likelihood that students will be able to successfully complete the homework. Solutions to all homework problems are found in the back of the book, which students will much appreciate. The book also contains a glossary of all key terms and an index that enables students to examine how topics unfold throughout the text.

I believe that great teaching requires a strong sense of humor. For this reason, many of the arguments in this book are crazy, complicated, and quite funny. These arguments frequently contain ludicrously false premises, which is by design. Often students are expected to analyze the validity or invalidity of an argument, which is based solely on the quality of the argument's structure irrespective of the truth of its premises. Ludicrously false premises make students laugh while reinforcing in their minds that an unsound argument may very well be valid. In this way, students learn to first evaluate the structure of an argument (whether it is valid) before evaluating the truth of the premises (whether the argument is sound).

To be good writers, students need to be good readers and good thinkers. In their academic pilgrimages and throughout their lives, students will often encounter passages on subjects with which they have no familiarity. This is especially true of pre-law students. As a professor of philosophy and religion, I often write passages in this book dealing with the academic study of religion, of which I know introductory students will have no cognizance. So much the better. It is far more important to understand the role that each of an author's statements plays in their overall argument, why and how an author is making their points, and whether the author's overall argument is valid than it is to know anything about the subject the author treats, which often has negligible if any importance. Good readers and good thinkers are marked by their ability to successfully evaluate arguments on any subject, whether or not they know anything about that subject.

Now a few final notes on my pedagogical decisions. In order to simplify concepts for introductory students, this book sacrifices some of the technical precision undergraduates will encounter in advanced logic textbooks. I typically use the conventionally accepted names of logical laws and valid argument forms, although sometimes I use my own names. When I make a controversial logical point, I acknowledge the controversy in a footnote, which includes references to a scholarly work defending each side of the controversy.

In sum, this book makes learning modern logic fun for introductory students in general education courses. It is my sincere hope that your students will enjoy learning this material as much as mine have and become better critical thinkers, readers, and writers in the process.

1

The Basics of Symbolizing English Statements (Part 1)

Welcome to *Exploring Modern Logic!* This textbook aims to teach you the essentials of modern logic—otherwise known as symbolic logic—as simply as possible. It also aims to teach you how to use modern logic to solve common problems found in a variety of disciplines as simply as possible. Good sense dictates that the best place to start in learning symbolic logic is learning how to symbolize English statements.

There are many skills in life that people shy away from learning because they are incorrectly told that these skills are too hard to acquire. Using modern logic is one of these skills. When many people see symbols, they immediately tend to freak out. However, there is nothing to freak out about. In reality, symbolizing English statements is extremely easy and so nothing to be intimidated by, as long as you consistently follow two rules. First, when the book tells you to memorize something, you need to memorize it immediately. Do not go on to the next page of the book until you memorize it. This book only asks you to memorize what absolutely needs to be memorized. Second, do each homework problem in every section, only checking the answer to each homework problem in the back of the book after you complete that problem. That way, you can learn from your mistakes before going on to the next problem. Accordingly, the solution to every homework problem is given in the back of the book.

Propositions

The first piece of vocabulary to learn is the term *proposition.* A proposition is the content of a declarative sentence. A declarative sentence is a sentence that makes a statement, as opposed to sentences that ask questions (known as interrogative sentences), issue commands (known as imperative sentences), or express emotions (known as exclamatory sentences). Notice that the declarative sentence itself is not the proposition; rather, the content or meaning of the declarative sentence is the proposition. For this reason, the same proposition can be expressed in a number of different declarative sentences. Consider the following two sentences: "The chair is yellow" and "Der Stuhl ist gelb." Here the same proposition is expressed in two different languages, as both the English sentence and the German sentence have the same content. To give another illustration, consider the following three sentences: "All cockroaches are evil," "Cockroaches are evil," and "Every cockroach is evil." Using three different stylistic variants, these sentences all mean the same thing and so express the same proposition. Here we see a preview of coming attractions: In logic, saying "cockroaches are evil" means that every single cockroach, without exception, is evil; it does not mean "some cockroaches are evil." We'll see more on this topic later!

We now come to two very important laws of logic, both of which you need to memorize. The *law of noncontradiction* maintains that a proposition cannot be both true and false at the same time and in the same sense. For example, suppose I express the proposition "I ate lunch at Burger King today" at 12:29 p.m. on December 9, 2024. At that moment, the proposition cannot be both true and false; in fact, at that moment it is true. Now, had I uttered the same proposition at 10:59 a.m. on that same day, the proposition would be false, since I hadn't eaten lunch at Burger King yet! But notice that this yields no violation of the law of noncontradiction, which allows for the same proposition to be true at one time (or in one sense) and false at another time (or in another sense). The proposition just cannot be true and false at the same time and in the same sense.

But could a proposition be neither true nor false at the same time and in the same sense? In other words, could it be something in between true and false? The answer is no, as this scenario is prevented by the *law of excluded middle.* The law of excluded middle maintains that, at any given time and sense, a proposition is either true or false; there is no middle ground between truth and falsity. Suppose that two Christians are now evaluating the claim, "The Bible is divinely inspired." The first Christian takes divine inspiration to mean that God overrode the free wills of the biblical authors to make them write exactly what God wanted them to write, as opposed to approving what the biblical authors freely wrote on their own. The second Christian takes divine inspiration to mean that God approved what the biblical authors freely wrote on their own, as opposed to overriding their free wills to compel them to write exactly what God wanted them to write. Now the claim "The Bible is divinely inspired" may be true in one of these senses and therefore false in the other sense, or it may be false in both. But for whatever sense of "divinely inspired" one means, the claim "The Bible is divinely inspired" is either true or false and exactly one of the two.

Simple and Compound Propositions

All propositions fall into one of two types: simple and compound. A *simple proposition* can be written as a sentence that does not include any of the logical connectors "and," "or," "not," "if . . . , then . . . ," "if and only if" (typically spelled by logicians as the one word "iff")," "therefore," or their synonyms. Here are two examples of simple propositions:

a. "Paul Tillich was a leading twentieth-century Christian theologian."
b. "My stuffed tabby cat is named Guido."

So how do we symbolize a simple proposition?

We symbolize a simple proposition with a capital letter standing for a (or the) main idea in the proposition. It is important to realize that there is no wrong letter you can use, as long as you consistently use the same letter for the same proposition and avoid using the same letter for different propositions. The point of the letter is that it needs to remind you of the proposition. Using the triple equals sign ≡ to mean "is logically equivalent to," we can now symbolize each example of a simple proposition.

a. T ≡ "Paul Tillich was a leading twentieth-century Christian theologian."
b. G ≡ "My stuffed tabby cat is named Guido."

Clearly T stands for Tillich and G stands for Guido; however, you could use whatever other letter you like for each proposition as long as you use different letters. Throughout this book I will often italicize a letter to show that I will use that letter to stand for a proposition.

A *compound proposition* must be written as a sentence that includes at least one of the following logical connectors: “and,” “or,” “not,” “if . . . , then . . . ,” “if and only if (iff),” or a synonym of any of these. These logical connectors link two or more simple propositions. Notice that I did not list the logical connector “therefore” and its synonyms. If the logical connector is “therefore” or one of its synonyms, we have an argument on our hands, not a compound proposition. We will learn more about arguments later. So how do we symbolize a compound proposition?

We symbolize a compound proposition by symbolizing each simple proposition and logical connector making it up. Since we already know how to symbolize simple propositions, we now need to memorize the following symbols that stand for logical connectors and their synonyms.

a. ∨ (called *vee*) means “or” and its synonyms.
   1. Note that “or” in modern logic is inclusive unless otherwise noted, meaning “at least one of.”
   2. The exclusive “or,” meaning “exactly one of,” is symbolized ⊻.
b. · (called *dot*) means “and” and its synonyms.[1]
c. ~ (called *tilde*) means “not” and its synonyms.[2]
d. → (called *arrow*) means “if (what’s left of the arrow), then (what’s right of the arrow).”
e. ↔ (called *bidirectional arrow*) means “(what’s left of the arrow) if and only if (what’s right of the arrow).”
f. ∴ (called *therefore*) means “therefore” and its synonyms.

Symbolizing Compound Propositions

Consider the following compound proposition: “Kirk or Lara will attend Dwiane’s fifth-grade recognition ceremony.” This is a compound

1. Alternate symbols that also mean “and” include & and ∧. This textbook will consistently use · for “and.”

2. An alternate symbol that also means “not” is ¬. This textbook will consistently use ~ for “not.”

proposition because it contains the logical connector "or." But what simple propositions does "or" link? You might be tempted to say "or" links "Kirk" with "Lara will attend Dwiane's fifth-grade recognition ceremony." However, the first part of that answer cannot be right, since we know that "or" links simple propositions, and "Kirk" is not a simple proposition (as it is not a sentence) but simply a name. Instead, we need to ask whether "Kirk or Lara will attend Dwiane's fifth-grade recognition ceremony" is a stylistic variant of a longer sentence that links two simple propositions. We immediately see that it is a stylistic variant of "Kirk will attend Dwiane's fifth-grade promotion ceremony or Lara will attend Dwiane's fifth-grade recognition ceremony." Here we clearly see that "or" links the simple proposition "Kirk will attend Dwiane's fifth-grade promotion ceremony" with the simple proposition "Lara will attend Dwiane's fifth-grade recognition ceremony." So at the outset we learn an important rule of thumb: *always think of stylistic variants of compound propositions in their longhand form to reveal the simple propositions they connect.* Now for each simple proposition in the longhand form, symbolize it with a capital letter standing for its main idea. So let K ≡ "Kirk will attend Dwiane's fifth-grade promotion ceremony." Let L ≡ "Lara will attend Dwiane's fifth-grade promotion ceremony." We already know that ∨ means "or." Hence our compound proposition is symbolized as K ∨ L.

Suppose we consider this compound proposition: "Kirk and Lara will attend Dwiane's fifth-grade recognition ceremony." We immediately see that it is a stylistic variant of "Kirk will attend Dwiane's fifth-grade recognition ceremony and Lara will attend Dwiane's fifth-grade recognition ceremony." Since · means "and," our compound proposition is symbolized as K · L.

Let us now attempt to symbolize a different proposition: "Hegel subscribed to the dialectic method if Hegel wrote *The Phenomenology of Spirit*." The word "if" lets us know that this is a compound proposition, even though you do not explicitly see the word "then." Here we learn another important rule of thumb: *Whenever "if" (or one of its synonyms) is used to modify one clause in a sentence lacking "then," the word "then" is implied and modifies the other clause in the sentence, even if the other clause comes first.* In that case, we simply have a stylistic variant of an "if . . . , then . . ." statement, known as a *conditional statement* (or *conditional*), on our hands. Before symbolizing any conditional statement, we must put it in its proper logical sequence, which is always "if" followed by the clause it modifies first and "then" followed by the clause it modifies second, regardless of the spoken order of the original sentence. The clause that follows "if" (but not the word "if") is called the *antecedent* (Latin, "that which comes before"), and the clause that follows "then" (but not the word "then") is called the *consequent* (Latin, "that which comes afterward"). Thus we see that "Hegel subscribed to the dialectic method if Hegel wrote *The Phenomenology of Spirit*" is a stylistic variant of the properly logically sequenced statement "If Hegel wrote *The Phenomenology of Spirit*, then Hegel subscribed to the dialectic method." We can now symbolize the antecedent and the consequent. Let P ≡ "Hegel wrote *The Phenomenology of Spirit*," and let D ≡ "Hegel subscribed to the dialectic method." We remember that → means "if (what's left of the arrow), then (what's right of the arrow)." So the proposition is symbolized P → D.

Now let's symbolize an iff (also spelled "if and only if") statement: "Heather is an atheist if and only if she thinks the problem of evil disproves God's existence." Let A ≡ "Heather is an *a*theist," and let E ≡ "Heather thinks the problem of *e*vil disproves God's existence." (As will be customary in this text, I italicized the *a* in atheist and the *e* in evil to indicate where my capital letters came from.) We remember that ↔ means "(what's left of the arrow) if and only if (what's right of the arrow)." Hence the proposition is symbolized A ↔ E.

Consider the proposition: "Kant did not regard the attacks on his transcendental idealism to be sound." The word "not" makes the proposition compound, such that it could be clunkily rewritten as "Not 'Kant regarded the attacks on his transcendental idealism to be sound.'" Since the proposition says what is not, it is called a negation. There are two options for symbolizing negations: treating them as compound (which they technically are) or treating them as simple. Choose the first option for now, keeping the other one in your back pocket. Using the first option, let R ≡ "Kant *r*egarded the attacks on his transcendental idealism to be sound." So the compound proposition is symbolized ~R. However, if we use the second option of treating the proposition as simple, we may symbolize it N (for "*n*ot regard") or whatever else you wish. In that case, however, we must make sure to remember that N is a negative proposition. If we take this path, then the positive proposition "Kant regarded the attacks on his transcendental idealism to be sound" would be symbolized ~N. That is because a positive proposition is the negation of a negative proposition.

This brings us to an important law of logic, which you must memorize along with its abbreviation: *double negation (DN)*. Simply put, two negatives make a positive. So ~N ≡ Not "Kant did not regard the attacks on his transcendental idealism to be sound" ≡ "Kant regarded the attacks on his transcendental idealism to be sound."

When Is It True?

You may wonder when "or" statements, "and" statements, "not" statements, "if . . . , then . . . ," statements, and "iff" statements are true and when they are false. To easily see the conditions under which each statement is true and false, we use truth tables. Truth tables list all combinations of the possible truth-values (either T for "true" or F for "false") every simple proposition making up a compound proposition can take and then state the overall truth-value of the compound proposition on each combination.

Let's illustrate how a truth table works by considering the "or" statement A ∨ B. The truth table for A ∨ B looks like this:

A	B	A ∨ B
T	T	T
T	F	T
F	T	T
F	F	F

In the first column, we see the possible truth values of A. In the second column, we see the possible truth values of B. In the third column, we see the resulting truth values of A ∨ B on the combination of truth values of A and B in each respective row. In the first row, we see that when A is true and B is true, then A ∨ B is true. In the second row, we see that when A is true and B is false, then A ∨ B is true. This makes sense since "or" means "at least one of," and one simple proposition (A) making up A ∨ B is true. In the third row, we see that when A is false and B is true, then A ∨ B is true, since one of the two simple propositions making it up (B) is true. In the fourth row, we see that when A is false and B is false, then—and only then—A ∨ B is false. For not even one of the simple propositions making it up is true.

Now that we understand how truth tables work, consider the truth table for A · B.

A	B	A · B
T	T	T
T	F	F
F	T	F
F	F	F

Here we see that for A · B to be true, both of the simple propositions making it up must be true. If either or both of the simple propositions making up A · B is false, then the compound proposition A · B is false. To illustrate, if I said, "2 + 2 = 4 and 3 + 3 = 6," then I have uttered a true statement, since both of the simple propositions making it up are true. But if I said, "2 + 2 = 4 and 3 + 3 = 5," then I have uttered a false statement, since the second simple proposition making it up is false. Likewise, if I said, "2 + 2 = 3 and 3 + 3 = 6," I have uttered a false statement, since the first simple proposition making it up is false. And if I said, "2 + 2 = 3 and 3 + 3 = 5," then I have uttered a false statement, as both simple propositions making it up is false.

Let us examine the truth table for ~A.

A	~A
T	F
F	T

This truth table is very easy to understand. ~A always has the opposite truth value of A. For example, if I uttered a true statement like "2 + 2 = 4," then its negation, here "2 + 2 ≠ 4," must be false. And if I uttered a false statement like "2 + 2 = 3," then its negation, here "2 + 2 ≠ 3," must be true.

Of all the truth tables we will consider in this chapter, the one for A → B is the most confusing. The truth table for A → B looks like this:

A	B	A → B
T	T	T
T	F	F
F	T	T
F	F	T

Fortunately, the first two rows are straightforward. Suppose that I buy a cell phone and use it to call my brother. Then the statement, "If I buy a cell phone, then I call my brother," is clearly true. Moreover, the statement "If I buy a cell phone, then I don't call my brother," is clearly false. The third and fourth rows are where the confusion comes in. We know that I, in fact, buy the cell phone. What then do we make of the statement "If I don't buy a cell phone, then I call my brother"? Is it true or false? We can't settle the issue by appealing to whether I call my brother, since we have no idea whether I call my brother under a set of circumstances that does not obtain. What does it even mean to say that I call my brother under unreal circumstances?[3] To settle this issue, we by default define "If I don't buy a cell phone, then I call my brother"—and any other if-then statement with a false antecedent—as a true statement, regardless of whether its consequent is true (row three) or false (row four). But the statement's truth doesn't convey to us any real information. Accordingly, an if-then statement with a false antecedent is *vacuously true*, since its truth is simply a matter of definition and communicates no actual content. Amazingly, both "If I don't buy a cell phone, then I call my brother" and "If I don't buy a cell phone, then I don't call my brother" are vacuously true! How this situation manages to escape being prevented by the law of noncontradiction will be seen in chapter five.

The truth table concerning "iff" statements makes far more sense. So let us examine the truth table for $A \leftrightarrow B$.

A	B	$A \leftrightarrow B$
T	T	T
T	F	F
F	T	F
F	F	T

Imagine looking at a triangle that is equilateral (all three sides have the same length) and equiangular (all three angles are 60°). Per the first row, the statement "The triangle is equilateral iff the triangle is equiangular" is true. Per the last row, the statement "The triangle is not equilateral

3. Notice that this is a different question than whether I *would* call my brother under unreal circumstances if the circumstances *were* real. That is a question of counterfactual logic, and it is indeed meaningful. But counterfactual logic goes well beyond the scope of this book!

iff the triangle is not equiangular" is true. So we find that when the simple statements making up an "iff" statement have the same truth value (whether true or false), the "iff" statement is true. However, when the simple statements making up an "iff" statement have different truth values, the "iff" statement is false. Thus in the second row, the statement "The triangle is equilateral iff the triangle is not equiangular" is false. And per the third row, the statement "The triangle is not equilateral iff the triangle is equiangular" is false.

Pre-Homework Practice!

Let's try to symbolize some compound propositions together to make sure you have the symbols for your logical connectors memorized. Remember that it doesn't matter whether you use a different capital letter than I do for each simple proposition; what matters is that the simple propositions making up each compound proposition are symbolized accurately, in logical order, and with the proper connector. Try to symbolize each example before looking at the solution below it.

1. If I go to the store, then I buy "Toffee Philosophy" ice cream.
   a. Here I let S ≡ "I go to the *s*tore" and let I ≡ "I buy 'Toffee Philosophy' *i*ce cream," where the italicized letters show what my capital letters mean. You can use different letters. Linking the two together with →, the solution is S → I. (All the steps before the solution you can, and ultimately should, do in your head.)
2. Chip and Dale are in their cages.
   a. I first recognize that this is a stylistic variant of the longhand "Chip is in his cage and Dale is in his cage." Then I let C ≡ "*C*hip is in his cage" and let D ≡ "*D*ale is in his cage." Linking the two together with ·, the solution is C · D.
3. Chip or Dale is in his cage.
   a. Again, this is a stylistic variant of the longhand "Chip is in his cage or Dale is in his cage." Keeping the same letters as before and linking the two together with ∨, the solution is C ∨ D.
4. I'll vacuum your room if you pick up the dirty clothes on the floor.
   a. This is a stylistic variant of the properly logically sequenced "If you pick up the dirty clothes on the floor, then I'll vacuum your

room." I let P ≡ "If you *p*ick up the dirty clothes on the floor" and let V ≡ "I'll *v*acuum your room." Linking the two together with →, the solution is P → V.

5. Kirk plays trumpet or Kyle plays French horn.[4]
    a. I let T ≡ "Kirk plays *t*rumpet" and let H ≡ "Kyle plays French *h*orn." Linking the two together with ∨, the solution is T ∨ H.
6. Kirk plays trumpet and Kyle plays French horn.
    a. Keeping the same letters as before and linking the two together with ·, the solution is T · H.

Homework Assignment 1

Symbolize the following statements:

1. Laozi or an anonymous community composed the *Daodejing*.
2. I know something if and only if I have justified true belief in that thing.
3. Luther and Calvin opposed the Roman Catholic Church.
4. I'll buy eight two-liters of caffeine-free Diet Coke if they're on sale for $1 each.
5. I am not eating at Olive Garden tomorrow.

4. A good friend of mine, Kyle Hopkins, is associate professor of music and director of bands at McPherson College and principal horn in the Salina Symphony.

2

The Basics of Symbolizing English Statements (Part 2)

CONGRATULATIONS ON LEARNING THE symbols for all the logical connectors! The next skill to master is knowing all synonyms of the logical connectors so that you can successfully translate any synonym into the connector it stands for. At the outset of this chapter, let me emphasize the supreme importance of memorizing all synonyms of logical connectors right away. Refusing to memorize them is simply not a viable option. Throughout my academic career, I have seen more philosophy students fall apart early in logic courses by neglecting to memorize the synonyms of logical connectors than for any other reason. By contrast, those students who heed my advice, refusing to read further than this chapter until they have memorized all synonyms of logical connectors, almost invariably perform extremely well in logic courses, as they are setting themselves on the path to success.

Synonyms of Logical Connectors

There are many synonyms of the logical connector "and." They include "but," "also," "yet," "despite that," "notwithstanding the fact that," "although," "even though," "while," and any other word that carries the same meaning as something else in the list. Now at this point you might hesitate because "but" and many other synonyms in the list have a different rhetorical force than "and," signifying a contrast. *However, in logic, rhetorical force makes no difference.* This is because in logic, the only thing that makes a difference is something that affects the truth-value of the proposition. Indeed, a compound proposition containing "and" will have exactly the same truth-value if it is replaced by anything in the synonym list. Given this fact, it makes perfect sense that "I went to the closest grocery store and I didn't buy hair spray," which is true of my last visit to the store, is logically equivalent to "I went to the closest grocery store but I didn't buy hair spray," "I went to the closest grocery store even though I didn't buy hair spray," and so forth. For each of these statements is true of my last visit to the store.

Let's consider the simple proposition D ≡ "Larry is a *d*espicable human being" and the simple proposition V ≡ "I'm going to *v*ote for Larry." How would we symbolize the compound proposition "Despite that Larry is a despicable human being, I'm going to vote for him"? We begin by recognizing that "despite that" is a synonym of, and therefore logically means, "and." We then see that trading "despite that" for "and" yields this proposition that is out of proper sequence: "And Larry is a despicable human being, I'm going to vote for him." Hence we put the proposition in proper sequence: "I'm going to vote for Larry and Larry is a despicable human being." This has the same truth-value as the original proposition and is consequently logically equivalent to it. Accordingly, the proposition is symbolized V · D. By the same reasoning, V · D also symbolizes "I'm going to vote for Larry even though he is a despicable human being," for "even though" means "and." Here we observe the importance of memorizing the synonyms of logical connectors: When you see things like "despite that" and "even though," you won't get thrown, and you'll immediately think "This just means 'and.'"

"Either . . . or" means the same thing as "or," namely, "at least one of." "Either 2 + 2 = 4 or 3 + 3 = 6" is therefore a true statement, since "or" is inclusive. We could symbolize it F ∨ S, with F reminding us of 4 and S reminding us of 6. By contrast, the exclusive or, ⊻, is indicated by "or . . . and not both."

There are many synonyms of the logical connector "if." These include "whenever," "given," "given that," "on," "on the condition that," "assuming," "provided," "provided that," and any other word that carries the same meaning as something else in the list. The clause following these synonyms is the antecedent (the if-clause). If the antecedent doesn't come out to be a complete sentence when you replace something on the list with "if," turn the antecedent into a sentence in a contextually appropriate way. Now the other clause in the sentence, wherever it occurs, is the consequent (the then-clause). Remember to put a "then" before the consequent. So let's consider this example: "Given theism, we have an explanation of the origin of the universe." Replacing "given" with "if" and putting a "then" before the other clause, we have "If theism, then we have an explanation of the origin of the universe." But the antecedent, "theism," isn't a complete sentence. In the context of the larger sentence, however, it means "theism is true" (adding the words "is true"). So "Given theism, we have an explanation of the origin of the universe" ≡ "If theism is true, then we have an explanation of the origin of the universe." At this juncture, the symbolization becomes easy. Letting T ≡ "*T*heism is true" and letting O ≡ "We have an explanation of the *o*rigin of the universe," the symbolization turns out to be T → O.

Iff (if and only if) has the following synonyms: "if but only if," "when and only when," "just in case," "precisely when," "exactly when," and any other phrase that carries the same meaning as something else in the list. To illustrate, "What Dwiane learned in *m*ath class is true just in case the *P*eano axioms of arithmetic hold" ≡ M ↔ P.

Very Confusing Synonyms of Logical Connectors

Here is an extremely confusing fact that you must commit to memory: *"Only if" does not mean "if"! Rather, "only if" means "then," where the clause following "only if" is the consequent and the other clause is the antecedent.* Just like the synonyms for "if" imply that the other clause is the then-clause (the consequent) and force you to add the word "then," so the synonyms for "then" (like "only if") imply that the other clause is the if-clause (the antecedent) and force you to add the word "if." Moreover, the word "only" by itself—namely, without the definite article "the"—is another synonym for "then." Treat "only" just like "only if." So suppose I say to my son Dwiane, "I'll get you a chocolate shake at McDonald's only if you bring in the garbage can." How would we symbolize this statement? Replacing "only if" with "then" and adding "if" before the first clause, we find that my statement means "If I get you a chocolate shake at McDonald's, then you bring in the garbage can." Letting C ≡ "I get you a *c*hocolate shake at McDonald's" and letting G ≡ "You bring in the *g*arbage can," the symbolization turns out to be C → G.

We now come to the two most confusing synonyms of logical connectors: "the only . . . is . . ." and "the only . . . is if . . . ," both of which mean the same thing. Regarding "the only . . . is . . . ," consider the sentence "The only worldview that plausibly grounds objective moral values is theism." The rule to memorize is this: *"The" applies to the first clause of the sentence, and "only" applies to the second clause of the sentence. "The" never logically goes with "only"; you need to keep "the" where it is and move "only" to the other clause.* So rephrase the sentence in your head: "The worldview that plausibly grounds objective moral values is only theism." Now remembering that "only" means "then," we see that this is a disguised if-then statement, such that the first clause is the if-clause (requiring you to add the word "if"). Rephrasing this sentence again in a contextually appropriate way, we find that it means "If a worldview plausibly grounds objective moral values, then that worldview is theism." We can symbolize this compound proposition O → T, where O ≡ "a worldview plausibly grounds *o*bjective moral values" and T ≡ "that worldview is *t*heism." So in short, *"the only . . . is . . ."* ≡ *"the . . . is only . . ."* ≡ *"if . . . , then . . ."* Regarding "the only . . . is if . . . ," consider the sentence "The only way I'll get you a chocolate shake at McDonald's is if you bring in the garbage can." Since "the" never goes with "only," we move "only" to the second clause of the sentence, giving us an "only if": "The way I'll get you a chocolate shake at McDonald's is only if you bring in the garbage can." "The only . . . is if . . ." is particularly tricky because it looks like the "if" is alone, simply meaning "if." But that is an illusion, since "only" goes with "if," and "only if" means "then"! Hence we see that *"the only . . . is if . . ."* ≡ *"the . . . is only if"* ≡ *"if . . . , then . . ."* So in your head, you can rephrase the sentence in a contextually appropriate way to yield "If I get you a *c*hocolate shake at McDonald's, then you bring in the *g*arbage can," symbolized C → G.

More Synonyms of Logical Connectors

The words "unless," "without," and "save for" each mean "if not" as well as "or." We will focus on the "if not" meaning for now. After translating the word "if," make sure to apply the "not" to the ensuing clause to get the antecedent (the if-clause). The other clause is the consequent (the then-clause). It is not negated. You will insert the word "then" before the consequent. You may need to reorder the antecedent and consequent to put them in their proper logical sequence (if . . . , then . . .). For example, "I'll stay home tonight unless I have a Hutchinson Municipal Band performance" ≡ "If I don't have a Hutchinson Municipal Band *p*erformance, then I'll *s*tay home tonight" ≡ ~P → S. Notice that the tilde (~) only applies to the P.

Two tricky double negatives to remember are "not . . . unless . . . " and "not . . . without . . ." These negatives cancel each other out and simply mean "if . . . , then . . . ," where "if" modifies the clause that originally had "not" and "then" modifies the clause that originally had "unless" or "without." Be sure to remove the "not" and "unless" or "without," so getting rid of the double negative. Therefore "I'm not playing cornhole without a pleasant temperature outside" ≡ "If I play *c*ornhole, then there is a pleasant *t*emperature outside" ≡ C → T.

Pre-Homework Practice!

Before moving on to your homework, let's try to symbolize some compound propositions together that contain synonyms of logical connectors. Here you can check how well you have the symbols for your logical connectors and the synonyms of those logical connectors memorized. Try to symbolize each example before looking at the solution below it. Of course, you can use different capital letters to symbolize each simple proposition than I do; but the letters you use should be in the same order as the letters I use to represent each simple proposition.

1. On the condition that I can play a double high G, I'll win first chair in the trumpet section.
    a. "On the condition that" is a synonym of "if" and thus modifies the antecedent, which means the second clause is the consequent (preceded by the word "then"). So the statement can be rewritten "If I can play a double high *G*, then I'll win *f*irst chair in the trumpet section" ≡ G → F.
2. Although my favorite golfer will probably never win again, I'll watch him play in the US Open.
    a. "Although" is a synonym of "and." Reordering the sentence and replacing "him" with "my favorite golfer," the statement can be rewritten "I'll *w*atch my favorite golfer play in the US Open and my favorite golfer will probably *n*ever win again" ≡ W · N.
3. Molina was not a Protestant theologian.
    a. This sentence could be clunkily rewritten "Not 'Molina was a *P*rotestant theologian'" ≡ ~P.

4. I'll raise your grade only if you get an A on the final exam.
    a. "Only if" means "then," such that we put "if" in front of the first clause. Accordingly, the statement can be rewritten "If I *r*aise your grade, then you get an *A* on the final exam" ≡ R → A.
5. Humanity is lost in the abyss of meaninglessness without having the experience of enlightenment.
    a. "Without" means "if not," such that we put "then" in front of the first clause. Reordering and contextually rewriting the sentence, we get "If humanity does not have the *e*xperience of enlightenment, then humanity is *l*ost in the abyss of meaninglessness" ≡ ~E → L. Be sure to remember the ~ ("not") before E.
6. I'm not petting the wolf spider unless you pet it first.
    a. "Not . . . unless . . ." is a double negative that means "if . . . , then . . ." Hence the statement can be rewritten "If I *p*et the wolf spider, then *y*ou pet it first" ≡ P → Y.
7. I'll sign my name on the dotted line just in case you pay me $500.
    a. "Just in case" means "iff." So we can rewrite the statement "I'll *s*ign my name on the dotted line iff you *p*ay me $500" ≡ S ↔ P.

Assuming you've memorized the synonyms of the logical connectors, you are now ready to proceed to your second homework assignment. Remember to check the answer to each homework problem in the back of the book before moving on to the next problem; this is the best way to learn from your mistakes.

Homework Assignment 2

Symbolize the following statements:

1. The only color of sneakers I will wear is yellow.
2. Although Agi was dumber than a freaking brick, Agi was entertaining.
3. Hubmaier proposed a free state church ecclesiology, assuming my research is sound.
4. I'll practice my trumpet tonight even though I'm extremely tired.

5. God could not have middle knowledge without relying on God's intuition.
6. Unless a person can reason logically, they cannot think critically.
7. Beethoven was the greatest classical musician of all time only if Mozart died before he turned forty years old.
8. Either Anselm was a realist or Aquinas was a conceptualist.

3

Necessary Conditions and Sufficient Conditions

Knowing what necessary conditions and sufficient conditions are and understanding the difference between them are two of the most practical lessons you will take away from this book. The terms "necessary" and "sufficient" are often used in the law and therefore show up in legal contexts with which we all deal, such as contracts, wills, deeds, agreements, affidavits, and other legal documents. To put it another way, before you sign a contract (like a mortgage), you need to understand the terms "necessary" and "sufficient"! For people often get confused between these terms. If a professor says to you, "Taking the final exam is a necessary condition (or is necessary) for passing this class" and you take the final exam, that doesn't mean you're going to pass the class! If you just show up for the exam without any preparation and think all is well, you may be sadly mistaken. By contrast, if that same professor says to you, "Earning a 95 percent course average is a sufficient condition (or is sufficient) for getting an A in the class," that doesn't mean you won't get an A with a 90 percent. So how do we correctly understand the terms "necessary" and "sufficient"?

Necessary Conditions

A *necessary condition* is a prerequisite for something to happen. It states what must be true for something to happen. But it does not, by itself, guarantee that the thing will happen. Synonyms of "is necessary for" that you need to memorize include "is required for," "must be true," "is implied by," "is ensured by," "is entailed by," "is guaranteed by" (which is not the same thing as "guarantees"), "is triggered by," and phrases that mean the same thing as the preceding. For example, being a student at McPherson College (the institution where I teach) is necessary for taking my Modern Logic class. A prerequisite for the class is that you're a McPherson College student; in other words, you must be a student at McPherson College to take my Modern Logic class. But being a McPherson College student doesn't guarantee that you'll take my Modern Logic class! It's not required of all McPherson College students, and most of them don't take it. However, if you're not a McPherson College student, then you can't take my Modern Logic class. Therefore "Being a McPherson College student is necessary for taking my Modern Logic class" ≡ "If you're not a McPherson College student, then you can't take my Modern Logic class." This leads to an important logical principle: *for any propositions* A *and* B, A *is necessary for* B ≡ *"if not* A, *then not* B*"* ≡ ~A → ~B.

However, we can say even more. Suppose you can take my Modern Logic class. Then what do we know about you? That you're a McPherson College student! You couldn't take the class without being one. So "Being a McPherson College student is necessary for taking my Modern Logic class" ≡ "If you can take my Modern Logic class, then you're a McPherson College student." So it is also true that A *is necessary for* B ≡ *"if* B, *then* A*"* ≡ B → A. Here we observe that the consequent, or then-clause, of any if-then statement is a necessary condition for its antecedent, or if-clause. Writing it all out in a chain, we find that A *is necessary for* B ≡ *"if not* A, *then not* B*"* ≡ ~A → ~B ≡ *"if* B, *then* A*"* ≡ B → A.

This leads to a very important law of logic, called *contraposition* (abbreviated *Cont*). The law of contraposition (Cont) holds that *for any propositions* X *and* Y, X → Y ≡ ~Y → ~X. ~Y → ~X is called the *contrapositive* of X → Y. The contrapositive of any if-then (conditional) statement is logically equivalent to the original statement; it's saying the same thing in other words by expressing it in an opposite, or contrary, light. Only if-then (conditional) statements have contrapositives. Whenever you see a conditional statement, you should always—at least mentally—form its contrapositive. Here is an easy-to-remember rule for forming a contrapositive: simultaneously flip and negate. This means to flip the antecedent (if-clause) and the consequent (then-clause)—but not the words "if" and "then," which stay exactly where they originally were—while negating both clauses. Hence the new if-clause is the negated consequent of the original conditional, and the new then-clause is the negated antecedent of the original conditional. We see this rule played out in the earlier example, where the contrapositive of "If you're not a McPherson College student, then you can't take my Modern Logic class" is "If you can take my Modern Logic class, then you're a McPherson College student" and vice versa. Notice that when negating both clauses of the original conditional, you run into double negatives, which are just positives.

Sufficient Conditions

A *sufficient condition* is enough for something to happen. It guarantees that something happens. So if the sufficient condition occurs, the something in question must be true. Synonyms of "is sufficient for" that you need to memorize include "requires," "is enough for," "implies," "ensures," "entails," "guarantees," "triggers," "depends on," and terms that mean the same thing as the preceding. To illustrate, having the deed to your house in your file cabinet is sufficient for your owning the house. Having the deed to your house in your file cabinet is enough for you to own the house; it guarantees that you own the house. But owning the house does not guarantee that you have the deed in your file cabinet. Maybe you have the deed in your desk drawer or in a safety deposit box at the bank. However, if you have the deed to your house in your file cabinet, then you own the house. This leads to an important logical principle: *for any propositions* A *and* B, A *is sufficient for* B ≡ A → B. Here we observe that the antecedent of any if-then statement is a sufficient condition for its consequent. Remember that any A → B can equivalently be written ~B → ~A (Cont), where Cont indicates the contrapositive.

Suppose we have the proposition A ↔ B. As the bidirectional arrow indicates, A ↔ B means both (1) A → B and (2) B → A. (1) shows that A is sufficient for B. (2), because its contrapositive (its logical equivalent) is ~A → ~B, shows that A is necessary for B. For these reasons, "is necessary and sufficient for" is a synonym of "iff." Hence "Getting at least a 59.5 percent is necessary and sufficient for *p*assing this class" ≡ G ↔ P.

Can It Be Interchanged?

When we see a logical connector, a good question to ask is whether we can switch the simple propositions on either side of the connector without changing the meaning of the overall statement. The answer is: for some connectors, yes; for other connectors, no. Let's focus first on the connectors which allow switches without affecting the meaning.

The simple propositions making up an "and" statement—known as *conjuncts*—can be interchanged. Put them in whatever order you prefer. Accordingly, "I'm reading and I'm writing" ≡ "I'm writing and I'm reading." This means that *for any propositions* A *and* B, A · B ≡ B · A. We can add as many propositions as we wish to a chain formed only by ·, and they can be arranged however we like. So for any propositions A, B, and C, (A · B · C) ≡ (A · C · B) ≡ (B · C · A) ≡ (B · A · C) ≡ (C · A · B) ≡ (C · B · A). Notice how, when dealing with a statement made up of three or more simple propositions, I use parentheses to help us from getting confused!

Likewise, the simple propositions making up an "or" statement—known as *disjuncts*—can be interchanged. Put them in whatever order you prefer. Accordingly, "I'm reading or I'm writing" ≡ "I'm writing or I'm reading." This means that *for any propositions* A *and* B, A ∨ B ≡ B ∨ A. We can add as many propositions as we wish to a chain formed only by ∨, and they can be arranged however we like. So for any propositions A, B, and C, (A ∨ B ∨ C) ≡ (A ∨ C ∨ B) ≡ (B ∨ C ∨ A) ≡ (B ∨ A ∨ C) ≡ (C ∨ A ∨ B) ≡ (C ∨ B ∨ A). What we have seen about "and" and "or" statements leads us to the logical *law of commutation*, abbreviated *Com*. This law says that conjuncts can be interchanged with each other and that disjuncts can be interchanged with each other.

You should also note that simple propositions on either side of a bidirectional arrow can be interchanged. Since the arrow goes both ways, it doesn't matter on which side we put each simple proposition. So *for any propositions* A *and* B, A ↔ B ≡ B ↔ A. We can add as many propositions as we wish to a chain formed only by ↔, and they can be arranged however we like. So for any propositions A, B, and C, (A ↔ B ↔ C) ≡ (A ↔ C ↔ B) ≡ (B ↔ C ↔ A) ≡ (B ↔ A ↔ C) ≡ (C ↔ A ↔ B) ≡ (C ↔ B ↔ A).

Now let's focus on a connector which does not allow switches, as switching the simple propositions on either side totally changes the meaning of the statement. The connector which prohibits switches is the if-then connector, →. The simple propositions making up an if-then statement—the antecedent and the consequent—*cannot* be interchanged! For example, "If Chip squeaks, then Dale squeaks" is not the same as saying "If Dale squeaks, then Chip squeaks." The second statement is known as the *converse* of the first statement. Confusing a statement for its converse is appropriately called the *converse error*. Thus *for any propositions* A *and* B, A → B ≢ B → A, where ≢ means "is not logically equivalent to." Why? Remember that A → B entails that A is sufficient for B and that B is necessary for A. But B → A is not the same, for it entails that B is sufficient for A and that A is necessary for B. In short, the converse error is an error because it confuses a necessary condition for a sufficient condition.

Pre-Homework Practice!

Let's do two examples together to see if you have your synonyms of "necessary" and "sufficient" memorized. Try to symbolize each example before looking at the solution below it.

1. My buying a yellow Lamborghini depends on my winning the lottery.
   a. "Depends on" is synonymous with "is sufficient for." So this example can be rewritten "My buying a yellow Lamborghini is sufficient for my winning the lottery" ≡ "If I *b*uy a yellow Lamborghini, then I *w*on the lottery" ≡ B → W.
2. A valid driver's license is required for you to vote.
   a. "Is required for" means "is necessary for." So this example can be rewritten "A valid driver's license is necessary for you to vote" ≡ "If you don't have a valid driver's *l*icense, then you can't *v*ote" ≡ ~L → ~V.

Now we'll do two examples to check if you remember the statements whose simple propositions can and cannot be interchanged. The question for each pair of statements is: Are these statements equivalent?

3. Joelle and Courtney and Kellie went to the movies; Kellie and Joelle and Courtney went to the movies.
   a. *Yes*. "And" is interchangeable.
4. If Aimee went to the movies, then Mandi went to the movies; if Mandi went to the movies, then Aimee went to the movies.
   a. *No*. "If . . . , then . . ." is not interchangeable.

Homework Assignment 3

Symbolize the following statements:

1. My earning all-state honors in trumpet is necessary for my invitation to perform in the United States Collegiate Wind Band.
2. Tillich's being an outspoken religious socialist was sufficient for Hitler to want him dead.
3. Two things are symmetric to each other precisely when they geometrically mirror one another.
4. The article's passing double-blind peer review requires its publication in the journal.
5. Your wearing clothes must be true for you to eat in that restaurant.

Are these statements logically equivalent? Why or why not?

6. If I go to McDonald's, then I'll drink myself into oblivion; if I drink myself into oblivion, then I'll go to McDonald's.
7. Snowy or Lady or Paddy Paws was the name of my first cat; Lady or Paddy Paws or Snowy was the name of my first cat.

4

Combining and Complexifying

COMPOUND PROPOSITIONS CAN BE made up of an unlimited number of simple propositions and different logical connectors. In this chapter we will combine different logical connectors in our compound propositions and then increase the complexity of our compound propositions. The good news is that you will not see in this book (or probably anywhere else) any more complicated propositions than those you will encounter here. This means once you learn to symbolize the propositions in this chapter, be very encouraged, because you will have the ability to symbolize any future proposition you encounter. So let's get started combining different logical connectors!

Mixing Things Up with ∨, ·, ~

Suppose we encounter the compound proposition "The jazz band will either play *Watermelon Man* or something other than a Miles Davis chart." We first notice that "something other than a Miles Davis chart" is another way of saying of "not a Miles Davis chart." Since "either . . . or" is synonymous with "or," we can rewrite our compound proposition "The jazz band will play *Watermelon Man* or not a Miles Davis chart." Expanding this to see both simple propositions making up our compound proposition more clearly, we arrive at "The jazz band will play W*atermelon Man* or the jazz band will not play a Miles *D*avis chart," symbolized W ∨ ~D. Now take the compound proposition "Stella doesn't *l*ove you or she doesn't *h*ate you." Since both sides of the "or" are negated, this is symbolized ~L

$\vee \sim D$. Here a word of warning is in order: $\sim L \vee \sim D \not\equiv \sim(L \vee D)$. We will see why in the next chapter.

Consider the compound proposition "Notwithstanding the fact that Sam didn't get his paper selected for presentation, he will still attend the conference." We recognize "notwithstanding the fact that" as a synonym of "and." So our compound proposition can be rewritten "Sam will still *a*ttend the conference and Sam didn't get his *p*aper selected for presentation" $\equiv A \cdot \sim P$. Since $\cdot$ ("and") is interchangeable, $A \cdot \sim P \equiv \sim P \cdot A$. As long as you put $\cdot$ between them, you can join A and $\sim P$ either way you like. However, notice an important fact: $\sim P \cdot A$ is not the same thing as $\sim(P \cdot A)$. $\sim$ ("not") only applies to the entity immediately beside it, which is here P.

Imagine I said, "I don't like *g*uns and I don't like *b*ombs." This can be symbolized $\sim G \cdot \sim B$. Here we notice two key points. First, $\sim G \cdot \sim B \not\equiv \sim(G \cdot B)$, as the next chapter will make clear. Second, "not . . . and not . . ." $\equiv$ "neither . . . nor . . ." Despite that "nor" and "or" rhyme, "neither . . . nor . . ." *does not mean* "not . . . or . . . ," and "neither . . . nor . . ." *does not mean* "not . . . or not . . ." Rhyming doesn't have anything to do with logical relationships! (For instance, "glad" and "clad" rhyme but obviously have nothing logically to do with each other.) Rather, "neither . . . nor . . ." means "not . . . and not . . ." So "I don't like guns and I don't like bombs" could equally well read "I like neither guns nor bombs," as the latter is a stylistic variant of the former.

Adding $\rightarrow$ into the Mix!

Let's begin with a neat trick that can help us later! The logical law called *material implication (MI)* affirms that *for any* A *and* B, $A \rightarrow B \equiv \sim A \vee B$. So "If I take alcohol with my medication, I'll end up in the hospital" is the same as saying "Either I don't take alcohol with my medication or I'll end up in the hospital." To practice this trick, let's symbolize and then apply MI to the following statement: "I'll eat cannoli unless I go to Red Lobster." Since "unless" means "if not" and the other clause is the consequent preceded by "then," the statement can be rewritten "If I don't go to *R*ed Lobster, then I'll eat *c*annoli" $\equiv \sim R \rightarrow C$. Now we apply MI, getting a double negative on the left-hand side: $\sim\sim R \vee C$, which by DN is just $R \vee C$. Translating back into English, this means "I'll go to Red Lobster or I'll eat cannoli." Since "or" is interchangeable, it also means "I'll eat cannoli or I'll go to Red Lobster." In sum, we find that "I'll eat cannoli unless I go to Red Lobster" means the same thing as "I'll eat cannoli or I'll go to Red Lobster." Comparing the two sentences, now we see why "unless" can be translated either as "if not" or "or."

Increasing the Complexity

We are now in a position to put everything together we've learned so far in the book and to increase the complexity of our compound propositions. Consider the statement "Whenever I listen to *Brass Roots*, my sadness goes away." Here we know two things. First, "whenever" means "if," making the second clause the consequent preceded by "then." Second, "my sadness goes away" is another way of saying "I am not sad." Hence our statement can be rewritten "If I listen to B*rass Roots*, then I am not *s*ad" ≡ B → ~S. Let's now consider another example: "If I don't teach *E*thics today, I won't get to use any of my *c*razy thought experiments." This statement is straightforward and can be symbolized ~E → ~C. However, I raise it to illustrate an important point: ~E → ~C is not the same as ~(E → C). The next chapter will clarify why.

Now consider the statement "Either I'll drink Diet Sam's Cola or something other than Diet Dr Pepper, assuming Walmart has what I want in stock." We first notice that "assuming" is a synonym of "if," meaning that the first clause is the consequent to be preceded by the word "then." Accordingly, the statement can be rewritten "If Walmart has what I want in stock, then either I'll drink Diet Sam's Cola or something other than Diet Dr Pepper." Here we see an important fact: Clauses of if-then statements—antecedents and consequents—can themselves be compound propositions. When they are, any "if" or "then" applies to the entirety of the compound proposition it modifies. In this example, the consequent contains two simple propositions ("I'll drink Diet Sam's Cola"; "I'll drink something other than Diet Dr Pepper") joined with "or." To show this, we must use careful placement of parentheses. Since "either . . . or" just means "or" and "I'll drink something other than Diet Dr Pepper" just means "I won't drink Diet Dr Pepper," we can rephrase the statement as "If *W*almart has what I want in stock, then I'll drink Diet *S*am's Cola or I won't drink Diet *D*r Pepper" ≡ W → (S ∨ ~D). Note how important the parentheses are! Without them, we wouldn't know that the entirety of S ∨ ~D is the then-clause. If we incorrectly symbolized our statement as W → S ∨ ~D, this could be understood as either (W → S) ∨ ~D or W → (S ∨ ~D), which are two radically different propositions meaning very different things.

Just as clauses of if-then statements can themselves be compound propositions, so can clauses of any other statements (e.g., "and" statements, "or" statements, "iff" statements, "not" statements). Before we get to other statements, let's consider the conditional "If I have a Schilke 14A4A and a *B*ach 3C, then I'll *m*ake it through the concert or I'll *p*ass out from playing too high." Both our antecedent and our consequent are compound, which we will need to indicate through parentheses. Hence the statement is symbolized (S · B) → (M ∨ P). As our next example will illustrate, the clauses of if-then statements can themselves be if-then statements. Consider the statement "Provided that God does not exist only if nominalism is true, abstract expressionism is not the best art style given the skill of many impressionist painters." This is clearly the most difficult example we've encountered thus far. As I said at the beginning of the chapter, if you can symbolize something like this, you can symbolize anything! So let's break down this very complicated statement piece by piece. First, "provided that" is a synonym of "if," meaning that "God does not exist only if nominalism is true" is the antecedent and that "abstract expressionism is not the best art style given the skill of many impressionist painters" is the consequent. So our first rewrite of the statement is as follows: "If 'God does not exist only if nominalism is true,' then 'abstract expressionism is not the best art style given the skill of many impressionist painters.'" Now let's look at the antecedent. Since "only if" means "then" and that the first part is the if-clause, the left-hand side of our statement can be rewritten "If 'if God does not exist, then nominalism is true.'" Looking at the consequent, "given" means "if" and that the first part is the then-clause. So the right-hand side of the statement can be rewritten "then 'if many impressionist painters have skill, then abstract expressionism is not the best art style.'" Putting this all together, we have our final rewrite of the statement: "If 'if *G*od does not exist, then *n*ominalism is true,' then 'if many *i*mpressionist painters have skill, then abstract *e*xpressionism is not the best art style.'" Making sure to note the single-quotations with parentheses to show that we have a nested if-then statement (i.e., an if-then statement made up of one or more if-then statements), our symbolization is (~G → N) → (I → ~E).

Turning now to an "or" statement (known as a *disjunction*), consider "Either Darwin didn't originate the idea of biological evolution if Anaximander did or zeppoli taste spicy." The first alternative, or disjunct, is "if

Anaximander originated the idea of biological evolution, then Darwin didn't originate the idea of biological evolution," and the second alternative is "zeppoli taste spicy." In other words, the statement affirms that at least one of these alternatives is true. Since "either . . . or" means "or," we can rewrite the statement "'If *A*naximander originated the idea of biological evolution, then *D*arwin didn't originate the idea of biological evolution' or zeppoli taste spicy," where the single quotes surrounding the first disjunct prevent us from getting confused. Replacing the single quotes with parentheses in our symbolization, we get (A → ~D) ∨ Z. Now consider this more complex "or" statement: "I'm not driving my car without a full gas tank, or I'll chance it given that I like to take risks." Regarding the first disjunct, hopefully you remember that "not . . . without . . ." is a double negative meaning "if . . . , then . . ." So the first disjunct is "If I'm driving my car, then I have a full gas tank." Regarding the second disjunct, "given that" means "if" and that the first part is the then-clause. So the second disjunct is "If I like to take risks, then I'll chance it." Accordingly, our "or" statement is telling us that at least one of these conditional statements is true. Putting all of this together, our overall "or" statement is "'If I'm *d*riving my car, then I have a full *g*as tank' or 'If I like to take *r*isks, then I'll *c*hance it'" ≡ (D → G) ∨ (R → C).

A self-explanatory synonym that we haven't yet seen is "both . . . and," which simply means "and." This synonym is often used when we need to keep each of our conjuncts clear. To illustrate, take the statement "It's the case both that bluejays are mean and that chickadees are the smallest birds if hummingbirds aren't." Our conjuncts are "bluejays are mean" and "chickadees are the smallest birds if hummingbirds aren't," each of which our "and" statement informs us is true. Putting the second conjunct in its logical order, our statement can be rewritten "*B*luejays are mean and 'if *h*ummingbirds aren't the smallest birds, then *c*hickadees are the smallest birds'" ≡ B · (~H → C). Let's now consider a statement that teaches us a very important lesson: "The word *K*ansas comes from a Native American term meaning 'wind people' or both 2 + 2 = *8* and 3 + 3 = 5." This is symbolized K ∨ (E · F), as the "both . . . and" indicates that the entirety of "2 + 2 = 8 and 3 + 3 = 5" is the disjunct of the larger "or" statement. Our lesson is that ∨ and · *cannot* be associated, namely regrouped, with each other. Let's reflect on why. An "or" statement is true if at least one of its disjuncts is true. Since the second disjunct (2 + 2 = 8 and 3 + 3 = 5) is clearly false, the truth of the statement depends on the truth of "The word Kansas comes from a Native American term meaning 'wind people.'" Since that disjunct is true, the overall "or" statement is true. But suppose we had wrongly symbolized the statement (K ∨ E) · F. This would indicate the very different statement "Either the word Kansas comes from a Native American term meaning 'wind people' or 2 + 2 = 8, and 3 + 3 = 5." Now an "and" statement (known as a *conjunction*) is true iff all its conjuncts are true; even one false conjunct renders the statement false. Since 3 + 3 ≠ 5, the "and" statement is false. This again illustrates the importance of careful placement of parentheses.

Keeping this point in mind, let's try "The Godfather is an awesome mob movie, even though I'm not hungry or I'm not thirsty." Recalling that "even though" means "and," we thus have the statement "The Godfather is an awesome mob movie, and 'I'm not *h*ungry or I'm not *t*hirsty'" ≡ G · (~H ∨ ~T). Now take the disjunction "Either clarinets sound cool provided they're woodwinds or Olympic figure skating is difficult." We recognize that of the two disjuncts (parts of the "or" statement), the first is a compound proposition, indicated by the term "provided" ≡ "if." So we can rewrite the disjunction "'If clarinets are *w*oodwinds, then they sound *c*ool' or *O*lympic figure skating is difficult" ≡ (W → C) ∨ O. Finally, consider the statement "Ric Flair is the greatest pro wrestler of all time, assuming that Nixon was impeached if he didn't resign." What kind of statement is it? The words "assuming that" mean "if," indicating that we have a conditional statement on our hands. The second half is the antecedent, and the first half is the consequent. So we now have as our first rewrite "If 'Nixon was impeached if he didn't resign,' then Ric Flair is the greatest pro wrestler of all time." This is another nested if-then, with a conditional making up the antecedent. Properly ordering the antecedent, we have as our final rewrite "If 'if Nixon didn't *r*esign, then Nixon was *i*mpeached,' then Ric *F*lair is the greatest pro wrestler of all time" ≡ (~R → I) → F.

Pre-Homework Practice!

Hopefully you've found in this chapter that you have the ability to symbolize anything if you have your synonyms of logical connectors memorized and you're careful with parentheses. With these skills mastered, there's no need to be intimidated by the complexity of any statement. Notice how symbolizing complex statements "cuts them down to size" and makes them easy to work with by exposing their logical structure.

For the following examples, try to symbolize each before looking at the solution below it.

1. I'm not going to San Diego without my blue hair dryer, despite that tuna fish sandwiches are better than hamburgers.
   a. "Despite that" means "and," making our overall statement a conjunction. The first conjunct is a conditional, where "not . . . without . . ." is a double negative meaning "if . . . , then . . ." Hence the statement can be rewritten "'If I go to *S*an Diego, then I have my *b*lue hair dryer' and *t*una fish sandwiches are better than hamburgers" ≡ (S → B) · T.
2. Either the Cardinals aren't my favorite baseball team or God exists on secular humanism.
   a. The "either . . . or" reveals our overall statement to be a disjunction. The second disjunct is a conditional, as "on" means "if." Hence "God exists on secular humanism" means "if secular humanism is true, then God exists." So the disjunction can be rephrased "The *C*ardinals aren't my favorite baseball team or 'if *s*ecular humanism is true, then *G*od exists'" ≡ ~C ∨ (S → G).
3. Amida Buddha offers entrance into the Pure Land, or Jōdo Buddhism is false and Hōnen didn't know what he was talking about.
   a. Here we simply have to remember that "or" and "and" cannot be associated. The overall statement is a disjunction, with the first disjunct a simple proposition and the second disjunct a compound proposition (namely, a conjunction), which we will note with parentheses. With this in mind, "*A*mida Buddha offers entrance into the Pure Land, or *J*ōdo Buddhism is false and *H*ōnen didn't know what he was talking about" ≡ A ∨ (~J · ~H).
4. It's true both that thundersnow is the most spectacular weather phenomenon and that not Euclid or not Anaximander was the second earliest pre-Socratic philosopher.
   a. The "both . . . and" shows our overall statement to be a conjunction, where the second conjunct is again compound (this time, a disjunction). Fully expanding the disjunction, we can rewrite the statement "*t*hundersnow is the most spectacular weather phenomenon and '*E*uclid was not the second earliest

pre-Socratic philosopher or *A*naximander was not the second earliest pre-Socratic philosopher" ≡ T · (~E ∨ ~A).

5. If multiplicity is false given the Line Paradox, then panentheism is true whenever Bob Dole was president.
    a. Here we have a nested if-then, whose antecedent and consequent are themselves conditionals. Turning to the antecedent, "given" means "if," such that "multiplicity is false given the Line Paradox" means "if the Line Paradox is true, then multiplicity is false." Turning to the consequent, "whenever" means "if," such that "panentheism is true whenever Bob Dole was president" means "if Bob Dole was president, then panentheism is true." Hence our statement can be rewritten "If 'if the *L*ine Paradox is true, then *m*ultiplicity is false,' then 'if Bob *D*ole was president, then *p*anentheism is true'" ≡ (L → ~M) → (D → P).

Homework Assignment 4

Symbolize the following statements:

1. Something's being true ensures its being a fact, assuming Wittgenstein was wrong.
2. Bernard of Clairvaux and Molina correctly analyzed counterfactuals only if the grounding objection fails.
3. Given that open theism entails God's not having exhaustive foreknowledge, my car is white only if it's not green.
4. If Calvinism is true and Arminianism is false, libertarian human freedom does not exist.
5. Either the church has a presbyterian style of government or Wynton Marsalis and someone other than Dizzy Gillespie professionally recorded *Autumn Leaves.*

5

Negating

THE ABILITY TO NEGATE conjunctions (and-statements), disjunctions (or-statements), and conditionals (if-then statements) is vitally important to logical thinking. Often people go wrong by incorrectly negating one or more of these types of statements. The first thing to know about negations is that they are the *contradictories* of the statements being negated. The contradictory of any statement has the opposite truth-value of the original statement under any circumstances. If there are circumstances in which both the original statement and its alleged negation can simultaneously be true or can simultaneously be false, then you've got the wrong negation. For example, suppose I told you that I have three white chairs and one blue chair in my office. You might think the negation of this proposition is that I don't have three white chairs and I don't have one blue chair in my office. But this would be mistaken. The truth is that I have two white chairs and one blue chair in my office. So the original proposition is false, and the alleged negation is false (since it says I don't have one blue chair in my office). But a negation must always have the opposite truth-value of the original statement. If the original statement is true, the negation must be false; and if the original statement is false, the negation must be true. So how do we correctly negate the three statement types mentioned above?

Negating · and ∨ Statements

We will first learn how to negate conjunctions and disjunctions. But first, a word of warning: this is not how to negate conditionals! Negating conditionals is quite different from negating conjunctions and disjunctions. Negating conjunctions and disjunctions is governed by *DeMorgan's Laws (DeM)*, distributive laws which state that you must distribute the "not" (~) across all of your terms. The trick is that · and ∨ are themselves terms! The negation of "and" is "or," and the negation of "or" is "and." Expressed symbolically, ~· ≡ ∨ and ~∨ ≡ ·. Applying DeM, we see that the correct negation of "I have three white chairs and one blue chair in my office" is "I don't have three white chairs in my office *or* I don't have one blue chair in my office." These two statements are in fact contradictories—notice how the first statement is false and the second statement is true (since I don't have three white chairs in my office). Consequently, DeMorgan's Laws can be stated as follows. *First,* ~(A · B) ≡ ~A ∨ ~B. *Second,* ~(A ∨ B) ≡ ~A · ~B.

So let's practice symbolizing statements to determine their meaning. Suppose I said, "It is not the case that I'm eating at *B*urger King and I'm buying a new pair of *j*eans." Letting B ≡ "I'm eating at Burger King" and J ≡ "I'm buying a new pair of jeans," the symbolization of this statement is ~(B · J). But what does this statement mean? Let's figure it out by distributing the ~ across all three of the terms (not two, since · is a term): ~B ∨ ~J. Now we translate the symbolization back into English: "I'm not eating at Burger King or I'm not buying a new pair of jeans." As long as I'm not doing even one of those two things, the statement is true. This is what "It is not the case that I'm eating at Burger King and I'm buying a new pair of jeans" means.

Imagine a theologian said, "It's false that *p*enal substitution or the *R*ansom to Satan theory adequately explains the atonement." This may be symbolized ~(P ∨ R). Now we distribute the ~ across all three of the terms to figure out the meaning (DeM): ~P · ~R. Finally, we clarify the meaning of the theologian's statement by translating back into English: "Penal substitution doesn't adequately explain the atonement and the Ransom to Satan theory doesn't adequately explain the atonement." Accordingly, we observe that a three-step procedure is used to figure out what negated conjunctions and disjunctions mean. First, we symbolize. Second, we apply the relevant DeMorgan's Law. Third, we translate back into English.

Using this procedure, we can determine the meaning of even the most confusing disjunctions and conjunctions. Let's see how by applying it to two confusing examples. First, suppose I told you, "It's not true that an *e*lm tree or something other than a *w*alnut tree is in my backyard." We observe that "something other than a walnut tree" is a tricky way of saying "not a walnut tree." Accordingly, the statement is symbolized ~(E ∨ ~W). Now we apply DeM: ~E · W. Notice that ~~W ≡ W by DN. Finally, we translate back into English to make the statement's meaning clear: "An elm tree isn't in my backyard and a walnut tree is in my backyard." If you saw my backyard, you would know that this statement is true!

Second, suppose I remarked after drinking too much apricot brandy, "The contradictory of my not being a *m*ember of the Church of the Brethren and my *l*iking Caesar salad is true." What on earth am I trying to convey? We begin by inquiring what it means for the contradictory of a proposition—here "I am not a member of the Church of the Brethren and I like Caesar salad"—to be true. This simply means that the negation, or "not," of the proposition is true (or, more simply, that the proposition is false). Accordingly, we symbolize my remark as ~(~M · L). Now we apply DeM: M ∨ ~L. Notice that ~~M ≡ M by DN. Now we learn my crazy statement's meaning by translating back into English: "I'm a member of the Church of the Brethren or I don't like Caesar salad." Since I am, in fact, a member of the Church of the Brethren, my crazy statement is accurate (even though I do like Caesar salad).

Negating → Statements

Negating if-then statements (i.e., conditionals) is different from negating conjunctions and disjunctions. It is very important to note that negating conditionals is *not* covered by DeMorgan's Laws. Rather, *the formula for negating a conditional (NC) is as follows:* ~(A → B) ≡ A · ~B. In plain English, the negation of "if A, then B" is "A and not B." Here we see that the negation of an if-then statement is not an if-then statement; it is an "and not" statement. When negating a conditional, the "if" and "then" go away, the antecedent (the if-clause) stays the same, an "and" is inserted, and the consequent (the then-clause) is denied.

That the negation, i.e., contradictory, of an if-then statement is not another if-then statement is the reason why, in chapter one, it did not violate the law of noncontradiction to say, given that I in fact buy a cell phone on which I call my brother, that both "If I don't buy a cell phone, then I call my brother" and "If I don't buy a cell phone, then I don't call my brother" are true. (They're vacuously true, but true nonetheless.) For $\sim(A \rightarrow B) \not\equiv (A \rightarrow \sim B)$. Hence the first statement is not the contradictory of the second statement and the second statement is not the contradictory of the first, such that they can both be true without violating the law of noncontradiction. Rather, the contradictory of "If I don't buy a cell phone, then I call my brother" (a true statement) is "I don't buy a cell phone and I don't call my brother" (a false statement since both conjuncts are false). Likewise, the contradictory of "If I don't buy a cell phone, then I don't call my brother" (a true statement) is "I don't buy a cell phone and I call my brother" (a false statement since the first conjunct is false). Notice how the correct contradictory of each conditional has the opposite truth-value of the original.

As with negated conjunctions and negated disjunctions, the best way to figure out the meaning of negated conditionals is by using a three-step procedure. However, we alter the second step by applying NC instead of DeM. So let's take the statement "It's not true that if something *e*xists, then it has a *c*ause." First we symbolize: $\sim(E \rightarrow C)$. Then we apply NC: $E \cdot \sim C$. Now we translate back into English: "Something exists and it does not have a cause." Any theist would agree with this sentiment, since they affirm that God exists and is uncaused. Most non-theists would also concur, contending that the laws of logic exist and are uncaused. Now let's try another example: "It is not the case that if Allen *V*izzutti is my favorite trumpet player, then Arturo *S*andoval is my third favorite trumpet player." First we symbolize: $\sim(V \rightarrow S)$. Then we apply NC: $V \cdot \sim S$. Now we translate back into English: "Allen Vizzutti is my favorite trumpet player and Arturo Sandoval is not my third favorite trumpet player." That statement is true, as Arturo Sandoval is my second favorite trumpet player (and Wynton Marsalis is my third favorite trumpet player).

Suppose I said, "That if I don't go to *C*asey's, I'll eat a *f*illed Long John donut for breakfast is a lie." What do I mean? To figure it out, we first symbolize: $\sim(\sim C \rightarrow F)$. Then we apply NC: $\sim C \cdot \sim F$. (Since $\sim C$ was the conditional's antecedent and the antecedent stays the same, it remains $\sim C$ in the conjunction.) Now we translate back into English: "I don't go to Casey's and I won't eat a filled Long John donut for breakfast." Imagine that I went on to claim, "The contradictory of the statement that if *K*rista dyes her hair, then she is not a natural *b*lond is true." Recall that the contradictory of a statement is the "not" of that statement. So let's figure out what the contradictory means. First we symbolize: $\sim(K \rightarrow \sim B)$. Then we apply NC: K · B. Notice that ~~B ≡ B by DN. Now we translate back into English: "Krista dyes her hair and she is a natural blond."

Pre-Homework Practice!

Before proceeding to your homework, let's figure out the meaning of four negations together. Try to symbolize each example before looking at the solution below it.

1. It isn't true that I have a globe and a Wii in my living room.
   a. Letting G ≡ "I have a globe in my living room" and W ≡ "I have a Wii in my living room," we first symbolize: ~(G · W). Then we apply DeM: ~G ∨ ~W. Now we translate back into English: "*I don't have a globe in my living room or I don't have a Wii in my living room.*"
2. That the doctrine of justification by faith was originally formulated by Luther or not by Paul is a lie.
   a. Letting L ≡ "The doctrine of justification by faith was originally formulated by Luther" and P ≡ "The doctrine of justification by faith was originally formulated by Paul," we first symbolize: ~(L ∨ ~P). Then we apply DeM: ~L · P. Now we translate back into English: "*The doctrine of justification by faith was not originally formulated by Luther and it was originally formulated by Paul.*"
3. It is not the case that if I'm middle-class, then I'll buy a Toyota.
   a. Letting M ≡ "I'm middle-class" and T ≡ "I'll buy a Toyota," we first symbolize: ~(M → T). Then we apply NC: M · ~T. Now we translate back into English: "*I'm middle-class and I won't buy a Toyota.*"
4. The contradictory of the statement that if I don't give water to the guinea pigs, they'll die of dehydration is true.
   a. Letting W ≡ "I give water to the guinea pigs" and D ≡ "The guinea pigs will die of dehydration," we first symbolize: ~(~W → D). Then we apply NC: ~W · ~D. Now we translate back into English: "*I don't give water to the guinea pigs and they won't die of dehydration.*"

Homework Assignment 5

Figure out the meaning of the following statements both in symbols and in English. (In other words, carry out the appropriate three-step procedure, and report as your answer steps two and three.)

1. It's not true that I wear purple sneakers or I drive a Ferrari.
2. It's a lie that if I go to Subway, I won't buy a Footlong.
3. The contradictory of the statement that Madonna or someone besides Prince recorded *Purple Rain* is true.
4. It is not the case that I'm sitting on my couch and I'm in my office.
5. It's false that if Hans Küng didn't write *Christ and the Modern Mind*, then Küng was an agnostic.

6

Logical Equivalences

LOGICAL EQUIVALENCES SHOW US how the same proposition can be expressed in multiple ways. Knowing our logical equivalences helps us to identify when propositions are stated in complex or confusing ways and to simplify them accordingly. We already know one logical equivalence: contraposition (Cont), which explains that any if-then statement is equivalent to an if-then statement where the antecedent and consequent are simultaneously flipped and negated, leaving the words "if" and "then" intact. So let's learn about the other equivalences, some of which permit us to express propositions in highly entertaining ways!

Helpful Equivalences

The *law of association (Assoc)* allows us to group together $\vee$ and $\cdot$ statements in whatever order we like. This follows from Com. Accordingly, *the law holds that* $A \vee (B \vee C) \equiv (A \vee B) \vee C$, *and that* $A \cdot (B \cdot C) \equiv (A \cdot B) \cdot C$. To illustrate with "or," we can express "I read *The Social Construction of Virtue*, or I read either Calvin's *Institutes* or Luther's *Bondage of the Will*" as "I read either *The Social Construction of Virtue* or Calvin's *Institutes*, or I read Luther's *Bondage of the Will*." The two statements mean exactly the same thing; it doesn't matter how we group our disjuncts. To illustrate with "and," we can express "I'm staring at a deer, and I'm staring at both a cardinal and a leaf" as "I'm staring at both a deer and a cardinal, and I'm staring at a leaf." These are two ways of articulating precisely the same sentiment, as we can group our conjuncts in whatever way we prefer. But a word of warning: Assoc only works when you've got the same symbol—either $\vee$ or $\cdot$—across the board. If you have a combination of symbols, such as $A \vee (B \cdot C)$ or $A \cdot (B \vee C)$, these cannot be regrouped. In other words, $A \vee (B \cdot C) \not\equiv (A \vee B) \cdot C$, and $A \cdot (B \vee C) \not\equiv (A \cdot B) \vee C$.

The *law of idempotence (Idem)* is just common sense with $\vee$ and $\cdot$. *Regarding* $\vee$, *it holds that for any* A, $A \equiv A \vee A$. Thus "I'm going to the store or I'm going to the store" means the same thing as "I'm going to the store." We could add as many additional ($\vee$ A)s as we wanted; the law still applies. *Regarding* $\cdot$, *the law holds that for any* A, $A \equiv A \cdot A$. Clearly, "I'm going to band rehearsal and I'm going to band rehearsal" means the same thing as "I'm going to band rehearsal." We could add as many additional ($\cdot$ A)s as we wanted; the law still applies.

The *law of absorption (Abs) comes in three forms. Form 1 maintains that* $A \rightarrow B \equiv A \rightarrow (A \cdot B)$. This makes good sense. Obviously, "If Jesus was crucified, then the Quran's description of Jesus' fate needs reinterpretation in order to be plausible" ≡ "If Jesus was crucified, then Jesus was crucified and the Quran's description of Jesus' fate needs reinterpretation in order to be plausible." Form 1 draws on the fact that for any A, $A \rightarrow A$. Obviously, if Jesus was crucified, then Jesus was crucified! *Form 2 maintains that* $A \equiv A \cdot (A \vee B)$. *Form 3 maintains that* $A \equiv A \vee (A \cdot B)$.[1] I must confess that forms 2 and 3 of Abs are my favorite logical equivalences. They are, in effect, logical black holes. We can put in whatever we want for B, true or false. It makes no difference; B just gets swallowed up!

Let's illustrate how forms 2 and 3 of Abs work. Form 2 states that "I like triple brownie ice cream" is logically equivalent to saying "I like triple brownie ice cream and either I like triple brownie ice cream or leprechauns exist." (Here our B ≡ "Leprechauns exist.") Form 3 states that "I like triple brownie ice cream" is logically equivalent to saying "I like triple brownie ice cream or both I like triple brownie ice cream and I'm going to Burger King for lunch." (Here our B ≡ "I'm going to Burger King for lunch.") At this point you might ask: Why do these weird forms (2 and 3) of the law of absorption work? They work because of what it means for two statements to be logically equivalent. Two statements are logically equivalent iff they have the same truth-value under any circumstances. Each is true whenever the other is true, and each is false whenever the other is false.

1. I am indebted to Epp, *Discrete Mathematics*, 14 for forms 2 and 3 of the law of absorption.

If we look at the above examples, it is obvious that they fulfill this condition. Suppose it is true that I like triple brownie ice cream. For this reason, it is also true that I like triple brownie ice cream and either I like triple brownie ice cream or leprechauns exist (even though leprechauns don't exist). Moreover, it is true that I like triple brownie ice cream or both I like triple brownie ice cream and I'm going to Burger King for lunch. Even if I don't go to Burger King for lunch, my liking triple brownie ice cream makes the overall statement true, since we only need one of the two disjuncts of an "or" statement to be true for the overall statement to be true. Now suppose it is false that I like triple brownie ice cream. Therefore, it is also false that I like triple brownie ice cream and either I like triple brownie ice cream or leprechauns exist. For an "and" statement to be true, both of its conjuncts must be true, and here neither one of them is. Likewise, it is false that I like triple brownie ice cream or both I like triple brownie ice cream and I'm going to Burger King for lunch. Here my not liking triple brownie ice cream makes both disjuncts of the "or" statement false, regardless of whether I go to Burger King for lunch. So whether the statement "I like triple brownie ice cream" is true or false, the statement expressed in forms 2 and 3 of Abs will have the identical truth-value.

We can demonstrate that these two weird forms of Abs work for any statements you might dream up by using a truth table. For any A and B, if A always has the same truth value as A · (A ∨ B) and as A ∨ (A · B), then we have proof that A ≡ A · (A ∨ B) and A ≡ A ∨ (A · B). To see if they always have the same truth value, the columns in the truth table for A, A · (A ∨ B), and A ∨ (A · B) must match. Here we will draw a truth table with six columns, one for A, one for B, one for (A ∨ B), one for (A · B), one for A · (A ∨ B), and one for A ∨ (A · B). The material in the third and fourth columns are just review from chapter one. So long as columns one, five, and six match, forms 2 and 3 of Abs are universally true. These columns are italicized below.

A	B	(A ∨ B)	(A · B)	A · (A ∨ B)	A ∨ (A · B)
T	T	T	T	*T*	*T*
T	F	T	F	*T*	*T*
F	T	T	F	*F*	*F*
F	F	F	F	*F*	*F*

As we can see, columns one (for A), five (for A · (A ∨ B)), and six (for A ∨ (A · B)) match. In the first row, A · (A ∨ B) is true because both A and (A ∨ B) are true, and A ∨ (A · B) is true because at least one (here both) of A and (A · B) is true. In the second row, A · (A ∨ B) is true because both A and (A ∨ B) are true, and A ∨ (A · B) is true because A is true. In the third row, A · (A ∨ B) is false because A is false, and A ∨ (A · B) is false because both A and (A · B) are false. In the fourth row, A · (A ∨ B) is false because at least one (here both) of A and (A ∨ B) is false, and A ∨ (A · B) is false because both A and (A · B) are false. Hence for any A and B, A ≡ A · (A ∨ B) and A ≡ A ∨ (A · B), with the content of B—true or false—always getting swallowed up.

We previously emphasized that · and ∨ cannot be interchanged. So, you might ask, what can we do with them? We can distribute them, using the *law of distribution (Dist). This law has two forms. Form 1 states that* A · (B ∨ C) ≡ (A · B) ∨ (A · C). Here the A · gets distributed to and grouped with B and C, leaving the ∨ intact. *Form 2 states that* A ∨ (B · C) ≡ (A ∨ B) · (A ∨ C). Here the A ∨ gets distributed to and grouped with B and C, leaving the · intact.[2] To give an example of form 1, "Alvin Plantinga is a brilliant American philosopher and N. T. Wright or Marcus Borg is a brilliant British New Testament scholar" ≡ "Both Alvin Plantinga is a brilliant American philosopher and N. T. Wright is a brilliant British New Testament scholar, or both Alvin Plantinga is a brilliant American philosopher and Marcus Borg is a brilliant British New Testament scholar."[3] To give an example of form 2, "John Dominic Crossan or both William Lane Craig and Michael Licona wrote *The Historical Jesus: The Life of a Mediterranean Jewish Peasant*" ≡ "John Dominic Crossan or William Lane Craig wrote *The Historical Jesus: The Life of a Mediterranean Jewish Peasant*, and John Dominic Crossan or Michael Licona wrote *The Historical Jesus: The Life of a Mediterranean Jewish Peasant*."[4]

2. You can think of distribution this way: The only thing that, when distributed, can change ∨ or · is ~. Distributing ~ to · makes it ∨, and distributing ~ to ∨ makes it ·. However, when A · is distributed to ∨, it just bounces off the ∨, such that the ∨ stays the same. Likewise, when A ∨ is distributed to ·, it just bounces off the ·, such that the · stays the same.

3. The example is true: Plantinga is a brilliant American philosopher, and Wright is a brilliant British New Testament scholar. Borg is a brilliant New Testament scholar, but he is American, not British.

4. This example is also true. Crossan wrote *The Historical Jesus*.

Pre-Homework Practice!

Let's try our hand together on five pairs of statements. With each pair, we will ask two questions. First, are the statements logically equivalent? Second, why or why not? Attempt to figure out the answers before looking at the solutions below each pair.

1. I like shopping for hand-painted ties; I like shopping for hand-painted ties or both I like shopping for hand-painted ties and 3 + 8 = 20.
   a. *Yes, the statements are logically equivalent. This is by form 3 of Abs*. To see this, let S ≡ "I like shopping for hand-painted ties" and T ≡ "3 + 8 = 20." The second statement is symbolized S ∨ (S · T), which—per form 3 of Abs—is logically equivalent to S, our first statement. Notice how T gets swallowed up in our logical black hole!
2. Swimming is fun and bull-riding or painting is fun; swimming is fun or bull-riding and painting is fun.
   a. *No, the statements are not logically equivalent. This is because · and ∨ cannot be interchanged.*
3. If God loves me, then God loves me and my cognitive faculties are fundamentally reliable; if God loves me, then my cognitive faculties are fundamentally reliable.
   a. *Yes, the statements are logically equivalent. This is by form 1 of Abs*. To see this, let G ≡ "God loves me" and C ≡ "My cognitive faculties are fundamentally reliable." The first statement is symbolized G → (G · C), which is logically equivalent to G → C, our second statement.
4. Cornhole should be an Olympic sport or both my blue chair and my red chair are comfortable; cornhole should be an Olympic sport or my blue chair is comfortable, and cornhole should be an Olympic sport or my red chair is comfortable.
   a. *Yes, the statements are logically equivalent. This is by form 2 of Dist*. To see this, let C ≡ "Cornhole should be an Olympic sport," B ≡ "My blue chair is comfortable," and R ≡ "My red chair is comfortable." Thus the first statement is symbolized C ∨ (B · R). Now we distribute: (C ∨ B) · (C ∨ R), which is our second statement.

5. Propositions are abstract objects and either propositions are abstract objects or I am a Tiger Woods fan; propositions are abstract objects.
    a. *Yes, the statements are logically equivalent. This is by form 2 of Abs*. To see this, let P ≡ "Propositions are abstract objects" and T ≡ "I am a Tiger Woods fan." The first statement is symbolized P · (P ∨ T), which—per form 2 of Abs—is logically equivalent to P, our first statement. Again, T vanishes into the logical black hole.

Homework Assignment 6

Are these statements logically equivalent? Why or why not?

1. If something is literally true, then it is metaphorically true; if something is literally true, then it is literally true and it is metaphorically true.
2. Obsessive-compulsive disorder is an anxiety disorder or both 7 + 6 = 14 and 9 + 3 = 1; obsessive-compulsive disorder is an anxiety disorder and 7 + 6 = 14, or 9 + 3 = 1.
3. I will eat dinner tonight and my brother's name is either Scotty or Brad; I will eat dinner tonight and my brother's name is Scotty, or I will eat dinner tonight and my brother's name is Brad.
4. Steel chairs are effective foreign objects in professional wrestling and either steel chairs are effective foreign objects in professional wrestling or donkeys have wings; steel chairs are effective foreign objects in professional wrestling.
5. I've spoken at the American Academy of Religion annual meeting multiple times or both computers have eyes and dogs have tails; I've spoken at the American Academy of Religion annual meeting multiple times or computers have eyes, and I've spoken at the American Academy of Religion annual meeting multiple times or dogs have tails.

7

Symbolizing Quantified Statements (Part 1)

IN THE FIRST SIX chapters, we have been working with simple and compound statements. However, we have not yet seen how to symbolize statements that express quantities, such as "All field goals are worth three points" or "Some pictures are not pleasant to look at." Such statements are appropriately known as quantified statements, and learning to symbolize them will occupy this chapter and chapter eight. Quantified statements come in four types: "all . . . are . . ." statements; "no . . . is . . ." statements; "some . . . are . . ." statements; and "some . . . are not . . ." statements. Among the most important skills in dealing with quantified statements is expressing them as one of these four types, which we will call "properly formed quantified statements." The verb of a properly formed quantified statement is crucial. It must be "are" or "is" (both forms of the linking verb "to be"), known as the *copula*. It can't be anything else! So if we have an improperly formed quantified statement where the verb is something else, the statement must be rewritten to make the verb "are" or "is." Thus "All cats meow" must be rewritten "All cats are meowers." Or again, "Some students swim" must be rewritten "Some students are swimmers." It is helpful to symbolize quantified statements and the statements surrounding them in a different way than we have symbolized simple and compound statements when at least one of the surrounding statements relies on the "all"-ness, the "no"-ness, the "some"-ness, or the "some . . . are not . . ."-ness of the quantified statement.

"All" Statements

"All" statements are disguised if-then statements applicable to anything that satisfies the antecedent (i.e., meets the condition of the if-clause). They are *universal affirmative statements.* Thus "all clarinets are woodwinds" is the same as saying, "For any *x*, if *x* is a clarinet, then *x* is a woodwind." Notice how the variable *x* is lowercase, since lowercase is used to denote individual items. Moreover, *x* is italicized because it is a variable. So how do we symbolize "for any *x*, if *x* is a clarinet, then *x* is a woodwind"? We denote "for any *x*" with (*x*). We denote "*x* is a clarinet" with C*x*, where C_ ≡ "_ is a clarinet." The first letter of the predicate term (here "clarinet") is capitalized and comes first, with a lowercase letter immediately following it that satisfies the predicate. Likewise, we denote "*x* is a woodwind" with W*x*, where W_ ≡ "_ is a woodwind." Putting this all together, we have (*x*)(C*x* → W*x*) as the symbolization of "all clarinets are woodwinds." Notice the careful placement of the second set of parentheses, since the "for all *x*" applies to the whole if-then.

Imagine some crazy clarinet player named their clarinet Bob. Suppose we then said, "Bob is a clarinet." Since Bob is an individual item, we symbolize it with b. Notice that b is not italicized, since it is a constant rather than a variable. And since C_ means "_ is a clarinet," we can symbolize "Bob is a clarinet" as Cb.

Here we should check that you're following the new symbolization style so far. Try to symbolize "All musicologists are history lovers." Recall that this means, "For any *x*, if *x* is a musicologist, then *x* is a history lover." "For any *x*" is symbolized (*x*). "*x* is a musicologist" is symbolized M*x*, where M_ ≡ "_ is a musicologist." "*x* is a history lover" could be symbolized as either H*x* or L*x*, whichever you choose. We'll take H*x* for the sake of convenience, where H_ ≡ "_ is a history lover." In sum, "All musicologists are history lovers" ≡ (*x*)(M*x* → H*x*). Moreover, if in this context we said, "Dr. Kernodle is a musicologist," we could symbolize it as Mk.[1]

"No" Statements

"No" statements are disguised "if-then not" statements applicable to anything that satisfies the antecedent (i.e., meets the condition of the

1. Indeed, Tammy Kernodle is a world-renowned musicologist who teaches at Miami University. I was privileged to have Dr. Kernodle as a professor when I was an undergraduate at Miami.

if-clause). They are equivalent to saying "All . . . are not . . ." and are *universal negative statements*. So "no flute is a quadruped" means "all flutes are not quadrupeds," i.e., for any *x*, if *x* is a flute, then *x* is not a quadruped. Now we can use the same method discussed when symbolizing "all" statements. Let F_ ≡ "_ is a flute," and let Q_ ≡ "_ is a quadruped." Given what we already know about ~, ~Q_ would then mean "_ is not a quadruped." Putting this all together, we get (*x*)(F*x* → ~Q*x*) as the symbolization of "No flute is a quadruped." And if some crazy flute player named their flute Pierre, then "Pierre is a flute" ≡ Fp.

Let's now try to symbolize "No Muslim is a believer in Muhammad's deity." Recall that this means "All Muslims are not believers in Muhammad's deity." In other words, for any *x*, if *x* is a Muslim, then *x* is not a believer in Muhammad's deity. (*x*) means "for any *x*." Let M*x* ≡ "*x* is a Muslim," and let B*x* ≡ "*x* is a believer in Muhammad's deity." ~B*x* would then mean "*x* is not a believer in Muhammad's deity." Accordingly, "No Muslim is a believer in Muhammad's deity" ≡ (*x*)(M*x* → ~B*x*). And if we said, "Shabir Ally is not a believer in Muhammad's deity," this would be symbolized ~Ba.[2]

"Some" Statements

"Some" statements are disguised "and" statements that apply to at least one thing. They are *particular affirmative statements*. "Some" means "at least one." Notice that "one" is "at least one." Don't let the plural verb ("Some . . . are . . .") mislead you! If there's even one thing that the statement applies to, then the statement is true. Thus "Some trumpets are made by Carol Brass" is the same as saying, "There exists an *x* such that *x* is a trumpet and *x* is made by Carol Brass." Let T_ ≡ "_ is a trumpet" and C_ ≡ "_ is made by Carol Brass." So how do we say, "There exists an *x*"? We use the existential quantifier ∃_, which means "There exists a _." We then put the *x* in the blank and enclose the thing in parentheses. Putting this all together, we have: (∃*x*)(T*x* · C*x*) as the symbolization of "Some trumpets are made by Carol Brass." Notice the careful placement of the second set of parentheses, since the "there exists an *x*" applies to the whole and-statement.

Following the same reasoning, how would we symbolize "Some cats are tabbies"? Well, remember that this sentence means "There exists an

2. Ally is a prominent Muslim scholar who serves as president of the Islamic Information & Dawah Centre International in Toronto.

x such that *x* is a cat and *x* is a tabby." ($\exists x$) means "there exists an *x*." Let C*x* ≡ "*x* is a cat" and T*x* ≡ "*x* is a tabby." Thus "Some cats are tabbies" ≡ $(\exists x)(Cx \cdot Tx)$.

"Some . . . Not" Statements

"Some . . . not" statements are disguised "and not" statements that apply to at least one thing. They are *particular negative statements.* Using what we already learned, we know that "Some pianos are not made by Carol Brass" is the same as saying, "There exists an *x* such that *x* is a piano and *x* is not made by Carol Brass." We previously saw that ($\exists x$) means "there exists an *x*." Let P_ ≡ "_ is a piano" and C_ ≡ "_ is made by Carol Brass." If we wanted to say "_ is not made by Carol Brass," this would be symbolized ~C_. Now the statement "Some pianos are not made by Carol Brass" is easy to symbolize: $(\exists x)(Px \cdot {\sim}Cx)$.

Let's now try our hand at symbolizing the statement "Some books are not published by Eerdmans." This means "There exists an *x* such that *x* is a book and *x* is not published by Eerdmans." "There exists an *x*" is symbolized ($\exists x$). Let B*x* ≡ "*x* is a book" and P*x* (you could also use E*x*) ≡ "*x* is published by Eerdmans." Then ~P*x* ≡ "*x* is not published by Eerdmans." As a result, "Some books are not published by Eerdmans" ≡ $(\exists x)(Bx \cdot {\sim}Px)$.

Pre-Homework Practice!

Before you turn to the homework, we will test our skills with five examples. Try to symbolize each one and then check your answer against the solution below it.

1. All philosophical theologians like structure.
   a. We first observe that this is not a properly formed quantified statement. However, that problem can be solved easily by rewriting the statement as "All philosophical theologians are structure-likers." This means, "For any *x*, if *x* is a philosophical theologian, then *x* is a structure-liker." Letting P*x* ≡ "*x* is a philosophical theologian" and S*x* ≡ "*x* is a structure-liker," our solution is $(x)(Px \rightarrow Sx)$.

2. Kirk is a philosophical theologian.
    a. Using the nomenclature from the first example, the solution is Pk. Note that k is not italicized since Kirk (me) is a constant.
3. No guinea pigs eat computers.
    a. We begin by turning this into a properly formed quantified statement, rewriting it as "No guinea pigs are computer-eaters." In other words, "All guinea pigs are not computer-eaters" ≡ "For any *x*, if *x* is a guinea pig, then *x* is not a computer-eater." Letting G*x* ≡ "*x* is a guinea pig" and C*x* ≡ "*x* is a computer-eater," our solution is (*x*)(G*x* → ~C*x*).
4. Some roosters wake people up.
    a. Turning this into a properly formed quantified statement, we obtain "Some roosters are wakers-up of people." In other words, "There exists an *x* such that *x* is a rooster and *x* is a waker-up of people." Letting R*x* ≡ "*x* is a rooster" and W*x* ≡ "*x* is a waker-up of people," the solution is (∃*x*)(R*x* · W*x*).
5. Some metals don't rust.
    a. When properly formed, the statement would read, "Some metals are not rusters" ≡ "There exists an *x* such that *x* is a metal and *x* is not a ruster." Letting M*x* ≡ "*x* is a metal" and R*x* ≡ "*x* is a ruster," *our solution is* (∃*x*)(M*x* · ~R*x*).

Homework Assignment 7

Symbolize the following quantified statements:

1. Some statistical generalizations are not accurate.
2. All objective moral duties possess a metaphysical ground.
3. Love is an objective moral duty.
4. No laptops have souls.
5. Some trees are petrified.

8

Symbolizing Quantified Statements (Part 2)

IN THIS CHAPTER WE will explore synonyms of "all," "no," "some," and "some . . . not." It is very important to be able to recognize these synonyms and think about the statement at hand as one of these four. We will also introduce a new and final quantifier, one that uses more than a single variable (and is therefore "multivariate").

Synonyms of "All"

Each of the following is an alternate way of saying, "All clarinets are woodwinds" and is therefore symbolized $(x)(Cx \rightarrow Wx)$.

1. Every clarinet is a woodwind.
2. Each clarinet is a woodwind.
3. Clarinets are woodwinds.
    a. This synonym is tricky. Often when we say something like this, we don't intend to convey that, for example, every single clarinet is a woodwind. Nevertheless, this is logically what our statement means. Saying "clarinets are woodwinds" means that clarinets as a class—and therefore each clarinet in that class—is a woodwind. If there were even one clarinet that was not a woodwind, then our statement would be false.

4. Only woodwinds are clarinets.
    a. This synonym is even trickier. It is a synonym of "All clarinets are woodwinds" because "only" means "then" and that the other clause is the if-clause. In other words, "For any *x*, if *x* is a clarinet, then *x* is a woodwind."

Synonyms of "No"

Each of the following is an alternate way of saying, "No dog is human" and is therefore symbolized $(x)(\mathrm{D}x \rightarrow {\sim}\mathrm{H}x)$.

1. All dogs are not human.
2. Dogs are not human.
    a. This synonym is tricky. Even if we're not specifically thinking of all dogs, our statement applies to dogs as a class and therefore includes every single one.
3. Not even one dog is human.
4. There does not exist a dog that is human.
    a. This synonym is tricky. But it makes sense if we think it through. If there does not exist a dog that is human, then no dog is human.
5. There does not exist a human dog.
    a. This synonym is also tricky but, like the previous example, makes sense if we think it through. If there is no human dog, then no dog is human.
6. No dogs are human.
7. Only non-humans are dogs.
    a. This synonym is even trickier. Since "only" means "then" and that the other clause is the if-clause, we're saying here that "for any *x*, if *x* is a dog, then *x* is a non-human."

Synonyms of "Some"

Each of the following is an alternate way of saying, "Some trumpets are made by Carol Brass" and is therefore symbolized $(\exists x)(\mathrm{T}x \cdot \mathrm{C}x)$.

1. A trumpet is made by Carol Brass.
    a. Remember that, to get "some," all we need is one.
2. There exists a trumpet made by Carol Brass.
3. Carol Brass made a trumpet.
    a. This synonym is tricky but makes sense if we think it through. If Carol Brass made a trumpet, then there exists an *x* such that *x* is a trumpet and *x* is made by Carol Brass.
4. Many trumpets are made by Carol Brass.
5. Several trumpets are made by Carol Brass.
    a. "Many" and "several" mean "at least two," which meet the condition of "at least one" and are therefore synonymous with "some."
6. Carol Brass made many trumpets.
    a. This synonym is tricky. Since "many" is "some," affirming that Carol Brass made some trumpets is the same as affirming that some trumpets are made by Carol Brass.
7. At least one trumpet is made by Carol Brass.

Synonyms of "Some . . . Not"

Each of the following is an alternate way of saying, "Some rock tumblers are not quiet" and is therefore symbolized $(\exists x)(Rx \cdot {\sim}Qx)$.

1. A rock tumbler is not quiet.
2. There exists a non-quiet rock tumbler.
3. Many rock tumblers are not quiet.
4. Several rock tumblers are not quiet.
5. At least one rock tumbler is not quiet.
6. Not all rock tumblers are quiet.
    a. This is a tricky but very important synonym which makes sense if we think it through. If not all rock tumblers are quiet, then some rock tumblers are not quiet.
7. Not every rock tumbler is quiet.

   a. This is another tricky but very important synonym. If not every rock tumbler is quiet, then there exists a rock tumbler that is not quiet.

8. It's not the case that only quiet things are rock tumblers.
   a. This synonym is trickiest. Given that "only" means "then" and that the other clause is the if-clause, our sentence is conveying that it's not the case that for any *x*, if *x* is a rock tumbler, then *x* is quiet. In other words, it's not the case that all rock tumblers are quiet, which means that some rock tumblers are not quiet.

"Only Some": The Multivariate Quantifier!

One final but very important quantifier is "only some." "Only some" means, "Some are and some others aren't." So "Only some people are kind" ≡ "Some people are kind and some other people aren't kind." Because we're dealing with two categories of people, we need to use two variables: *x* and *y*. This prevents us from confusing the kind people with the unkind people. In other words, "There exists a *x* and there exists a *y* such that both *x* is a person and *x* is kind and *y* is a person and *y* is unkind." Putting it all together, we get $(\exists x)(\exists y)((Px \cdot Kx) \cdot (Py \cdot {\sim}Ky))$. Notice that for as many variables as there are, they all come at the beginning.

Practice on All Quantifiers and Their Synonyms

The only way to get good at recognizing the synonyms of quantifiers is lots of practice. So let's review the most important synonyms we've seen thus far. Consider first the statement "Cats are not wolves." This means, "All cats are not wolves," i.e., "No cat is a wolf," and is accordingly symbolized $(x)(Cx \rightarrow {\sim}Wx)$. Suppose we now said, "A pillow is soft." This is symbolized $(\exists x)(Px \cdot Sx)$ and means the same thing as "Some pillows are soft." If we assert, "Only bad doctrines are heresies," we mean, "All heresies are bad doctrines" ≡ $(x)(Hx \rightarrow Bx)$. If someone comments, "Not all books are tedious to read," they're maintaining that some books are not tedious to read, which is symbolized $(\exists x)(Bx \cdot {\sim}Tx)$. Regarding the trumpet mouthpieces I own, it is the case that "Only some mouthpieces give a thin tone quality." In other words, some mouthpieces give a thin tone quality, and other mouthpieces don't give a thin tone quality. So we need two variables for the two classes of mouthpieces, indicating that there exists an *x* and there exists a y such that x is a mouthpiece and x gives a thin tone quality and that y is a mouthpiece and y does not give a thin tone quality. This is symbolized $(\exists x)(\exists y)((Mx \cdot Tx) \cdot (My \cdot \sim Ty))$.

Having once lived in a studio apartment infested with cockroaches, I believe that "Not even one cockroach deserves to live in my house." In other words, I think that "No cockroach deserves to live in my house" ≡ $(x)(Cx \rightarrow \sim Dx)$. If I complain, "There exists a not-in-tune piano," I mean "There exists a piano that is not in tune," i.e., "Some pianos are not in tune," which is symbolized $(\exists x)(Px \cdot \sim Tx)$. If a wine connoisseur insists that "Only some wines are expensive," they mean "Some wines are expensive and some wines aren't expensive," leading us to use two variables for the different kinds of wine. Thus, the sentence is symbolized $(\exists x)(\exists y)((Wx \cdot Ex) \cdot (Wy \cdot \sim Ey))$. Given my experiences at the annual C.A.R.S. Club Car and Motorcycle Show at McPherson College, I know that "Restored antique cars look great." By this I mean, "All restored antique cars are great-looking" ≡ $(x)(Rx \rightarrow Gx)$. If it is true that "Several ants bite," then at least two, and therefore some, ants bite, yielding the symbolization $(\exists x)(Ax \cdot Bx)$.

Pre-Homework Practice!

You should now have a good handle on the synonyms of quantifiers and on the multivariate quantifier "only some." For the following examples, try to symbolize each before looking at the solution below it.

1. The Supreme Court wrote a decision.
   a. This sentence entails that there exists a x such that x is a decision and x is written by the Supreme Court, namely, $(\exists x)(Dx \cdot Wx)$. Hopefully you recognize that this sentence is a synonym for "Some decisions are written by the Supreme Court."
2. Many clouds aren't thick.
   a. Since many—at least two—clouds aren't thick, some clouds are not thick. This is symbolized $(\exists x)(Cx \cdot \sim Tx)$.
3. Each garden plant is cultivated.
   a. This is synonymous with "All garden plants are cultivated" ≡ $(x)(Gx \rightarrow Cx)$.

4. Not even a single house was built by Rubens.
   a. This is an alternate way of saying, "No house was built by Rubens" ≡ $(x)(\text{H}x \rightarrow \sim\text{B}x)$.
5. A bird chirps.
   a. In other words, there exists a x such that x is a bird and x is a chirper, namely, $(\exists x)(\text{B}x \cdot \text{C}x)$. This is synonymous with the properly formed quantified statement "Some birds are chirpers."
6. Only some rich people are snobs.
   a. This means, "Some rich people are snobs and some other rich people aren't snobs" ≡ $(\exists x)(\exists y)((\text{R}x \cdot \text{S}x) \cdot (\text{R}y \cdot \sim\text{S}y))$.

Homework Assignment 8

Symbolize the following quantified statements:

1. Not every keyboard is made by Yamaha.
2. Only some Bibles are translated from Latin.
3. Only stringed instruments are violins.
4. Not a single jar of peanut butter tastes like Sprite.
5. There exists a living falcon.

9

Traditional Square of Opposition

We have seen in the last two chapters how to symbolize quantified statements. In this chapter we explore the question: How do we negate quantified statements? Negating quantified statements is a very important skill to learn. Many people—especially in popular media—incorrectly negate quantified statements. So let's begin by getting out of the way how *not* to negate quantified statements, all of which are errors—if you didn't know any better—you would be tempted to make! First, the negation of "All A are B" is not "All A are not B," i.e., "No A is B." Second, the negation of "No A is B" is not "No A is not B," i.e., "All A are B." Third, the negation of "Some A are B" is not "Some A are not B." Fourth, the negation of "Some A are not B" is not "Some A are B." Avoid these errors like the plague!

Correctly Negating Quantified Statements

The rules for how to correctly negate quantified statements, as well as many other logical rules, are conveniently packaged together in the *Traditional Square of Opposition (Sq).*[1] When citing any of these rules, all you need to write is Sq. I cannot overemphasize the importance of

1. Many logicians dispute aspects of the Traditional Square of Opposition and instead advocate the so-called Modern Square of Opposition. These aspects are technical and do not affect everyday reasoning. To the contrary, I believe that all aspects of the Traditional Square of Opposition are correct, such that it should therefore be advocated in modern logic. For the reasons why I think this way, see Seuren, "Saving." Compare this with the case against the Traditional Square presented in Kneale and Kneale, *Development*, 55–61.

memorizing the Traditional Square of Opposition. If you do, you will likely find yourself using it—to your benefit—for the rest of your life, since almost no one can avoid negating quantified statements. The four corners of the square take their names from the first two vowels of the Latin verb for "to affirm" (*affirmo*) and the first two vowels of the Latin verb for "to negate" (*nego*). The first vowel of each designates a universal quantified statement, and the second vowel of each designates a particular quantified statement. So A ≡ universal affirmative ≡ All A are B ≡ $(x)(Ax \rightarrow Bx)$. E ≡ universal negative ≡ No A are B ≡ $(x)(Ax \rightarrow \sim Bx)$. I ≡ particular affirmative ≡ Some A are B ≡ $(\exists x)(Ax \cdot Bx)$. O ≡ particular negative ≡ Some A are not B ≡ $(\exists x)(Ax \cdot \sim Bx)$.

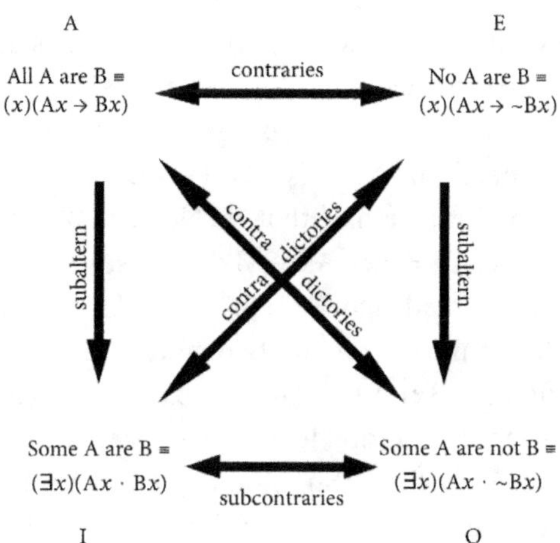

Let's get clear on the meaning of some other vocabulary found in the square. As we already learned, the contradictory of a statement is the "not" (~) of that statement. Two statements are *contraries* when if one is true, the other is false, but they can both be false. Two statements are *subcontraries* when if one is false, the other is true, but they can both be true. A *subaltern* of a statement is another statement that is logically implied by the original statement *but does not imply* the original statement.

Eight Things Sq Teaches Us

Sq teaches us a lot. First, viewing the upper left to bottom right, we find that the contradictory (~) of "All A are B" ≡ $(x)(Ax \rightarrow Bx)$ is "Some A are not B" ≡ $(\exists x)(Ax \cdot \sim Bx)$. In other words, $\sim(x)(Ax \rightarrow Bx) \equiv (\exists x)(Ax \cdot \sim Bx)$. This makes sense: "Not all cats meow" ≡ "Some cats don't meow." Note well that "not all" is *radically different* from "all . . . are not."

Second, viewing the bottom right to upper left, we find that the contradictory (~) of "Some A are not B" ≡ $(\exists x)(Ax \cdot \sim Bx)$ is "All A are B" ≡ $(x)(Ax \rightarrow Bx)$. In other words, $\sim(\exists x)(Ax \cdot \sim Bx) \equiv (x)(Ax \rightarrow Bx)$. This makes sense: "It's false that some cats don't meow" ≡ "All cats meow."

Third, viewing the upper right to bottom left, we find that the contradictory (~) of "No A is B" ≡ $(x)(Ax \rightarrow \sim Bx)$ is "Some A are B" ≡ $(\exists x)(Ax \cdot Bx)$. In other words, $\sim(x)(Ax \rightarrow \sim Bx) \equiv (\exists x)(Ax \cdot Bx)$. This makes sense: "It's false that no cats meow" ≡ "Some cats meow."

Fourth, viewing the bottom left to upper right, we find that the contradictory (~) of "Some A are B" ≡ $(\exists x)(Ax \bullet Bx)$ is "No A is B" ≡ $(x)(Ax \rightarrow \sim Bx)$. In other words, $\sim(\exists x)(Ax \cdot Bx) \equiv (x)(Ax \rightarrow \sim Bx)$. This makes sense: "It's false that some cats meow" ≡ "No cats meow."

Fifth, viewing the top left to top right, we find that if "All A are B" ≡ $(x)(Ax \rightarrow Bx)$ is true, then "No A is B" ≡ $(x)(Ax \rightarrow \sim Bx)$ is false. Viewing the top right to top left, we find that if "No A is B" ≡ $(x)(Ax \rightarrow \sim Bx)$ is true, then "All A are B" ≡ $(x)(Ax \rightarrow Bx)$ is false. However, both "All A are B" ≡ $(x)(Ax \rightarrow Bx)$ and "No A are B" ≡ $(x)(Ax \rightarrow \sim Bx)$ could be false. All of this is what it means for the two statements to be contraries. In other words, $(x)(Ax \rightarrow Bx) \rightarrow \sim(x)(Ax \rightarrow \sim Bx)$ and $(x)(Ax \rightarrow \sim Bx) \rightarrow \sim(x)(Ax \rightarrow Bx)$. Thus we can validly deduce from step 1 to step 2: (1) $(x)(Ax \rightarrow Bx)$ (2) $\therefore \sim(x)(Ax \rightarrow \sim Bx)$ (Sq, 1) and (1) $(x)(Ax \rightarrow \sim Bx)$ (2) $\therefore \sim(x)(Ax \rightarrow Bx)$ (Sq, 1). This makes sense: "(1) All cats meow. (2) Therefore, it is false that no cats meow." Likewise, "(1) No cats meow. (2) Therefore, it is false that all cats meow." However, in actual fact they're both false: some cats meow and some don't! (For instance, some cats have had their vocal cords removed, and some cats have nonfunctioning vocal cords.) Notice that steps 1 and 2 *cannot* be reversed!

Sixth, viewing the bottom left to bottom right, we find that if "Some A are B" ≡ $(\exists x)(Ax \cdot Bx)$ is false, then "Some A are not B" ≡ $(\exists x)(Ax \cdot \sim Bx)$ is true. Viewing the bottom right to bottom left, we find that if "Some A are not B" ≡ $(\exists x)(Ax \cdot \sim Bx)$ is false, then "Some A are B" ≡ $(\exists x)(Ax \cdot Bx)$ is true. However, both "Some A are B" ≡ $(\exists x)(Ax \cdot Bx)$ and "Some A are not B" ≡ $(\exists x)(Ax \cdot \sim Bx)$ could be true. All of this is what it means for the two statements to be subcontraries. In other words, $\sim(\exists x)(Ax \cdot Bx) \rightarrow (\exists x)(Ax \cdot \sim Bx)$ and $\sim(\exists x)(Ax \cdot \sim Bx) \rightarrow (\exists x)(Ax \cdot Bx)$. Thus we can validly deduce from step 1 to step 2: (1) $\sim(\exists x)(Ax \cdot Bx)$ (2) $\therefore (\exists x)(Ax \cdot \sim Bx)$ (Sq,

1) and (1) $\sim(\exists x)(Ax \cdot \sim Bx)$ (2) $\therefore$ $(\exists x)(Ax \cdot Bx)$ (Sq, 1). This makes sense: "(1) It is false that some cats meow. (2) Therefore, some cats don't meow." Likewise, "(1) It is false that some cats don't meow. (2) Therefore, some cats meow." However, in actual fact they're both true: some cats meow and some don't. Notice that steps 1 and 2 *cannot* be reversed!

Seventh, viewing the top left to bottom left, we find that "All A are B" $\equiv (x)(Ax \rightarrow Bx)$ implies that "Some A are B" $\equiv (\exists x)(Ax \cdot Bx)$. In other words, $(x)(Ax \rightarrow Bx) \rightarrow (\exists x)(Ax \cdot Bx)$. Thus we can validly deduce from step 1 to step 2: (1) $(x)(Ax \rightarrow Bx)$ (2) $\therefore$ $(\exists x)(Ax \cdot Bx)$ (Sq, 1). This makes sense: "1. All cats breathe. 2. Therefore, some cats breathe." But steps 1 and 2 *cannot* be reversed! For example, we cannot validly reason, "1. Some television sets are black and white. 2. Therefore, all television sets are black and white." All of this is what it means for "Some A are B" to be a subaltern of "All A are B," as the latter implies the former but the former does not imply the latter.

Eighth, viewing the top right to bottom right, we find that "No A is B" $\equiv (x)(Ax \rightarrow \sim Bx)$ implies "Some A are not B" $\equiv (\exists x)(Ax \cdot \sim Bx)$. In other words, $(x)(Ax \rightarrow \sim Bx) \rightarrow (\exists x)(Ax \cdot \sim Bx)$. Thus we can validly deduce from step 1 to step 2: (1) $(x)(Ax \rightarrow \sim Bx)$ (2) $\therefore$ $(\exists x)(Ax \cdot \sim Bx)$ (Sq, 1). This makes sense: "1. No blade of grass has lungs. 2. Therefore, some blades of grass do not have lungs." But steps 1 and 2 *cannot* be reversed! For example, we cannot validly reason, "1. Some students are not athletes. 2. Therefore, no student is an athlete." All of this is what it means for "Some A are not B" to be a subaltern of "No A is B," as the latter implies the former but the former does not imply the latter.

Pre-Homework Practice!

Let's see if you can use Sq and if you understand how the logical relationships it embodies work. Try to answer the following questions on your own before looking at the answers beneath each one.

1. What is the contradictory of "All print books contain paper"?
    a. *Some print books don't contain paper.* To see this, follow the diagonal from the top left to bottom right.
2. What is the contradictory of "No print books contain paper"?
    a. *Some print books contain paper.* To see this, follow the diagonal from the top right to bottom left.
3. What is the contradictory of "Some print books contain paper"?

   a. *No print books contain paper.* To see this, follow the diagonal from the bottom left to top right.

4. What is the contradictory of "Some print books don't contain paper"?
   a. *All print books contain paper.* To see this, follow the diagonal from the bottom right to top left.

5. Is this a valid argument? Why or why not? (1) Some print books don't contain paper. (2) Therefore, no print books contain paper.
   a. *No. The steps are reversed.* (1) is a subaltern of (2), which means that (2) implies (1) but (1) does not imply (2).

6. Is this a valid argument? Why or why not? (1) It's false that no print books contain paper. (2) Therefore, all print books contain paper.
   a. *No. The steps are reversed.* (1) and (2) are contraries, which means that if one is true, the other is false. But if one is false, then we know nothing about the other.

Homework Assignment 9

1. What is the contradictory of "Some people aren't ultimately going to heaven"?
2. What is the contradictory of "Some people are ultimately going to heaven"?
3. What is the contradictory of "All people are ultimately going to heaven"?
4. What is the contradictory of "No person is ultimately going to heaven"?
5. Is this a valid argument? Why or why not? (1) It's false that some triangles aren't three-sided. (2) Therefore, some triangles are three-sided.
6. Is this a valid argument? Why or why not? (1) All rainbows are nice to look at. (2) Therefore, it's false that no rainbow is nice to look at.

10

Arguments and Their Parts

In logic, an argument does not mean two people getting angry with each other. Rather, an argument is a series of steps—pieces of evidence called *premises*—offered in support of a conclusion. The *conclusion* is the central point of an argument. It's what the argument is trying to persuade us of. Put another way, the conclusion is the statement that at least one other statement supports and that supports no other statement. Now an argument may have one or more subconclusions reached on the way to the conclusion. A *subconclusion* is a statement that at least one other statement supports and that supports at least one other statement. Moreover, an argument may be accompanied by *background information*. While this may put the argument in context, it is not part of the argument and must be separated from it.

Valid and Invalid Arguments

A *valid* argument is one where the conclusion follows inescapably from the premises. This means that if the premises are true (which they may or may not be), there is no way out of the conclusion. Let me issue a *very important* warning to prevent you from making mistakes when figuring out whether an argument is valid. When determining validity, *do not* concern yourself with the truth of the premises or the conclusion. Even if you know one or more premises or the conclusion is false, *it makes no difference!* The argument could still be valid. Validity *only* concerns the structure of the argument, namely, how well the argument is built. Iff it is built such that the conclusion follows inescapably from the premises, it is valid.

By contrast, an *invalid* argument is one where the conclusion does not follow inescapably from the premises. In other words, if the premises are true (which they may or may not be), there is at least one way out of the conclusion. Here we see a key contrast between valid and invalid arguments. Valid arguments are truth-preserving, where the condition of having all true premises guarantees the truth of the conclusion. On the other hand, invalid arguments are not truth-preserving, since the condition of having all true premises does not guarantee the truth of the conclusion.

Sound and Unsound Arguments

A *sound* argument is one which is *both* valid *and* where all the premises are true. Sound arguments are perfect arguments. They are *both* built well *and* accurate. In a sound argument, it's not just that there's no way out of the conclusion hypothetically (i.e., if the premises are true); rather, there's no way out of the conclusion in reality. Therefore, in a sound argument, the conclusion must be true. Obviously, a sound argument is a good argument. By contrast, an *unsound* argument is one which is invalid *or* contains at least one false premise *or* both. In an unsound argument, the conclusion may or may not be true. But not all unsound arguments are bad. However, if an unsound argument contains at least one false premise, it is bad.

So how could an unsound argument be good? This occurs when the conclusion follows highly probably (think ≥ 95 percent)—but not inescapably—from the premises, and it has all true premises. Key synonyms of "highly probably" include "almost all," "virtually all," "all but very few," "the vast majority of," and the like. Iff an argument is structured in such a way that the conclusion follows highly probably but not inescapably from the premises, it is *strong*. Just like validity, strength has *nothing to do* with the truth of the premises. It only concerns the way the argument is built. An argument that is *both* strong *and* has all true premises is called *cogent*. In such an argument, the conclusion is very probably true, but not inescapably true. A cogent argument is good, but not perfect like a sound argument is. However, any argument that is *both* unsound *and* uncogent is bad. Accordingly, any argument with a false premise is bad. This is a deal-breaker. Another deal-breaker is where the argument is structured in such a way that the conclusion does not even follow highly probably from the premises. An argument with this kind of structure is called *weak*. All weak arguments are bad, *even if* all the premises are true.

To sum up, there are two ways an argument could be good: it is sound, or it is cogent. There are three ways an argument could be bad: it is weak, it has at least one false premise, or it is both weak and has at least one false premise.

Practice!

Let's work on evaluating the structure *and only* the structure of some easy arguments (i.e., having no background information or subconclusions). Remember that there are three structure terms, where every argument is *exactly one* of these three: valid, strong, weak. Consider this argument: "All trees have leaves. There is a tree in my front yard. Therefore, it has leaves." This argument is valid, since if we assume that all trees really do have leaves and that there really is a tree in my front yard, there is no way out of the conclusion that this tree has leaves. Now consider this similar argument: "Almost all trees have leaves. There is a tree in my front yard. Therefore, it has leaves." Recall that "almost all" is a synonym of "highly probably." So if we assume that almost all trees really do have leaves and that there really is a tree in my front yard, it is highly probable, but not guaranteed, that this tree has leaves. Therefore, the argument is strong. But now consider another similar argument: "Most trees have leaves. There is a tree in my front yard. Therefore, it has leaves." "Most" simply means more than half, and we have no idea how much more. It could be just barely more than half. So for all we know, even if we assume that most trees really have leaves, there could well be, say, a 50.0000000001 percent probability that any given tree has leaves. Thus even if we assume that there really is a tree in my front yard, we are nowhere close to having at least 95 percent confidence that this tree has leaves. Consequently, the argument is weak.

Suppose my son Dwiane says to me, "You buy me food from McDonald's or Burger King. You don't buy me food from Burger King. Therefore, you buy me food from McDonald's." What should I make of this argument? Notice that if we assume that I really do buy him food from McDonald's or Burger King and that I really don't buy him food from Burger King, then it's a lock that I buy him food from McDonald's. Therefore Dwiane's argument is valid. But now suppose Dwiane slightly altered his argument to say, "You buy me food from McDonald's or Burger King. You buy me food from McDonald's. Therefore, you don't buy me food from Burger King." How does this argument fare? Suppose we grant that I buy him food from McDonald's or Burger King and that I buy him food from McDonald's. Does it follow at all from this that I don't buy him food from Burger King? No, because in logic the word "or" means "at least one"—it could be more than one! So Dwiane's premise that "You buy me food from McDonald's or Burger King" simply means that "You buy me food from at least one of the following: McDonald's, Burger King." I could well buy him food from both fast-food restaurants. So Dwiane's argument is weak: even if both premises are true, the conclusion doesn't follow. This is because the structure of Dwiane's argument violates the law of logic regarding the meaning of "or" in going from premises to conclusion. The moral of this story is that any argument whose structure violates one or more laws of logic is weak.

Imagine that I buy a lottery ticket but, realist as I am, remark, "It's 99.9 percent certain that I won't win the lottery. Therefore, I won't win the lottery." This argument is strong, since it is structured in such a way that there's at least a 95 percent certainty that I won't win the lottery. Now suppose someone quips quite pessimistically after a job interview, "It's 49.9 percent certain that I won't get the job. Therefore, I won't get the job." This argument is weak, since its structure permits nowhere close to 95 percent certainty that the person won't get the job. Suppose McPherson College's head football coach observes, "Not all students are athletes. Therefore, some students are not athletes." His observation is valid, since the conclusion follows from the premise by Sq. Indeed, going from the top left to the bottom right, we know that the "not," or contradictory, of "All students are athletes" is "Some students are not athletes." But now suppose he says, "Not all students are athletes. Therefore, no students are athletes." Seeing the Traditional Square of Opposition in your mind's eye, you find that "All students are athletes" and "No students are athletes" are contraries, such that knowing that the first is true allows you to infer that the second is false. However, knowing that the first is false does not allow you to infer that the second is true. This argument violates Sq and is therefore weak. Imagine now that the coach tries to revise his argument as follows: "Some students are athletes. Therefore, some students are not athletes." Has his argument improved? Well, unfortunately not. For we know from Sq that "Some students are athletes" and "Some students are not athletes" are subcontraries, such that knowing that the first is false allows you to infer that the second is true. But knowing that the first is true does not allow you to infer the second is true. Hence his revision violates Sq in a different way and is, accordingly, still weak.

But now suppose that I come along and state, "It is false that some students are athletes. Therefore, some students are not athletes." My argument is valid, as the conclusion follows from the premise by Sq. Let's turn to consider this argument: "If I were rich, then I would buy a yellow Lamborghini. Therefore, if I were to buy a yellow Lamborghini, then I would be rich." This argument commits the converse error, the error of thinking that $A \rightarrow B$ means $B \rightarrow A$. So it violates a law of logic and is therefore weak. Imagine that I drank four shots of apricot brandy and said, "All cats are dogs. Therefore, some cats are dogs." How should we evaluate this argument's structure? We must first remember that structure has nothing to do with whether the premise is true! Even if we know the premise is false (as we do here), we are evaluating the status of the conclusion if the premise were true. And indeed, if it were the case that all cats are dogs, it would follow from Sq that some cats are dogs, since the latter is a subaltern of the former. So my argument is valid! My intoxicated state has only rendered me unable to give a sound argument but has not affected my ability to craft a valid argument. And if I sober up and contend, "It's a lie that some students are not athletes. Therefore, all students are athletes," my argument is valid. For if it's a lie that some students are not athletes, then the contradictory of "Some students are not athletes" is true. So, moving from bottom right to top left in Sq, we find that this contradictory is indeed "All students are athletes."

Pre-Homework Practice!

Here the issue facing each of the following arguments is whether it is valid, strong, or weak. Test your understanding of these concepts before checking your answer below each argument.

1. There exists an evil angel. Therefore, all angels are evil.
   a. This is *weak*, as it violates Sq. For "There exists an evil angel" ≡ "Some angels are evil" is the subaltern of "All angels are evil." A subaltern does not imply the statement from which it is derived (i.e., of which it is a subaltern).

2. Whatever exists has a reason for being. I exist. Therefore, I have a reason for being.
    a. This is *valid*. For if we suppose that the two premises are true, then there's no way out of the conclusion.
3. Virtually all houses on Trinity Street are painted green. Therefore, the house at 724 Trinity Street is painted green.
    a. This is *strong*. "Virtually all"—a synonym of "highly probably"—means at least 95 percent. So from the premise, we can be at least 95 percent confident that the conclusion is true.
4. It's not the case that some traffic cones are not orange. Therefore, all traffic cones are orange.
    a. This is *valid*, as it obeys Sq. Moving in Sq from bottom right to top left, we see that the "not," or contradictory, of "Some traffic cones are not orange" is "All traffic cones are orange."
5. It's very probable that if one's doctor says one doesn't have cancer, one doesn't have cancer. My doctor says I don't have cancer. Therefore, I don't have cancer.
    a. This is *strong*, as "very probable" means at least 95 percent. So if we assume that both premises are accurate, we can be at least 95 percent confident of the conclusion.

Homework Assignment 10

For each of the following arguments, is it valid, strong, or weak?

1. Either I'm going to the store or I won't have anything to drink. I'm not going to the store. Therefore, I won't have anything to drink.
2. If reciprocity is a virtue, then I'm a good person. Therefore, if I'm a good person, reciprocity is a virtue.
3. Only some shoes are yellow. Therefore, some shoes are not yellow.
4. The vast majority of non-smokers don't get lung cancer. I don't smoke. Therefore, I won't get lung cancer.
5. Virtually all professional historians agree that Lincoln was assassinated. So if I'm a professional historian, I believe Lincoln was assassinated.
6. Some hamsters don't like strawberry jam. So no hamsters like strawberry jam.

11

Modus Ponens and *Modus Tollens*

The most powerful application of logic is demonstrating the validity or invalidity of arguments. Accordingly, a *proof* in logic proves that an argument is valid. If you have a valid argument, then you'll need to use other skills to prove whether the premises are true, thereby making the argument sound. In other words, if you can logically prove something, you can say, "OK, the argument is built as well as it can be. Now are the premises true?" Several laws of logic help us in spotting valid arguments right away. These laws need to be memorized. Moreover, knowing structural fallacies people often confuse for these laws helps us in spotting weak arguments right away. These fallacies need to be memorized.

Modus Ponens

The four laws of logic we will examine in this chapter are forms, or argument patterns. Any argument that possesses one of these forms is valid. The first law is *modus ponens (MP)*, Latin for "the way of affirming." *Modus ponens* arguments take the following structure, where the letters A and B are arbitrary (and so could be replaced by any other letters):

1. $A \rightarrow B$	1. If I'm in my basement, then I'm enjoying myself.
2. A	2. I'm in my basement.
3. $\therefore$ B	3. Therefore, I'm enjoying myself.

You can plug in anything for A and B that you like (true or false); the argument will be valid. The three steps do not need to appear in this order. An argument that contains these steps in any order is proven valid by MP. Here we will call attention to a neat trick alluded to in chapter one which is quite helpful in identifying valid arguments: treating a negation as a simple proposition. In other words, A and/or B can be negative statements! If so, you just have to remember that ~A and/or ~B are positive statements. So the following argument is valid by MP: (1) If I don't have a headache, then I have a toothache (A → B, where A ≡ "I don't have a headache"); (2) I don't have a headache (A); (3) Therefore, I have a toothache (∴ B).

People often confuse for *modus ponens* a fallacy that resembles it but goes wrong in its second step. This fallacy is called *affirming the consequent*. The name comes from the fact that, instead of correctly affirming step 1's if-clause (antecedent) in step 2, step 2 incorrectly affirms step 1's then-clause (consequent). The fallacy proceeds in step 3 (the conclusion) to wrongfully infer step 1's antecedent instead of its consequent. Affirming the consequent is weak and therefore both invalid and bad; *don't do this*! Again, the letters A and B are arbitrary.

1. A → B	1. If I'm in my basement, then I'm enjoying myself.
2. B	2. I'm enjoying myself.
3. ∴ A	3. Therefore, I'm in my basement.

Any argument that contains these steps in any order is proven to be a bad argument. Using the neat trick described above, we observe that the following argument affirms the consequent and is therefore bad: (1) If I don't have a headache, then I have a toothache (A → B); (2) I have a toothache (B); (3) Therefore, I don't have a headache (∴ A). Like the converse error (i.e., weakly and thus invalidly and badly reasoning (1) A → B (2) ∴ B → A), affirming the consequent confuses a necessary condition for a sufficient condition.

Universal *Modus Ponens*

The second law depicting a valid form is *universal modus ponens (UMP)*, the quantified version of *modus ponens* that applies this reasoning pattern to universal affirmative statements (i.e., "All A are B" statements). Universal *modus ponens* arguments take the following structure, where the letters A, B, and c are arbitrary (and so could be replaced by any other letters):

1. $(x)(Ax \rightarrow Bx)$	1. All even numbers are pleasant to me.
2. Ac	2. 6 is an even number.
3. ∴ Bc	3. Therefore, 6 is pleasant to me.

You can plug in anything for A_, B_, and c that you like (true or false); the argument will be valid.[1] Again, the three steps do not need to appear in this order. An argument that contains these steps in any order is proven valid by UMP. A quantified version of our neat trick allows A_ and/or B_ to be negative predicates. If so, you just have to remember that ~A_ and/or ~B_ are positive predicates. So the following argument—though crazy—is valid by UMP: (1) All non-shoes are healthy ($(x)(Ax \rightarrow Bx)$, where A_ ≡ "_ is not a shoe"); (2) Great Value Diet Root Beer is not a shoe (Ac, where c ≡ "Great Value Diet Root Beer"); (3) Therefore, Great Value Diet Root Beer is healthy (∴ Bc).

A related fallacy to avoid is *universal affirming the consequent*, the quantified version of affirming the consequent. Universal affirming the consequent is weak and therefore both invalid and bad; *don't do this!*

1. $(x)(Ax \rightarrow Bx)$	1. All even numbers are pleasant to me.
2. Bc	2. My blue hair dryer is pleasant to me.
3. ∴ Ac	3. Therefore, my blue hair dryer is an even number.[2]

Employing the quantified version of our neat trick, we find that the following argument universally affirms the consequent and is therefore bad: (1) All odd numbers are not pleasant to me ($(x)(Ax \rightarrow Bx)$, where B_ ≡ "_ is not pleasant to me"); (2) Rain is not pleasant to me (Bc, where c ≡ "rain"); (3) Therefore, rain is an odd number (∴ Ac). Like its namesake, universal affirming the consequent confuses a necessary condition for a sufficient condition. It commits the same confusion as the *universal converse error*, which weakly and thus invalidly and badly reasons (1) $(x)(Ax \rightarrow Bx)$ (2) ∴ $(x)(Bx \rightarrow Ax)$.

1. Epp, *Discrete Mathematics*, 100.
2. Epp, *Discrete Mathematics*, 104.

Modus Tollens

The third law depicting a valid form is *modus tollens (MT)*, Latin for "the way of denying." *Modus tollens* arguments take the following structure, where the letters A and B are arbitrary (and so could be replaced by any other letters):

1. A → B	1. If I'm in my basement, then I'm enjoying myself.
2. ~B	2. I'm not enjoying myself.
3. ∴ ~A	3. Therefore, I'm not in my basement.

You can plug in anything for A and B that you like (true or false); the argument will be valid. The three steps do not need to appear in this order. An argument that contains these steps in any order is proven valid by MT. Using our neat trick, we observe that this argument is valid by MT: (1) If I'm reading Nietzsche's *Beyond Good and Evil*, then I'm not happy (A → B, where B ≡ "I'm not happy"); (2) I'm happy (~B ≡ Not "I'm not happy," which by DN is just the positive statement "I'm happy"); (3) Therefore, I'm not reading Nietzsche's *Beyond Good and Evil* (~A).

People often confuse for *modus tollens* a fallacy that resembles it but goes wrong in its second step. This fallacy is called *denying the antecedent*. The name comes from the fact that, instead of correctly denying step 1's then-clause (consequent) in step 2, step 2 incorrectly denies step 1's if-clause (antecedent). The fallacy proceeds in step 3 (the conclusion) to wrongfully infer step 1's negated consequent instead of its negated antecedent. Denying the antecedent is weak and therefore both invalid and bad; *don't do this!* Again, the letters A and B are arbitrary.

1. A → B	1. If I'm in my basement, then I'm enjoying myself.
2. ~A	2. I'm not in my basement.
3. ∴ ~B	3. Therefore, I'm not enjoying myself.

Our neat trick shows us that this argument also denies the antecedent and is therefore bad: (1) If Sally hasn't read the first volume of Craig's *Systematic Philosophical Theology*, then she's not a philosopher (A → B, where A ≡ "Sally hasn't read the first volume of Craig's *Systematic Philosophical Theology*" and B ≡ "Sally is not a philosopher"); (2) Sally has read the first volume of Craig's *Systematic Philosophical Theology* (~A ≡ Not "Sally hasn't read the first volume of Craig's *Systematic Philosophical*

Theology" ≡ "Sally has read the first volume of Craig's *Systematic Philosophical Theology*" by DN); (3) Therefore, Sally is a philosopher (~B ≡ Not "Sally is not a philosopher" ≡ "Sally is a philosopher" by DN). Denying the antecedent confuses a sufficient condition for a necessary condition. It commits the same confusion as the *inverse error*, which weakly and thus badly reasons (1) A → B (2) ∴ ~A → ~B.

Universal *Modus Tollens*

The fourth law depicting a valid form is *universal modus tollens (UMT)*, the quantified version of *modus tollens* that applies this reasoning pattern to universal affirmative statements. Universal *modus tollens* arguments take the following structure, where the letters A, B, and c are arbitrary:

1. (*x*)(A*x* → B*x*)	1. All even numbers are pleasant to me.
2. ~Bc	2. Getting sunburned is not pleasant to me.
3. ∴ ~Ac	3. Therefore, getting sunburned is not an even number.

You can plug in anything for A_, B_, and c that you like (true or false); the argument will be valid.[3] The three steps do not need to appear in this order. An argument that contains these steps in any order is proven valid by UMT. Using the quantified version of our neat trick, we observe that this argument is valid by UMT: (1) All non-plants are not leafy ((*x*)(A*x* → B*x*), where A_ ≡ "_ is not a plant" and B_ ≡ "_ is not leafy"); (2) My birch tree is leafy (~Bc, where ~B_ ≡ Not "_ is not leafy" ≡ "_ is leafy" by DN and c ≡ "my birch tree"); (3) My birch tree is a plant (~Ac, where ~A_ ≡ Not "_ is not a plant" ≡ "_ is a plant" by DN).

A related fallacy to avoid is *universal denying the antecedent*, the quantified form of denying the antecedent. Universal denying the antecedent is weak and therefore both invalid and bad; *don't do this!* Here again, the letters A, B, and c are arbitrary.

1. (*x*)(A*x* → B*x*)	1. All even numbers are pleasant to me.
2. ~Ac	2. My blue hair dryer is not an even number.
3. ∴ ~Bc	3. Therefore, my blue hair dryer is not pleasant to me.[4]

3. Epp, *Discrete Mathematics*, 102.
4. Epp, *Discrete Mathematics*, 107.

The quantified version of our neat trick shows that the following argument universally denies the antecedent and is therefore bad: (1) All non-sacred music is unspiritual ($(x)(Ax \rightarrow Bx)$, where A_ ≡ "_ is not sacred music" and B_ ≡ "_ is unspiritual"); (2) *Warrior* is sacred music (~Ac, where ~A ≡ Not "_ is not sacred music" ≡ "_ is sacred music" by DN and c ≡ "*Warrior*"); (3) Therefore, *Warrior* is spiritual (~Bc, where ~B ≡ Not "_ is unspiritual" ≡ "_ is spiritual" by DN). Like its namesake, universal denying the antecedent confuses a sufficient condition for a necessary condition. It commits the same confusion as the *universal inverse error*, which weakly and thus badly reasons (1) $(x)(Ax \rightarrow Bx)$ (2) $\therefore$ $(x)(\sim Ax \rightarrow \sim Bx)$.

Getting Rid of Background Information and Reordering Steps

Two of the most vital skills in effectively symbolizing arguments are getting rid of any background information that may accompany the argument and reordering the steps of the argument in logical sequence if the steps are not already in logical sequence. Since background information is not part of an argument, it is *not* symbolized and must be disregarded as logically irrelevant. The best way of spotting background information and discerning the logical sequence of an argument is through your knowledge of the logical laws depicting valid forms and your knowledge of the related fallacies. Background information will neither fit into a valid form nor fit into a related fallacy. Moreover, the valid forms show you the proper sequence of an argument. Fallacies expose improper sequences that arguments often take. But in either case, your prior knowledge will enable you to discern the sequence of an argument.

Moreover, knowing indicator words is often very helpful in determining an argument's structure. Note well that an argument does not need to contain any indicator words. In every argument, the conclusion is the main point, namely, the one position that's being argued for and that does not serve as support for any other position. The premises are the pieces of evidence in support of the conclusion. If there is a subconclusion (and there can be more than one), it will be a deduction from various premises that serves as evidence in support of the conclusion. With that said, indicator words quickly clue you in on the role a statement in an argument plays. Indicator words for premises encompass "since" and its synonyms, i.e., "because," "for," "after all," "it follows from," "for example," "to illustrate," and so forth. In any sentence that goes "[Clause 1], since [Clause 2]" or "Since [Clause 2], [Clause 1]," [Clause 2] is always a premise and [Clause 1] is either the conclusion or a subconclusion. The same is true with consecutive sentences: "[Clause 1]. For/after all/ to illustrate/etc. [Clause 2]." Indicator words for either a conclusion or a subconclusion encompass "therefore" and its synonyms, i.e., "thus," "hence," "for this reason," "it follows that," "that proves," "accordingly," "consequently," "as a result," "it stands to reason that," and so forth. Let's take four of the valid arguments already discussed in this chapter and see what they could look like when they contain background information and have their steps differently arranged.

Consider argument 1: "Studies have shown that people tend to enjoy their basements. I'm in my basement. The carpet is so comfortable! And I'm enjoying myself, for if I'm in my basement, then I'm enjoying myself. I'm glad my basement is properly insulated." The sentence "And I'm enjoying myself, *for* if I'm in my basement, then I'm enjoying myself" is, from the logician's perspective, pure gold. The indicator word "for" tells you that what follows it, "I'm in my basement, then I'm enjoying myself," is a premise and that what precedes it, "I'm enjoying myself," is either a conclusion or a subconclusion. Since "I'm enjoying myself" doesn't support any further conclusion, it is the conclusion. So now we've identified a premise and a conclusion. Using our knowledge of MP, we can see that "I'm in my basement," the second sentence, is the missing premise which completes the argument. Accordingly, argument 1 is nothing more than a dressed-up version of the following properly logically sequenced argument: "(1) If I'm in my *b*asement, then I'm *e*njoying myself. (2) I'm in my basement. (3) Therefore, I'm enjoying myself," namely, (1) B → E; (2) B; (3) ∴ E. Again, this is MP and therefore valid. All the other sentences in argument 1—"Studies have shown that people tend to enjoy their basements"; "The carpet is so comfortable"; "I'm glad my basement is properly insulated"—are background information and so must be disregarded. We know they constitute background information because they do not fit into any valid form (or into any fallacy).

Consider argument 2: "I've always enjoyed the philosophy of mathematics and the various abstract objects comprising the mathematical domain. Indeed, all even numbers are pleasant to me. Hence 6 is pleasant to me. After all, 6 is an even number. Heck, I also like all odd numbers!" Here we see two indicator words: "hence" and "after all." The "hence" tells us that "6 is pleasant to me" is the conclusion (as it doesn't support any further conclusion), and the "after all" tells us that "6 is an even number" is a premise. Given our knowledge of the various forms, is there any other premise in this argument that, if considered alongside the conclusion and the identified premise, would give us a valid argument? Indeed there is: "All even numbers are pleasant to me." This is the missing, and first, premise in UMP. As a result, argument 2 simply goes as follows when arranged in proper logical sequence: "(1) All *e*ven numbers are *p*leasant to me; (2) *6* is an even number; (3) Therefore, 6 is pleasant to me," namely, (1) $(x)(Ex \rightarrow Px)$; (2) Es (s ≡ "six"); (3) ∴ Ps. Again, this is UMP and therefore valid. The remaining sentences in argument 2—"I've always enjoyed the philosophy of mathematics and the various abstract objects comprising the mathematical domain" and "Heck, I also like all odd numbers"—are pieces of irrelevant background information which do not fit into any valid form (or into any fallacy).

Consider argument 3, a modification of argument 1: "Studies have shown that people tend to enjoy their basements. Sadly, I'm not enjoying myself. However, the carpet in my basement is so comfortable! But I'm not in my basement, for if I'm in my basement, then I'm enjoying myself. I'm glad my basement is properly insulated." The key word in the fourth sentence is again "for." What comes after it, "If I'm in my basement, then I'm enjoying myself," is a premise, and what comes before it, "I'm not in my basement," is the conclusion. Using our knowledge of MT, the missing premise we need in order to get from the already identified premise to the conclusion is "I'm not enjoying myself." Consequently, argument 3 reads like this when arranged in proper logical sequence: "(1) If I'm in my *b*asement, then I'm *e*njoying myself; (2) I'm not enjoying myself; (3) Therefore, I'm not in my basement," namely, (1) B → E; (2) ~E; (3) ∴ ~B. Again, this is MT and therefore valid. As with argument 1, everything else stated above is background information that must be disregarded.

Finally, consider argument 4, a modification of argument 2: "I've always enjoyed the philosophy of mathematics and the various abstract objects comprising the mathematical domain. Indeed, all even numbers are pleasant to me. Hence getting sunburned is not an even number. After all, getting sunburned is not pleasant to me. Heck, I also like all odd numbers!" The word "hence" in the third sentence signals the conclusion, and the term "after all" in the fourth sentence signals a premise. As exposed by UMT, the only premise that would make this a valid argument is the second sentence, "All even numbers are pleasant to me." When arranged in proper logical sequence, argument 4 is nothing more than this: "(1) All *e*ven numbers are *p*leasant to me; (2) *G*etting sunburned is not pleasant to me; (3) Therefore, getting sunburned is not an even number," namely, (1) (*x*)(E*x* → P*x*); (2) ~Pg; (3) ∴ ~Eg. By UMT, this argument is valid. As with argument 2, the remaining sentences are background information to be ignored.

Pre-Homework Practice!

Try to symbolize each of these arguments (remember the neat trick!). Looking at your symbolization, is the argument valid or weak (and therefore bad), and why? Keep in mind that any MP, UMP, MT, or UMT argument is valid (as it follows a law of logic), and any argument that affirms the consequent, universally affirms the consequent, denies the antecedent, or universally denies the antecedent is weak and hence bad (as it violates a law of logic). Try to figure out the answer on your own before looking at the solution below each argument.

1. If I am getting cool in front of my fan, I don't have the air conditioner on. I have the air conditioner on. Therefore, I'm not getting cool in front of my fan.
   a. (1) C → D (C ≡ "I am getting cool in front of my fan" and D ≡ "I don't have the air conditioner on"); (2) ~D (≡ "I have the air conditioner on"; use DN in your mind's eye to see this); (3) ∴ ~C. *Valid. MT.*
2. Every single guinea pig has false beliefs. Dale is a guinea pig. Therefore, Dale has false beliefs.
   a. (1) (*x*)(G*x* → F*x*) (G_ ≡ "_ is a guinea pig" and F_ ≡ "_ is a haver of false beliefs"); (2) Gd (d ≡ "Dale"); (3) ∴ Fd. *Valid. UMP.*
3. Only readable books are books that make Doug smile. The *Institutes of the Christian Religion* is a readable book. So the *Institutes of the Christian Religion* is a book that makes Doug smile.
   a. (1) (*x*)(S*x* → R*x*) (S_ ≡ "_ is a book that makes Doug smile" and R_ ≡ "_ is a readable book"; remember that "only" means "then," making the other clause the if-clause); (2) Ri (i ≡ "the *Institutes of the Christian Religion*"); (3) ∴ Si. *Weak and therefore bad. Universal affirming the consequent.*
4. Jesus' parable of the mustard seed makes sense if the mustard seed is not a weed. The mustard seed is a weed. Therefore, Jesus' parable of the mustard seed doesn't make sense.

a. (1) N → S (N ≡ "The mustard seed is not a weed" and S ≡ "Jesus' parable of the mustard seed makes sense"); (2) ~N (≡ "The mustard seed is a weed"; use DN in your mind's eye to see this); (3) ∴ ~S. *Weak and therefore bad. Denying the antecedent.*

5. Provided that Kate gets time off, Kate takes a vacation. Kate gets time off. So Kate takes a vacation.

   a. (1) T → V (T ≡ "Kate gets time off" and V ≡ "Kate takes a vacation"); (2) T; (3) ∴ V. *Valid. MP.*

6. Paintings by Rembrandt are beautiful. The painting on the wall is not beautiful. Therefore, the painting on the wall is not by Rembrandt.

   a. (1) (*x*)(R*x* → B*x*) (R_ ≡ "_ is a painting by Rembrandt" and B_ ≡ "_ is beautiful"); (2) ~Bw (w ≡ "the painting on the wall"); (3) ∴ ~Rw. *Valid. UMT.*

Homework Assignment 11

Symbolize each argument. Is it valid or weak (and therefore bad)? Why?

> *(WARNING: Each problem contains background information, which is not part of the argument and must be disregarded; accordingly, background information is not symbolized. Use your knowledge of the logical laws depicting valid forms and of the related fallacies to determine what is, and is not, background information. Background information will neither fit into a valid form nor fit into a related fallacy. Moreover, the steps of each argument do not necessarily appear in order. You may need to reorder the steps to make them fit a valid form or a related fallacy.)*

1. Is it better for God to love everyone or to love only good people? According to some Muslims, it's better for God not to love people like Adolf Hitler. If the Quran literally states, "God loves the evildoers," then snow is not white. Clearly the Quran doesn't literally state, "God loves the evildoers," for snow is white. And thundersnow is freaking awesome!

2. That it's terrible to be body-slammed on brass tacks stands to reason. I've seen the bloody impact this makes on pro wrestlers. Brass tacks are so sharp! Indeed, pro wrestling is very dangerous. And

if it's terrible to be body-slammed on brass tacks, pro wrestling is very dangerous.

3. Each witness who testified at the trial lied under oath. Sadly, this led to an innocent man getting a life sentence. But Lara didn't testify at the trial! So Lara didn't lie under oath. This makes sense in light of Lara's virtuous character.
4. Everyone who shoots an associate of the Corleone family in the head just to watch him die works for Barzini. We all know that Francisco works for Barzini. After all, Francisco shot an associate of the Corleone family in the head just to watch him die. We've already seen that Francisco is a despicable scumbag. Maybe Michael Corleone will seek retribution for the shooting.

12

Disjunctive Syllogism and Hypothetical Syllogism

In this chapter we will be learning four more laws of logic that depict valid forms. Any argument that observes one of these laws is valid. Like the previous logical laws found in this book, it is very important to memorize the laws presented in this chapter. When evaluating passages, knowledge of these laws will be vital in separating background information from the arguments contained in these passages and, if necessary, in reordering the steps of the arguments when you symbolize them.

Disjunctive Syllogism

Disjunctive syllogism (DS) is a law of logic displaying a valid form ("syllogism" just means "valid form"). It is a process of elimination. The name "disjunctive" comes from the term "disjunction," which refers to an "or" statement. Recall that a disjunct is a simple proposition in an "or" statement. Hence, in A ∨ B, the statement as a whole is a disjunction, A is a disjunct, and B is a disjunct. So a disjunctive syllogism will contain an "or" statement—a disjunction—as its first premise and then proceed by using the meaning of the term "or." Accordingly, disjunctive syllogisms take the following structure, where the letters A and B are arbitrary.

1. $A \vee B$	1. $A \vee B$	1. Bob will eat at McDonald's or Arby's.
2. $\sim A$	2. $\sim B$	2. Bob won't eat at McDonald's.
3. $\therefore B$	3. $\therefore A$	3. Therefore, Bob will eat at Arby's.

You can plug in anything for A and B that you like (true or false); the argument will be valid. The steps do not need to appear in this order. An argument that contains these steps in any order is proven valid by DS. Importantly, we can make the disjunction (the series of "or"s in premise 1 as long as we want (i.e., $A \vee B \vee C \vee D \vee \ldots$). As long as we eliminate some option or options in the ensuing premises (however many there are), DS allows us to conclude the remaining option or disjunction (i.e., or-statement) of options. In other words, DS allows us to say, "Bob will eat at McDonald's or Arby's or Burger King. Bob won't eat at McDonald's. Therefore, Bob will eat at Arby's or Burger King."

As we saw in the last chapter, many valid forms are often mistaken for fallacies that look like these forms. For DS, the associated fallacy is *confusing inclusive or for exclusive or*. For example, we can't reason, (1) $A \vee B$; (2) A; (3) $\therefore \sim B$, because $\vee$ means "at least one of." It could be both! Likewise, we can't reason, (1) $A \vee B$; (2) B; (3) $\therefore \sim A$. Any argument that confuses inclusive or for exclusive for is weak and therefore both invalid and bad.

Domain Disjunctive Syllogism

Another law of logic displaying a valid form is *domain disjunctive syllogism (DDS)*. Domain disjunctive syllogism is the quantified form of disjunctive syllogism. Here we will restrict x to anything in a particular domain (set of things). We write, let $x \in D$.[1] Then:

1. $(x)(Ax \vee Bx)$	1. $(x)(Ax \vee Bx)$	1. Everyone on the bus will eat at McDonald's or Arby's.
2. $\sim Ac$	2. $\sim Bc$	2. The bus driver won't eat at McDonald's.
3. $\therefore Bc$	3. $\therefore Ac$	3. Therefore, the bus driver will eat at Arby's.

The letters A, B, and c are arbitrary. You can plug in anything for A_, B_, and c that you like (true or false); the argument will be valid. Indeed,

1. $\in$ means "be a member of," and *D* stands for "domain."

the steps do not need to appear in this order. An argument that contains these steps in any order is proven valid by DDS. DDS works in the same way as the regular disjunctive syllogism. Consequently, we can make the disjunction (premise 1) as long as we want (i.e., $(x)(\mathrm{A}x \lor \mathrm{B}x \lor \mathrm{C}x \lor \mathrm{D}x \lor \ldots)$). As long as we eliminate some option or options in the ensuing premises (however many there are), DDS allows us to conclude the remaining option or disjunction (i.e., or-statement) of options. In other words, DDS allows us to say, "Everyone on the bus will eat at McDonald's or Arby's or Burger King. The bus driver won't eat at McDonald's. Therefore, the bus driver will eat at Arby's or Burger King."

The related fallacy to avoid when dealing with quantified disjunctions is again confusing inclusive or for exclusive or. For example, we can't reason, let $x \in D$; (1) $(x)(\mathrm{A}x \lor \mathrm{B}x)$; (2) Ac; (3) $\therefore$ ~Bc, because the bus driver might get something from McDonald's and then get something from Arby's!

Recognizing a DDS argument or a quantified argument that confuses inclusive or for exclusive or depends on our letting x = anything in a particular domain (set) in our mind's eye and then symbolizing the argument. Let's test your understanding by symbolizing the following argument to determine its validity: "All *m*usicians in the orchestra *p*ractice hard or have *n*atural talent. The principal *t*rumpet player in the orchestra practices hard. Hence, the principal trumpet player in the orchestra doesn't have natural talent." Our symbolization looks like this: Let $x \in M$; (1) $(x)(\mathrm{P}x \lor \mathrm{N}x)$; (2) Pt; (3) $\therefore$ ~Nt. This argument is weak and therefore bad, as it commits the fallacy of confusing inclusive or for exclusive or.

Hypothetical Syllogism

The next logical law depicting a valid form is *hypothetical syllogism (HS)*, all of whose steps (premises and conclusion) are hypothetical—namely, conditional—statements, i.e., "if-then" statements. While we are used to a premise being a conditional statement, this is the first form we've encountered where the conclusion is also a conditional statement. A hypothetical syllogism takes the following structure, where the letters A, B, and C are arbitrary:

1. $A \rightarrow B$	1. If Kirk plays cornhole, then Lara sews.
2. $B \rightarrow C$	2. If Lara sews, then Dwiane rides his bike.
3. $\therefore A \rightarrow C$	3. Therefore, if Kirk plays cornhole, then Dwiane rides his bike.

You can plug in anything for A, B, and C that you like (true or false); the argument will be valid. The steps do not need to appear in this order. An argument that contains these steps in any order is proven valid by HS. The logician Richard Epstein helpfully calls HS "reasoning in a chain."[2] Keeping with Epstein's analogy, we will define a *link in the chain* as a proposition that occurs as the consequent of one if-then statement and the antecedent of another if-then statement. So B is the link in the chain. The *start of the chain* is the proposition that only occurs as the antecedent of one if-then statement which has a link in the then-clause. The *end of the chain* is the proposition that only occurs as the consequent of one if-then statement which has a link in the if-clause. We can have as many links in the chain as we like. HS allows us to conclude that if the start of the chain, then the end of the chain.

Accordingly, this argument is valid by HS: "If I *p*et Guido, then *A*gi hisses. If *A*gi hisses, then I *r*ead *The Paul Quest*. If I *r*ead *The Paul Quest*, then I *w*onder if justification is primarily an ecclesiological doctrine. If I *w*onder if justification is primarily an ecclesiological doctrine, then I *g*ive a lecture on justification. Therefore, if I *p*et Guido, then I *g*ive a lecture on justification." We would symbolize this argument as follows: (1) $P \rightarrow A$; (2) $A \rightarrow R$; (3) $R \rightarrow W$; (4) $W \rightarrow G$; (5) $\therefore P \rightarrow G$. Notice how A, R, and W are links in the chain: A is the consequent of (1) and the antecedent of (2); R is the consequent of (2) and the antecedent of (3); W is the consequent of (3) and the antecedent of (4). P is the start of the chain, since it only occurs as the antecedent of (1) and its related then-clause, A, is a link in the chain. G is the end of the chain, as it only occurs as the consequent of (4) and its related if-clause, W, is a link in the chain. Because (1) through (4) are interlocked together as a chain through the aforementioned three links, HS allows us to validly conclude in (5) that if P (the start of the chain), then G (the end of the chain).

2. Epstein, *Critical Thinking*, 153.

Universal Hypothetical Syllogism

The logical law enunciating a valid quantified form of hypothetical syllogism is *universal hypothetical syllogism (UHS)*. Employing the arbitrary letters A, B, and C, the form runs as follows:

1. $(x)(Ax \rightarrow Bx)$	1. All cornhole players are sewers.
2. $(x)(Bx \rightarrow Cx)$	2. All sewers are bike-riders.
3. $\therefore (x)(Ax \rightarrow Cx)$	3. Therefore, all cornhole players are bike-riders.

You can plug in anything for A_, B_, and C_ that you like (true or false); the argument will be valid. The steps do not need to appear in this order. An argument that contains these steps in any order is proven valid by UHS. Epstein calls this form "reasoning in a chain with all."[3] It works in the same way as HS. Here the link in the chain is B*x*, as it occurs as the consequent of premise 1 and the antecedent of premise 2.

Let's try to find and symbolize the argument in the following selection (which contains background information) to determine validity: "Trumpet virtuosi have long disagreed about the best way to play altissimo. Every *a*ltissimo player has their own *m*ethod. And everyone who has their own *m*ethod *l*ikes their method. It stands to reason that every *a*ltissimo player *l*ikes their own method." The phrase "it stands to reason" in the last sentence is a synonym of "therefore" and signals the conclusion. The fact that the conclusion is an "every," i.e., "all" (universal affirmative), statement should automatically make you think you may be looking at a universal hypothetical syllogism. This impression is borne out by the second and third sentences, which are also "every(one)," i.e., "all" (universal affirmative), statements. The second and third sentences are the two premises, where "having their own method" is the link in the chain. The first sentence is background information and not part of the argument. The argument goes: (1) $(x)(Ax \rightarrow Mx)$; (2) $(x)(Mx \rightarrow Lx)$; (3) $\therefore (x)(Ax \rightarrow Lx)$, which is UHS and therefore valid.

In English, premises and conclusion do not have to occur in logical order. With that in mind, consider this example: "The date of the book of Jonah's composition is a fascinating topic in biblical studies. Pastor Fred thinks Jonah was written in 730 BCE or 721 BCE. Many scholars think the issue will never be definitively settled. But Pastor Fred thinks Jonah

3. Epstein, *Critical Thinking*, 178.

was written in 721 BCE, since he doesn't think 730 BCE makes good sense." The first and the third sentences are background information and so can be disregarded. Hopefully you can spot the argument: (1) E ∨ L (E ≡ Pastor Fred thinks Jonah was written in the earlier date of 730 BCE; L ≡ Pastor Fred thinks Jonah was written in the later date of 721 BCE); (2) ~L (the clause that follows "since" in the last sentence); (3) ∴ E (the first clause of the last sentence). This argument is valid by DS.

Pre-Homework Practice!

Try to symbolize each of these arguments. Looking at your symbolization, is the argument valid or weak (and therefore bad), and why? Keep in mind that any DS, DDS, HS, or UHS argument is valid (as it follows a law of logic), and any argument that confuses inclusive or for exclusive or is weak and hence bad (as it violates a law of logic). Try to figure out the answer on your own before looking at the solution below each argument.

1. I like buying ice cream at Dillon's. I'll buy triple brownie ice cream on the condition that I go to Dillon's today. Triple brownie ice cream tastes so good! Only if I'll eat it as soon as I get home will I go to Dillon's today. For if I buy triple brownie ice cream, I'll eat it as soon as I get home.
    a. (1) D → T (second sentence, where D ≡ "I go to Dillon's today" and T ≡ "I'll buy triple brownie ice cream"); (2) T → E (last sentence, where E ≡ "I'll eat triple brownie ice cream as soon as I get home"); (3) ∴ D → E (third sentence). *Valid. HS.*
2. Every cat is either an inbred dog or a globe. My cat Paddy Paws is a globe. That proves it: My cat Paddy Paws is not an inbred dog!
    a. Let *x* ϵ *C* (C ≡ cats); (1) (*x*)(I*x* ∨ G*x*) (I_ ≡ "_ is an inbred dog" and G_ ≡ "_ is a globe"); (2) Gp (p ≡ Paddy Paws); (3) ∴ ~Ip. *Weak and therefore bad. Confusing inclusive or for exclusive or.*
3. Lifting weights regularly is healthy for you. Now we all know that Taylor Swift likes Swifties. All weight lifters are either Swifties or health fanatics. World champion weight lifter Lex is no health fanatic. It follows that Lex is a Swiftie!
    a. Let *x* ϵ *W* (*W* ≡ weight lifters); (1) (*x*)(S*x* ∨ F*x*) (S_ ≡ "_ is a Swiftie" and F_ ≡ "_ is a health fanatic"); (2) ~Fl (l ≡ Lex); (3) ∴ Sl. *Valid. DDS.*

4. I just got home from the football game with Chad. Boy, Chad's team stunk! Every football player on Chad's team is stupid. So all football players on Chad's team are made out of concrete. After all, only bricks are stupid. And bricks are made out of concrete.

   a. (1) $(x)(Fx \rightarrow Sx)$ (F_ ≡ "_ is a football player on Chad's team" and S_ ≡ "_ is stupid"); (2) $(x)(Sx \rightarrow Bx)$ (B_ ≡ "_ is a brick"); (3) $(x)(Bx \rightarrow Cx)$ (C_ ≡ "_ is made out of concrete"); (4) ∴ $(x)(Fx \rightarrow Cx)$. *Valid. UHS.*

Homework Assignment 12

Symbolize each argument. Is it valid or weak (and therefore bad)? Why?

1. I am not driving to Lindsborg without my music. I'm performing at a gig in Lindsborg. I'll play *Lean on Me* at the gig on the condition that I have my music. *Lean on Me* is a great Bill Withers song. Accordingly, if I drive to Lindsborg, I'll play *Lean on Me* at the gig. In any case, the jazz band will be grooving.
2. Eddie Murphy movies are so funny! Eddie Murphy starred in either *Beverly Hills Cop* or *Dirty Rotten Scoundrels*. Whichever one it is, I'm looking forward to watching both movies. But it's false that Eddie Murphy starred in *Dirty Rotten Scoundrels*. Nevertheless, the twist at the end of that movie is hilarious. So Eddie Murphy starred in *Beverly Hills Cop*.
3. Ever since its condemnation by the Christian church in the fourth century CE, Arianism has continued to rear its ugly head at various points throughout church history. Everyone who holds that Jesus is Michael the Archangel maintains that Jesus died exclusively for Adam's sin. That notion is patently unbiblical. Only people who hold that Jesus is Michael the Archangel are Jehovah's Witnesses. So all Jehovah's Witnesses maintain that Jesus died exclusively for Adam's sin. How do they think their own sins will be forgiven by God?
4. Everyone competing in the US Open is a professional golfer or an exceptionally talented amateur golfer. It doesn't look like any amateur golfers will make the thirty-six-hole cut this year. Justin Thomas, a competitor in the US Open, is not an exceptionally talented amateur golfer. Indeed, he's a former major champion. Accordingly, Justin Thomas is a professional golfer.

13

Reverse Hypothetical Syllogism, Existential Generalization, and Law of Identity

THIS CHAPTER WILL EXPLORE four laws of logic. Three of these are logical forms, and the fourth of these is a logical equivalence that enables us to draw two logical inferences. It is imperative to memorize the laws presented in this chapter, as they enable us to spot valid arguments very quickly. They also enable us, when reading passages containing arguments, to separate background information from the steps of the argument and to determine the logical sequence of the steps.

Reverse Hypothetical Syllogism

Reverse hypothetical syllogism (RHS) is another form all of whose steps are conditional statements, i.e., if-then statements. A reverse hypothetical syllogism takes the following structure, where the letters A, B, and C are arbitrary:

1. A → B	1. If Kirk plays cornhole, then Lara sews.
2. C → ~B	2. If Dwiane eats, then Lara doesn't sew.
3. ∴ C → ~A	3. Therefore, if Dwiane eats, then Kirk doesn't play cornhole.

You can plug in anything for A, B, and C that you like (true or false); the argument will be valid. The steps do not need to appear in this order. An argument that contains these steps in any order is proven valid by RHS. A reverse hypothetical syllogism relies on the contrapositive of premise 1 and HS for its validity. Recall that the contrapositive of $A \rightarrow B$ is $\sim B \rightarrow \sim A$. So substituting $A \rightarrow B$ for $\sim B \rightarrow \sim A$ in your mind's eye and mentally reversing the order of premises 1 and 2, you obtain $C \rightarrow \sim B$; $\sim B \rightarrow \sim A$; from which it follows by HS that $C \rightarrow \sim A$, with $\sim B$ serving as the link in the chain.

Consider this example: "Kirk doesn't *r*ead the new journal issue unless it comes in the *m*ail. Kirk's house is painted *b*rown only if the new journal issue doesn't come in the mail. It follows from this that if Kirk's house is painted brown, Kirk doesn't read the new journal issue." Let's do a sentence-by-sentence analysis. In the first sentence, "not . . . unless . . ." is a double negative and means "if . . . , then . . . ," such that the sentence may be rewritten "If Kirk *r*eads the new journal issue, then it comes in the *m*ail." We symbolize this as (1) $R \rightarrow M$. Regarding the second sentence, "only if" means "then" and that the other clause is the if-clause, enabling this sentence to be rewritten, "If Kirk's house is painted *b*rown, then the new journal issue doesn't come in the mail." This is symbolized as (2) $B \rightarrow \sim M$. In the third sentence, the phrase "it follows from this" is a synonym of "therefore," giving us (3) $\therefore B \rightarrow \sim R$. We see that this argument is RHS and therefore valid.

Reverse hypothetical syllogism is often confused with the logical fallacy which I call the *inverse error argument.* As a logical fallacy, the inverse error argument is weak and therefore bad; *don't commit it!* Here's what the inverse error argument looks like.

1. $A \rightarrow B$	1. If Kirk plays cornhole, then Lara sews.
2. $C \rightarrow \sim A$	2. If Dwiane eats, then Kirk doesn't play cornhole.
3. $\therefore C \rightarrow \sim B$	3. Therefore, if Dwiane eats, then Lara doesn't sew.

The inverse error argument is so called because the argument relies on the inverse error of thinking that $A \rightarrow B \equiv \sim A \rightarrow \sim B$. (Of course, $A \rightarrow B \equiv \sim B \rightarrow \sim A$, not the other way around.) Only by committing the inverse error can the argument wrongfully infer from $C \rightarrow \sim A$ that $C \rightarrow \sim B$.

Universal Reverse Hypothetical Syllogism

The quantified form of reverse hypothetical syllogism is *universal reverse hypothetical syllogism (URHS)*. Employing the arbitrary letters A, B, and C, the form runs as follows:

1. $(x)(Ax \rightarrow Bx)$	1. All cornhole players are readers.
2. $(x)(Cx \rightarrow \sim Bx)$	2. No potato chip is a reader.
3. $\therefore (x)(Cx \rightarrow \sim Ax)$	3. Therefore, no potato chip is a cornhole player.

You can plug in anything for A_, B_, and C_ that you like (true or false); the argument will be valid. The steps do not need to appear in this order. An argument that contains these steps in any order is proven valid by URHS. Epstein calls this form "the direct way of reasoning with no."[1] It works in the same way as RHS. URHS relies on the contrapositive of premise 1, namely $(x)(\sim Bx \rightarrow \sim Ax)$, and UHS for its validity. Upon substituting $(x)(Ax \rightarrow Bx)$ for $(x)(\sim Bx \rightarrow \sim Ax)$ in your mind's eye and mentally reversing the order of premises 1 and 2, you obtain $(x)(Cx \rightarrow \sim Bx)$; $(x)(\sim Bx \rightarrow \sim Ax)$; from which it follows by UHS that $(x)(Cx \rightarrow \sim Ax)$, with $\sim Bx$ serving as the link in the chain.

Let's take a look at this example: "Only *a*thletes are *p*rofessional golfers. All *c*ats are not athletes. Consequently, cats are not professional golfers." Giving a sentence-by-sentence analysis, recall that "only" means "then," such that the first sentence can be rewritten, "All professional golfers are athletes," symbolized (1) $(x)(Px \rightarrow Ax)$. The second sentence is easy to symbolize: (2) $(x)(Cx \rightarrow \sim Ax)$. Likewise, the third sentence is straightforward: (3) $(x)(Cx \rightarrow \sim Px)$. We see that this argument is URHS and therefore valid.

Universal reverse hypothetical syllogism is often confused with the logical fallacy which I call the *universal inverse error argument*. As a logical fallacy, the universal inverse error argument is weak and therefore bad; *make sure to avoid it!* The universal inverse error argument proceeds as follows:

1. $(x)(Ax \rightarrow Bx)$	1. All cornhole players are readers.
2. $(x)(Cx \rightarrow \sim Ax)$	2. No potato chip is a cornhole player.
3. $\therefore (x)(Cx \rightarrow \sim Bx)$	3. Therefore, no potato chip is a reader.

1. Epstein, *Critical Thinking*, 179.

Epstein calls this fallacy "arguing backwards with no."[2] I refer to it as the universal inverse error argument because the argument relies on the universal inverse error of thinking that $(x)(\mathrm{A}x \rightarrow \mathrm{B}x) \equiv (x)({\sim}\mathrm{A}x \rightarrow {\sim}\mathrm{B}x)$. (Of course, $(x)(\mathrm{A}x \rightarrow \mathrm{B}x) \equiv (x)({\sim}\mathrm{B}x \rightarrow {\sim}\mathrm{A}x)$, not the other way around.) Only by committing the universal inverse error can the argument wrongfully infer from $(x)(\mathrm{C}x \rightarrow {\sim}\mathrm{A}x)$ that $(x)(\mathrm{C}x \rightarrow {\sim}\mathrm{B}x)$.

Existential Generalization

Our next valid argument form is a logical law known as *existential generalization (EG)*. It allows us to make the obvious inference that if something has a property, then there exists an entity that has that property. Using the arbitrary letter A for a property and c for an individual entity, the form runs as follows:

1. Ac	1. Bob plays football.
2. ∴ $(\exists x)\mathrm{A}x$	2. Therefore, someone plays football.

In other words, Bob is a football player, so there exists an entity which is a football player. You will find this law very helpful in logical proofs where you need to prove an existential statement, namely, a statement that begins $(\exists x)$. Consider this example of EG: "Simone Biles is a gymnast. So there exists a gymnast." Going sentence-by-sentence, our symbolization is (1) Gb; (2) ∴ $(\exists x)\mathrm{G}x$. Because it is EG, this argument is valid.

Law of Identity

The *law of identity (Id)* comes in two forms, one obvious and the other less obvious. You will hardly ever use the obvious form, but the less obvious form is central to reasoning well and will be used quite frequently. The obvious form of Id states that $x = x$. Notice here I used the double equals sign, which means "is identical to." Clearly x is identical to x! The less obvious form of Id states that $(x)(y)((x = y) \equiv (P)(Px \leftrightarrow Py))$.[3] How do we read this complicated statement? We read it like this: For all x (i.e., (x)) and all y (i.e., (y)), x is identical to y (i.e., $(x = y)$) means that (i.e., $\equiv$)

2. Epstein, *Critical Thinking*, 179.

3. This less-obvious form was discovered by the famous philosopher and mathematician Gottfried Wilhelm Leibniz (1646–1716). See Leibniz, *Discourse on Metaphysics*, 14.

for every property *P* (i.e., (*P*)), *P* is true of *x* iff *P* is true of *y* (i.e., (*P*)(*Px* ↔ *Py*)). This law is crucial because it means that if we know that two entities are identical, then we can immediately conclude that the two entities have all the same properties. In other words, it allows us to reason: (1) c1 = c2; (2) ∴ (*P*)(*P*c1 ↔ *P*c2) (Id). Moreover, Id means that if we know that two entities have all the same properties, then we can immediately conclude that the two entities are identical. Thus it allows us to reason: (1) (*P*)(*P*c1 ↔ *P*c2) (2) ∴ c1 = c2 (Id).[4]

This law makes good sense. Suppose I see someone coming into the building where my office is located at 7:30 a.m. and you see someone coming into that same building at 7:30 a.m. How could we figure out if we saw the same person or two different people? We would start comparing the properties of the person I saw with the properties of the person you saw. If the person I saw and the person you saw both have blond hair, both weigh about 240 lbs., both have a red cap on, are both carrying a pink backpack, are both males, are both around eighteen years old, and share every other property we can think of, we can safely conclude that we saw the same person. In other words, the person I saw and the person you saw are identical. However, if there's even one property that the person I saw has and the person you saw lacks (e.g., the person I saw has a red cap on while the person you saw isn't wearing any cap) or even one property that the person you saw has and the person I saw lacks (e.g., the person you saw has blond hair while the person I saw has black hair), then we rightfully conclude that we saw two different people.

Accordingly, whenever you see a statement that two entities are identical such as "Samuel *C*lemens is Mark *T*wain," you can immediately replace that with "Samuel Clemens and Mark Twain have all the same properties." In other words, c = t can be immediately replaced by (*P*)(*P*c ↔ *P*t). Likewise, whenever you see a statement that two entities have all the same properties like "Eric Arthur *B*lair and George *O*rwell have all the same properties," you can immediately replace that with "Eric Arthur Blair is George Orwell." In other words, (*P*)(*P*b ↔ *P*o) can be immediately replaced by b = o.

4. While all logicians to my knowledge endorse the first inference drawn above, some logicians deny the second inference on the grounds that "thisness" or haecceity is not a property. For example, see Moreland and Craig, *Philosophical Foundations*, 179, 200. However, I maintain that "thisness" is a property, such that the second inference is valid and should be affirmed by modern logic. In defense of the second inference see Rodriguez-Pereyra, *Two Arguments*. This debate between logicians who deny and affirm the second inference does not affect everyday reasoning.

A fascinating real-world application of the less obvious form of Id concerns this question: Is the mind the same as the brain? Well, they are the same if and only if everything true of the mind is true of the brain and everything true of the brain is true of the mind. However, they are not the same if there is even one thing true of the mind but false of the brain or true of the brain but false of the mind.[5]

Pre-Homework Practice!

To make sure you have your logical laws memorized, try to name the logical law making each of the following arguments valid. Then check your answer against the abbreviation beneath each argument.

1. Every trombone is a brass instrument. No clarinet is a brass instrument. So no clarinet is a trombone.
    a. *URHS*
2. Kirk is a philosopher. Therefore, some philosophers exist.
    a. *EG*
3. Driving conditions are terrible on the condition that there's thundersnow outside. In Florida, driving conditions aren't terrible. Accordingly, in Florida, there isn't thundersnow outside.
    a. *RHS*
4. Everything true of Muhammad Ali is also true of Cassius Clay. And everything true of Cassius Clay is also true of Muhammad Ali. It follows that Muhammad Ali and Cassius Clay are the same person.
    a. *Id*

Now try to symbolize each argument below and give the abbreviation of the logical law making it valid. Afterward, check your answer against the solution beneath each argument.

5. I'm turning on my Christmas tree unless it's June. If it's the day emancipation was announced to enslaved persons in Texas, I'm not turning on my Christmas tree. So it's June if it's the day emancipation was announced to enslaved persons in Texas.

5. For wonderful discussions of whether the mind is the same as the brain, see Moreland, *Scaling*, 77–96; and Rickabaugh and Moreland, *Substance*.

   a. (1) ~J → C (J ≡ "It is June" and C ≡ "I'm turning on my Christmas tree"); (2) E → ~C (E ≡ "It's the day emancipation was announced to enslaved persons in Texas"); (3) ∴ E → J. *RHS.*

6. Tiger Woods is a golfer. So there are some golfers.

   a. (1) Gt (t ≡ Tiger Woods); (2) ∴ (∃*x*)G*x*. *EG.*

7. Squirrels dash out in front of moving cars. Rocks don't dash out in front of moving cars. It follows that rocks aren't squirrels.

   a. (1) (*x*)(S*x* → D*x*) (S_ ≡ "_ is a squirrel" and D_ ≡ "_ is a dasher out in front of moving cars"); (2) (*x*)(R*x* → ~D*x*) (R_ ≡ "_ is a rock"); (3) ∴ (*x*)(R*x* → ~S*x*). *URHS.*

8. Jesus is the Christ. So anything is true of Jesus just in case it's true of the Christ.

   a. (1) j = c (j ≡ Jesus and c ≡ the Christ); (2) ∴ (*P*)(*P*j ↔ *P*c). *Id.*

Homework Assignment 13

Symbolize each argument and give the abbreviation of the logical law making it valid.

1. Everything that's true of K'ung-fu-tzu is true of Confucius. So K'ung-fu-tzu is Confucius.
2. If a maximally great being does not exist, then the modal version of the ontological argument is not sound. But if there's no logical contradiction or category mistake in the concept of a maximally great being, then the modal version of the ontological argument is sound. Assuming there's no logical contradiction or category mistake in the concept of a maximally great being, then, a maximally great being exists.
3. Lara is a hospice chaplain. So a hospice chaplain exists.
4. Every single point in spacetime is subject to the gravitational field equations of the universe. No divine person is subject to the gravitational field equations of the universe. From this it follows that no divine person is a point in spacetime.

14

Laws of Conjunction, Addition, and Simplification

THIS CHAPTER WILL ADD three more laws of logic to your arsenal. These laws prove invaluable in distinguishing one or more subconclusions of an argument from its conclusion, or central point. Recall that an argument may have one or more subconclusions reached on the way to the conclusion. A subconclusion is a statement that at least one other statement supports and that supports at least one other statement. After learning the three laws, you will have the skills you need to begin annotating arguments. Annotating arguments entails symbolizing the steps of an argument in logical order alongside the logical laws which enable each inference to be drawn and the premises each law uses to draw the inference.

Law of Conjunction

The *law of conjunction (Conj)* depends on the fact that if two or more separate propositions are known to be true, then their conjunction (·) into one proposition must also be true. This law is easy to understand and assumes the following logical form:

1. A	1. Kirk was born in Ohio.
2. B	2. Lara was born in Texas.
3. ∴ A · B	3. Therefore, Kirk was born in Ohio, and Lara was born in Texas.

Conj is often used when a speaker is forced to admit an inconvenient truth. Consider this argument: "Joe is *c*rookeder than a dog's hind leg. But Joe has great *p*olicies. Despite Joe's blatant dishonesty, then, Joe's policies are terrific." Since "blatant dishonesty" is synonymous with "crookeder than a dog's hind leg" and since "despite" means "and," the argument is symbolized as follows: (1) C; (2) P; (3) C · P (Conj). An inconvenient truth that someone has to admit alongside a conclusion is often minimized with a synonym of "and" like "despite" or "nevertheless" that rhetorically tries to lead the hearer not to pay attention to it. Such rhetorical diversions are called *discounts* (because they try to discount an inconvenient truth). Whether inconvenient or not, any truth that logically can be or is conjoined to a conclusion is called *consistent* or *compatible with that conclusion.*

Law of Addition

The *law of addition (Add)* is based on the fact than an "or" statement is true if at least one of its disjuncts is true. For this reason, once we know a proposition is true, we can use it in a subsequent statement as a disjunct. Since this disjunct is already true, we can add anything the heck we want—true or false—as the other disjunct (or disjuncts), and the resulting statement will always be true simply by virtue of the original disjunct. The law takes this logical form:

1. A	1. Kirk was born in Ohio.
2. ∴ A ∨ B	2. Therefore, Kirk was born in Ohio, or dogs lay eggs.

Add, along with the two "black hole" forms of Abs, is very useful in constructing logical proofs where you need to introduce a brand new statement. To illustrate, suppose we know that I own a Canon printer. Then we can use Add to conclude that I own a Canon printer or B, where B can be anything (no matter how crazy). Since I do own a Canon printer, the truth-value of B is irrelevant to the truth of the overall statement.

There are two related fallacies to avoid when using Add. First is the fallacy of reversing the steps of Add, which I call the *fallacy of subtraction*. The fallacy of subtraction goes like this:

1. A ∨ B	1. 2 + 2 = 8 or George Washington was the first US president.
2. ∴ A	2. Therefore, 2 + 2 = 8.

The reason the steps cannot be reversed is that when you begin with a true disjunction (A ∨ B) and don't know what the letters stand for, you have no idea which disjunct (A; B) is true. It's a pure guess as to which one. Here we guessed wrong, as seen by the meaning of the letters! Since a logical form must be true under all circumstances and subtraction isn't, it cannot be a logical form but rather constitutes a fallacy. Avoid this like the plague!

Second is the fallacy of *confusing* ∨ *for* · *(i.e., confusing disjunction for conjunction)*. This deceptively resembles Add but wrongfully trades out ∨ for · in the second step:

1. A	1. Kirk was born in Ohio.
2. ∴ A · B	2. Therefore, Kirk was born in Ohio, and dogs lay eggs.

The problem with confusing ∨ for · should be obvious. To be true, a conjunction (·) requires each conjunct making it up to be true. If even one conjunct is false, the entire conjunction is false. As seen in Conj, we can only conjoin propositions that we already know to be true to a true proposition. We can't just conjoin anything we like, because the resulting conjunction has just as much chance of being false as it has to be true! As seen in the example above, the resulting conjunction is false. So make sure to avoid this fallacy!

Law of Simplification

The *law of simplification (Simp)* stems from the observation that any true conjunction must, by definition, be made up of all and only true conjuncts. So if we know that a conjunction is true, we can "pick off" any of the conjuncts and conclude that it is true. The logical form runs like this:

1. A · B	1. A · B	1. I read books and I watch TV.
2. ∴ A	2. ∴ B	2. Therefore, I read books. / Therefore, I watch TV.

Or consider this example: "I have Hubmaier's *Schriften* and Molina's *Concordia* in my library. Therefore, I have Molina's *Concordia* in my library." This is symbolized (1) S · C; (2) ∴ C (Simp).

With Conj, Add, and Simp in place, we can now analyze and construct arguments with both subconclusions and conclusions. Remember that the conclusion—known as the central point of the argument—is the statement which at least one statement supports and does not support any other statement. When analyzing an argument, keep in mind that the conclusion is not necessarily the statement that most of the argument is about. For something to be the conclusion, all you need is for one statement to support it and for it not to support any other statement. In other words, it's the end of your chain of reasoning. What is tricky is that most of an argument may actually be about the subconclusion. However, the subconclusion supports at least one other statement, minimally the conclusion!

Finding the Central Point of an Argument

We now turn to finding the central point of an argument. Let's begin by looking at this one: "Guinea pigs are annoying. After all, if guinea pigs poop all over the place, then they're annoying. And they do poop all over the place. Chip, a guinea pig, even pooped on me while I was holding him. So guinea pigs are annoying or 2 + 2 = 8!" The central point (conclusion) is "Guinea pigs are annoying or 2 + 2 = 8." The subconclusion is "Guinea pigs are annoying." Why? Consider the logical structure of this argument:

1. P → A	1. If guinea pigs *p*oop all over the place, then they're *a*nnoying.
2. P	2. Guinea pigs poop all over the place.
3. ∴ A (MP, 1, 2)	3. Guinea pigs are annoying. (This is the subconclusion.)
4. ∴ A ∨ E (Add, 3)	4. Guinea pigs are annoying or 2 + 2 = 8.

A ∨ E does not support any other statement—it is the end of our chain of reasoning—and is supported by (3). Notice that for all inferences—the subconclusion (3) and the conclusion (4)—I gave in parentheses the abbreviation of the logical law permitting the inference to be drawn, then a comma, and finally the steps used by the law to draw the inference. Laying out the logical structure of an argument in symbols alongside the information in parentheses for each inference is known as annotating an argument. Background information (in this argument "Chip, a guinea pig, even pooped on me while I was holding him") is not part of the logical structure of an argument and is therefore disregarded. You will be annotating arguments from this point forward in the course.

Now let's consider a second argument: "Bob drinks scotch. For if Bob doesn't drink apricot brandy and scotch, weeds are not hard to pull. And weeds are hard to pull. I tore a small layer of skin off my finger from pulling them! Therefore, Bob drinks apricot brandy and scotch. Yet I don't like scotch." What is the central point of this argument? It is "Bob drinks scotch." For consider the argument's logical structure:

1. ~(A · S) → ~W	1. If Bob doesn't drink *a*pricot brandy and *s*cotch, *w*eeds are not hard to pull.
2. W	2. Weeds are hard to pull.
3. ∴ A · S (MT, 1, 2)	3. Bob drinks apricot brandy and scotch. (This is the subconclusion.)
4. ∴ S (Simp, 3)	4. Bob drinks scotch.

Again, background information (here "I tore a small layer of skin off my finger from pulling them" and "Yet I don't like scotch") is disregarded as irrelevant. Just for review, let's make sure you understand why (3) is derived from MT on 1 and 2. (2) W, by DN, is the same as ~(~W). MT allows us to combine this with (1) to get ~(~(A · S)), which by DN is just A · S.

Pre-Homework Practice!

I hope you can see why having all your logical laws and their abbreviations memorized is absolutely critical to analyzing and annotating arguments. A sure-fire way to recognize background information is that it will not fit into any logical form with any other statement in an argument. So if there are any laws or abbreviations that you haven't yet memorized, *please be sure to do this now!*

Once you've done this, annotate (i.e., logically map out the structure of) each of these arguments to find its central point (conclusion) and its subconclusion. Then check your answer against the solution below each argument.

Argument 1

I am an Anabaptist. After all, assuming I hold to believers' baptism and just peacemaking, I'm an Anabaptist. I hold to believers' baptism and just peacemaking. It's really fascinating that I'm an Anabaptist or I like red onions. Why did I ask the server at Olive Garden to remove red onions from my salad? That remains to be explained.

1. $(B \cdot J) \rightarrow A$	1. Assuming I hold to *b*elievers' baptism and *j*ust peacemaking, I'm an *A*nabaptist.
2. $B \cdot J$	2. I hold to believers' baptism and just peacemaking.
3. $\therefore A$ (MP, 1, 2)	3. I am an Anabaptist. (This is the subconclusion.)
4. $\therefore A \vee R$ (Add, 3)	4. I'm an Anabaptist or I like *r*ed onions. (This is the central point, namely, the conclusion.)

Argument 2

Let me prove to you that I'm going to Hutchinson and playing at the concert tonight. Now I'm not doing what I just said only if I don't have a pane of clear glass to cover my music with. I do have a pane of clear glass to cover my music with. Yay! I'm going to Hutchinson. Playing at the concert is so much fun!

1. $\sim(H \cdot P) \rightarrow \sim G$	1. I'm not doing what I just said (i.e., going to *H*utchinson and *p*laying at the concert tonight) only if I don't have a pane of clear *g*lass to cover my music with.
2. G	2. I do have a pane of clear glass to cover my music with.
3. $\therefore H \cdot P$ (MT, 1, 2)	3. I'm going to Hutchinson and playing at the concert tonight. (This is the subconclusion.)
4. $\therefore H$ (Simp, 3)	4. I'm going to Hutchinson. (This is the central point, namely, the conclusion.)

Homework Assignment 14

Annotate each argument, identifying its subconclusion(s) and conclusion.

Argument 1

Whatever is a bicycle has two wheels. Dwiane really likes riding his bicycle. Only things used in the Olympics have two wheels. So bicycles are used in the Olympics. And it's a fact that either I don't need to practice the piano or bicycles are used in the Olympics. I haven't seriously practiced the piano since I was an undergraduate.

Argument 2

If Sid Vicious were to have challenged Vader for the World Title at Starrcade '93 or won the title at the event, then Sid Vicious would have beaten Ric Flair. But Sid Vicious lost to Ric Flair. I was so cheering for Ric Flair in that match! So it's false that Sid Vicious challenged Vader for the World title at Starrcade '93 or won the title at the event. Accordingly, Sid Vicious didn't challenge Vader for the World Title at Starrcade '93 and didn't win the title at the event. So Sid Vicious didn't win the World Title at Starrcade '93. Ric Flair's World title victory at Starrcade '93 is arguably the greatest match in Starrcade history.

15

Material Equivalence, Exportation, and Constructive Dilemma

IN THIS CHAPTER YOU will learn three additional laws of logic that prove quite valuable in annotating arguments. Two of these laws are logical equivalences, and the third is a logical form. Using these laws, you will refine your skills in annotating arguments, especially arguments with more than one subconclusion. Remember to memorize each law of logic as you learn it. When you encounter logical proofs in chapter 17, having your laws of logic memorized will be crucial.

Material Equivalence

The law of *material equivalence (ME)* comes in two forms, each of which explains the meaning of iff (↔). The first form states that A ↔ B ≡ (A → B) · (B → A). In other words, A iff B means that if A, then B (the "only if" part) and if B, then A (the "if" part). The second form states that A ↔ B ≡ (A · B) ∨ (~A · ~B). In other words, A iff B also means that both A and B are true or both A and B are false. When one is true, the other is true, and when one is false, the other is false. As with any logical equivalence, we can reason from one side of each form of material equivalence to the other side. So regarding the first form, it is valid to reason: (1) A ↔ B; (2) ∴ (A → B) · (B → A) (ME, 1) or (1) (A → B) · (B → A); (2) ∴ A ↔ B (ME, 1). And regarding the second form, it is valid to reason: (1) A ↔ B; (2) ∴ (A · B) ∨ (~A · ~B) (ME, 1) or (1) (A · B) ∨ (~A · ~B); (2) ∴ A ↔ B (ME, 1). The second form of ME is extremely useful when, in writing proofs, you need to convert an iff statement into an and-or statement and vice versa.

Here we will use our synonyms of iff in seeing how these reasoning patterns play out in ordinary English. Suppose I said, "A triangle is equi*l*ateral just in case it is equi*a*ngular. So if a triangle is equilateral, then it is equiangular; and if a triangle is equiangular, then it is equilateral." This argument is logically valid and would be annotated (1) L ↔ A; (2) ∴ (L → A) · (A → L) (ME, 1). Now suppose I said, "If I have a *H*ebrew Bible, then I have a *G*reek New Testament; and if I have a Greek New Testament, then I have a Hebrew Bible. Consequently, I have a Hebrew Bible exactly when I have a Greek New Testament." This argument is logically valid and would be annotated (1) (H → G) · (G → H); (2) ∴ H ↔ G (ME, 1). Suppose my wife Lara told me, "I'll be coming home *l*ate from work today if but only if I need to *w*rite a report. Hence I'll be coming home late from work today and I need to write a report; or I won't be coming home late from work today and I don't need to write a report." This argument is logically valid and would be annotated (1) L ↔ W; (2) ∴ (L · W) ∨ (~L · ~W) (ME, 1). Now suppose Lara told me, "Either I'll buy you both a trumpet *m*outhpiece and a trumpet *p*lunger mute or I'll buy you neither a trumpet mouthpiece nor a trumpet plunger mute. Accordingly, I'll buy you a trumpet mouthpiece when and only when I'll buy you a trumpet plunger mute." This argument is logically valid and would be annotated (1) (M · P) ∨ (~M · ~P); (2) ∴ M ↔ P (ME, 1).

Exportation

The *law of exportation (Ex)* is a logical equivalence affirming that (A · B) → C ≡ A → (B → C). For example, "If I go to McDonald's and get an Egg McMuffin, then I get two diet drinks" ≡ "If I go to McDonald's, then if I get an Egg McMuffin, then I get two diet drinks." Or again, "If I go to McDonald's, then if I get an Egg McMuffin, then I get two diet drinks" ≡ "If I go to McDonald's and get an Egg McMuffin, then I get two diet drinks." As a logical equivalence, we can use Ex in validly reasoning (1) (A · B) → C; (2) ∴ A → (B → C) (Ex, 1) or (1) A → (B → C); (2) (A · B) → C (Ex, 1). Ex is helpful when we know some information and want to prove that this triggers an if-then between two things. Suppose we know that if I go to McDonald's and get an Egg McMuffin, then I get two diet drinks. We also know that I go to McDonald's. Then we can conclude by Ex that if I get an Egg McMuffin, then I get two diet drinks. Ex is also helpful when we know some information about a nested if-then and want to prove the end of the chain. Suppose we know that if I go to McDonald's, then if I get an Egg McMuffin, then I get two diet drinks. We also know that I go to McDonald's and get an Egg McMuffin. Then we can conclude by Ex that I got two diet drinks.

We shall use our synonyms of "if . . . , then . . ." to see how Ex plays out in plain English. Imagine I argued, "Assuming I have a *w*hite pillow and a *r*ed pillow, I *s*leep comfortably at night. Thus I have a white pillow only if I sleep comfortably at night on the condition that I have a red pillow." (Remember that the second sentence means "Therefore, if I have a white pillow, then if I have a red pillow, then I sleep comfortably at night.") This reasoning is valid and is annotated (1) (W · R) → S; (2) ∴ W → (R → S) (Ex, 1). Now imagine I argued, "Given that I have a *p*ink highlighter, I have an *o*range highlighter whenever I have a *y*ellow highlighter. So I have both a pink and a yellow highlighter only if I have an orange highlighter." This reasoning is valid and is annotated (1) P → (Y → O); (2) (P · Y) → O (Ex, 1).

Constructive Dilemma

The law of *constructive dilemma (CD)* applies to a situation where we know that two if-then statements are true and that one of the two if-clauses is true, but we don't know which one. In this case, CD allows us to conclude that one of the two then-clauses is true, even though we don't know which one. The law assumes this logical form:

1. (A → C) · (B → D)	1. If I go to McDonald's, then I get a Big Mac, and if I go to Burger King, then I get a Whopper.
2. A ∨ B	2. I go to McDonald's or Burger King.
3. ∴ C ∨ D	3. Therefore, I get a Big Mac or a Whopper.

Consider this example: "Either a *R*epublican or a *D*emocrat will win the election. Assuming that a Republican wins, there will be a larger *f*ederal deficit, and a Democrat won't win unless the wealthy will pay a higher *t*ax rate. So either there will be a larger federal deficit or the wealthy will pay a higher tax rate." This argument is valid and is annotated (1) R ∨ D; (2) (R → F) · (D → T); (3) ∴ F ∨ T (CD, 2, 1). Notice that it's fine that the order of the premises is flipped, as long as we list them in the proper order in the parentheses accompanying the conclusion.

Here is another example: "*D*eontology is false unless *K*ant is a great moral philosopher, and *c*ontractarianism is false unless *R*awls is a great moral philosopher. Either deontology or contractarianism is true. So either Kant or Rawls is a great moral philosopher." (Recall that "is false unless" ≡ "is not true unless" ≡ "if . . . , then . . .") This argument is valid and is annotated (1) $(D \rightarrow K) \cdot (C \rightarrow R)$; (2) $D \vee C$; (3) ∴ $K \vee R$ (CD, 1, 2).

Annotating Arguments Using Laws Learned So Far

Let's see how to annotate two arguments to find the central point (conclusion) and the subconclusion(s) of each. Take this argument: "If Dave plays the *t*rumpet, then Barbara won't play the *p*iano without Dave and Barbara playing a *d*uet. Trumpet-piano duets are so much fun to listen to! Dave plays the trumpet even though Barbara plays the piano. Consequently, Dave and Barbara play a duet on the condition that Dave plays the trumpet while Barbara plays the piano. It turns out Dave and Barbara will play a duet. I hope they perform *Over the Rainbow*." Disregarding the background information (the second and sixth sentences) and remembering our synonyms of "if . . . , then . . ." and "and," the argument is annotated, sentence-by-sentence, as follows:

1. $T \rightarrow (P \rightarrow D)$
2. $T \cdot P$
3. ∴ $(T \cdot P) \rightarrow D$ (Ex, 1) Subconclusion
4. ∴ D (MP, 3, 2) Conclusion

Here we learn that MP is often used in conjunction with Ex. The same is true of MT.

Now take this argument: "I'm not eating either *b*russel sprouts or *j*alapeno peppers. Brussel sprouts taste horrible. And jalapeno peppers are way too hot. It follows that I'm not eating brussel sprouts and I'm not eating jalapeno peppers. So I'm eating brussel sprouts and jalapeno peppers, or I'm not eating brussel sprouts and I'm not eating jalapeno peppers. Accordingly, I'm eating brussel sprouts just in case I'm eating jalapeno peppers. Why the heck do foods exist that I don't like?" We can disregard the second, third, and seventh sentences as background information. Upon doing so, the sentence-by-sentence annotation of the argument proceeds like this:

1. ~(B ∨ J)
2. ∴ ~B · ~J (DeM, 1) Subconclusion
3. ∴ (B · J) ∨ (~B · ~J) (Add, 2) Subconclusion
4. ∴ B ↔ J (ME, 3) Conclusion

We get from 1 to 2 by distributing our ~ across all three of the terms, per DeM. We get from 2 to 3 by remembering that any proposition, true or false, can be added to a true proposition. Here the argument cleverly adds (B · J). Since ∨ is interchangeable, the two parts of the disjunction can be written in either order. And we get from 3 to 4 by using ME.

Pre-Homework Practice!

Annotate each of these arguments to find its conclusion (central point) and its subconclusion(s). In so doing, be sure to disregard any background information. Then check your answer against the solution below each argument.

Argument 1

The government runs only if people pay their taxes, and cows fly on the condition that they have wings. The idea of flying cows sounds awesome and yet quite problematic for farmers. Now the government runs or cows have wings. That proves it: People pay their taxes or cows fly. And either people pay their taxes or cows fly or I'm investing in gold. Gold is freaking gold! How can you go wrong with that investment?

1. (G → T) · (W → F)	1. The government runs only if people pay their *t*axes, and cows *fly* on the condition that they have *w*ings.
2. G ∨ W	2. The government runs or cows have wings.
3. ∴ T ∨ F (CD, 1, 2)	3. Therefore, people pay their taxes their or cows fly. (This is the subconclusion.)
4. ∴ T ∨ F ∨ I (Add, 3)	4. Therefore, people pay their taxes or cows fly or I'm *i*nvesting in gold. (This is the conclusion.)

Argument 2

I'm investing in gold exactly when cows fly. Think of all the money I'll rake in. So only when cows fly am I investing in gold, and I'm investing in gold provided that cows fly. It's a tremendous possible world where all this goes down. As a result, if I'm investing in gold, then cows fly.

1. $I \leftrightarrow F$	1. I'm *i*nvesting in gold exactly when cows *fly*.
2. $\therefore (I \rightarrow F) \cdot (F \rightarrow I)$ (ME, 1)	2. Therefore, only when cows fly am I investing in gold, and I'm investing in gold provided that cows fly. (This is the subconclusion.)
3. $\therefore I \rightarrow F$ (Simp, 2)	3. Therefore, if I'm investing in gold, then cows fly. (This is the conclusion.)

Homework Assignment 15

Annotate each argument, identifying its subconclusion(s) and conclusion.

Argument 1

I'm sitting in the dentist's office precisely when I need to accompany a family member to the dentist. I hate the dentist! Hence I'm sitting in the dentist's office and I need to accompany a family member to the dentist, or I'm not sitting in the dentist's office and I don't need to accompany a family member to the dentist. I haven't gone to the dentist for myself ever since I was in high school. And I've never had a cavity in the interim. Take that, dentists! For these reasons, either the sky is blue, or I'm sitting in the dentist's office and I need to accompany a family member to the dentist, or I'm not sitting in the dentist's office and I don't need to accompany a family member to the dentist.

Argument 2

I'm eating a tuna fish sandwich and drinking a protein shake only if I'm going to work out. Melanie makes the best tuna fish sandwiches. She gets the contents of two whole cans, dried and combined with Miracle Whip, into one sandwich. And I'm eating a tuna fish sandwich. Hence if I'm eating a tuna fish sandwich, then I'm drinking a protein shake only if I'm going to work out. So assuming I'm drinking a protein shake, I'm going to work out. But I don't enjoy working out. It follows that if I'm not going to work out, I'm not drinking a protein shake. Thinking of the taste of a protein shake makes me nauseated.

16

Practicing All Laws of Logic

THROUGHOUT THIS BOOK I'VE been stressing the importance of memorizing all the laws of logic. I want to congratulate you on making it this far through the course because you have now seen nearly all the laws of logic! You've also reached the halfway mark in the course. In this chapter you get to test yourself in making sure you have each of these logical laws memorized before we turn to writing proofs—a skill for which you will need the laws and their abbreviations memorized—in the next chapter. Hence this chapter will review every law of logic you have encountered in chapters one through fifteen.

Accordingly, this chapter will be organized differently than the previous chapters. I will first put the name of each law of logic in bold type. Without looking at what comes underneath the name (hiding it with a sheet of paper if necessary), either say or write on a sheet of paper the law in symbolic form along with its abbreviation. Remember there may be more than one version of each law—say or write them all. Thus you may want to have two separate sheets of paper on hand to assist your review. Afterward, check your answer against the law and abbreviation beneath its name. So let's get started!

Law of Contraposition

$A \to B \equiv {\sim}B \to {\sim}A$ (Cont)

Law of Commutation

$A \cdot B \equiv B \cdot A$

$A \vee B \equiv B \vee A$ (Com)

Material Implication

$A \rightarrow B \equiv \sim A \vee B$ (MI)

DeMorgan's Laws

$\sim(A \cdot B) \equiv \sim A \vee \sim B$

$\sim(A \vee B) \equiv \sim A \cdot \sim B$ (DeM)

Negating a Conditional

$\sim(A \rightarrow B) \equiv A \cdot \sim B$ (NC)

Law of Association

$A \vee (B \vee C) \equiv (A \vee B) \vee C$

$A \cdot (B \cdot C) \equiv (A \cdot B) \cdot C$ (Assoc)

Law of Idempotence

$A \equiv A \vee A$

$A \equiv A \cdot A$ (Idem)

Law of Absorption

$A \rightarrow B \equiv A \rightarrow (A \cdot B)$

$A \equiv A \cdot (A \vee B)$

$A \equiv A \vee (A \cdot B)$ (Abs)

Law of Distribution

$A \cdot (B \vee C) \equiv (A \cdot B) \vee (A \cdot C)$

$A \vee (B \cdot C) \equiv (A \vee B) \cdot (A \vee C)$ (Dist)

Traditional Square of Opposition

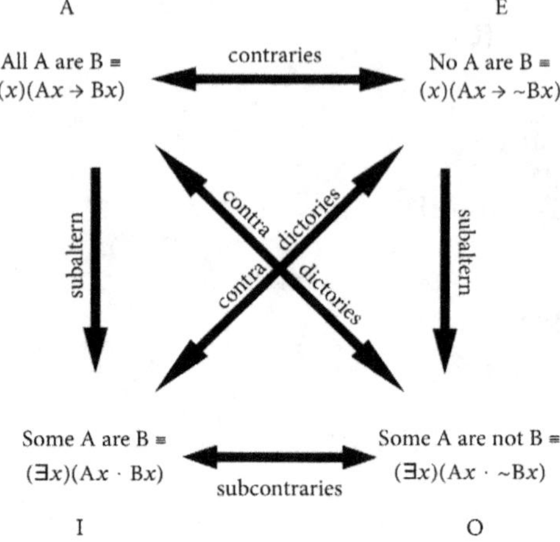

Modus Ponens

1. $A \rightarrow B$
2. A
3. $\therefore B$ (MP)

Universal *Modus Ponens*

1. $(x)(Ax \rightarrow Bx)$
2. Ac
3. $\therefore Bc$ (UMP)

Modus Tollens

1. $A \rightarrow B$
2. $\sim B$
3. $\therefore \sim A$ (MT)

Universal *Modus Tollens*

1. $(x)(Ax \rightarrow Bx)$
2. $\sim Bc$
3. $\therefore \sim Ac$ (UMT)

Disjunctive Syllogism

1. $A \vee B$
2. $\sim A$
3. $\therefore B$ (DS)

Domain Disjunctive Syllogism

Let $x \in D$. Then:

1. $(x)(Ax \vee Bx)$
2. $\sim Ac$
3. $\therefore Bc$ (DDS)

Hypothetical Syllogism

1. $A \rightarrow B$
2. $B \rightarrow C$
3. $\therefore A \rightarrow C$ (HS)

Universal Hypothetical Syllogism

1. $(x)(Ax \rightarrow Bx)$
2. $(x)(Bx \rightarrow Cx)$
3. $\therefore (x)(Ax \rightarrow Cx)$ (UHS)

Reverse Hypothetical Syllogism

1. $A \rightarrow B$
2. $C \rightarrow \sim B$
3. $\therefore C \rightarrow \sim A$ (RHS)

Universal Reverse Hypothetical Syllogism

1. $(x)(Ax \rightarrow Bx)$
2. $(x)(Cx \rightarrow {\sim}Bx)$
3. $\therefore$ $(x)(Cx \rightarrow {\sim}Ax)$ (URHS)

Existential Generalization

1. Ac
2. $\therefore$ $(\exists x)Ax$ (EG)

Law of Identity

$x = x$

$(x)(y)((x = y) \equiv (P)(Px \leftrightarrow Py))$ (Id)

Law of Conjunction

1. A
2. B
3. $\therefore$ $A \cdot B$ (Conj)

Law of Addition

1. A
2. $A \vee B$ (Add)

Law of Simplification

1. $A \cdot B$
2. $\therefore$ A (Simp)

Material Equivalence

$A \leftrightarrow B \equiv (A \rightarrow B) \cdot (B \rightarrow A)$

$A \leftrightarrow B \equiv (A \cdot B) \vee ({\sim}A \cdot {\sim}B)$ (ME)

Exportation

$(A \cdot B) \rightarrow C \equiv A \rightarrow (B \rightarrow C)$ (Ex)

Constructive Dilemma

1. $(A \rightarrow C) \cdot (B \rightarrow D)$
2. $A \vee B$
3. $\therefore C \vee D$ (CD)

Pre-Homework Practice!

We'll do a bit more reviewing in the pre-homework practice and in Homework Assignment 16. For each of the following logical laws, state it symbolically and give its abbreviation. Then check your answer against the law provided earlier in this chapter.

1. *Modus Ponens*
2. Disjunctive Syllogism
3. Reverse Hypothetical Syllogism
4. Addition
5. Identity

Homework Assignment 16

For each of the following logical laws, state it symbolically and give its abbreviation.

1. Traditional Square of Opposition
2. *Modus Tollens*
3. Hypothetical Syllogism
4. Constructive Dilemma
5. Exportation

17

Direct Proof (Part 1)

WITH THIS CHAPTER WE begin the second half of the course. The second half is primarily about applying the skills you learned in the first half of the course. One of the most important applications is writing proofs—proofs that various arguments are valid. You should have all the laws of logic memorized by now. The second half of the course assumes that you do. The goal of any proof is simple: find the series of subconclusions and other steps ending with the conclusion, thereby proving that the premises make the conclusion logically certain. So let's get started by exploring the structure of a logical proof and three strategies that will prove invaluable in writing them.

Structure of a Logical Proof

The prompt of a logical proof is a series of premises, the last of which puts the conclusion you need to prove, introduced by ∴, indented on the right. This line is underlined. This is the only place in the proof where ∴ should occur. For example:

1. P → Q
2. P ∴ Q ∨ (Q · R)

Now how do you write a proof? Underneath this line, you need to provide the list of steps (starting with whatever the next number in the series is, here 3) which end with the conclusion. So the conclusion will always be the last step in any proof. Each step needs to be annotated.

So what are the three key strategies in writing a proof? (1) Work forwards. In other words, ask: What can we infer right away from our premises? This will be the first step (or series of steps) in the proof. Write it (or them) down and annotate it (or them). (2) Work backwards. In other words, ask: Is the conclusion identical to or obviously logically derivable from something else? If so, this "something else" is the second to last step in the proof, with the conclusion as the last step of the proof. I'd write these down on a separate sheet of paper, because you don't know yet how much space you'll need between the first step and second to last step. (3) Connect the dots. Ask: Can we use a law of logic to get directly from the first step (or series of steps) to the second to last step? If so, annotate it, list all your steps, and you're done. If not, go back through the three strategies, treating your first step (or series of steps) as a new premise (or new premises) and your second to last step as your new conclusion. Keep going through the three strategies until you're done!

Let's use our strategies to write the proof above. (1) Using MP on premises 1 and 2, we can infer right away that Q is true. So that gives us 3. Q (MP, 1, 2). (2) We know from Abs that the conclusion is identical to Q, which we already have as step 3. Step 4, our conclusion, is 4. Q ∨ (Q · R) (Abs, 3). We didn't even need strategy (3) for this proof! Notice that we don't need to write ∴ before any of our steps, since it would be redundant (almost everything below the line is a subconclusion or a conclusion). Accordingly, we write our two new steps below the line as follows:

3. Q (MP, 1, 2)
4. Q ∨ (Q · R) (Abs, 3)

That's it! We've proved our conclusion and thereby completed our first proof.

Now let's work together through writing another proof, with the following prompt:

1. (*x*)(P*x* → ~Q*x*)
2. ~Pc → ~(Rk · Sk)
3. <u>Qc ∴ ~Rk ∨ ~Sk</u>

We'll now go through our three strategies. (1) Applying UMT to 1 and 3, we get ~Pc. This, along with its annotation (UMT, 1, 3), will be the first step (numbered 4) in the proof. (2) We see that by DeM that ~Rk ∨ ~Sk ≡ ~(Rk · Sk). So ~(Rk · Sk) will be the second to last step in the proof, with ~Rk ∨ ~Sk annotated (DeM, [insert the number of the step ~(Rk · Sk)]) as the last step. (3) So can we connect the dots by getting from ~Pc to ~(Rk · Sk)? Yes! By combining 2 with ~Pc through MP, we get ~(Rk · Sk)—the second to last step—which we can now annotate (MP, 2, 4). Having linked everything together, we write the proof underneath the line as follows:

3. ~Pc (UMT, 1, 3)
4. ~(Rk · Sk) (MP, 2, 4)
5. ~Rk ∨ ~Sk (DeM, 5)

And that completes our second proof! In this chapter we will focus on short proofs, which have four or fewer steps.

At this point three helpful tips are in order. First, Add and the two black hole forms of Abs allow you to add new propositions to a line. So if you need a new proposition, look here first! You should especially keep Add and the two black hole forms of Abs in mind when working backwards and connecting the dots. Ask yourself: In the premises and steps above, do I see anything that, through Add or Abs, could be transformed into the line I currently have? If so, you now have the line just prior to the line you previously had. Second, you can substitute equivalent expressions for equivalent expressions in a line of a proof! Just make the line with substitutions your next line and annotate it. Third, a clever use of DN can often get you out of a jam. DN occurs so frequently that it doesn't need to be cited.

Having seen a two-step and a three-step proof, let's try a four-step proof. Its prompt runs like this:

1. P · Q
2. Q → R ∴ (R ∨ S) · ((R ∨ S) ∨ T)

Applying strategy (1), we see two things. First, we can use Simp on 1 to get Q, which will be numbered 3. Q (Simp, 1). Second, we can use MP on 2 and 3 to get R, numbered 4. R (MP, 2, 3). Turning to strategies (2) and (3), we wonder: through Add and Abs, could (R ∨ S) · ((R ∨ S) ∨ T) be obtained from R? Working backwards per (2), we see through Abs that (R ∨ S) · ((R ∨ S) ∨ T) ≡ R ∨ S, where R ∨ S is the second to last line in the proof. Hence the conclusion's annotation will list Abs as the law in play. Connecting the dots with strategy (3), we see that we can get from

R to R ∨ S by Add. That links up everything! So our finished proof puts this under the line above:

3. Q (Simp, 1)
4. R (MP, 2, 3)
5. R ∨ S (Add, 4)
6. (R ∨ S) · ((R ∨ S) ∨ T) (Abs, 5)

Hopefully, the way to write proofs is making sense and continuing to get clearer for you. All that's needed to get it crystal-clear is more practice.

Let's do another proof, with the following prompt:

1. (*x*)(P*x* → Q*x*)
2. (∃*x*)(P*x* · Q*x*) → R
3. R → Sf ∴ (∃*x*)S*x*

We proceed through our three strategies. (1) We see by HS that we can connect 2 and 3 (with R as the link in the chain) to get (∃*x*)(P*x* · Q*x*) → Sf, which—properly annotated—will be our first step (numbered 4). (2) Could we get (∃*x*)S*x* from any step or any part of a step we currently have? Yes—we could get it from Sf by applying EG. So Sf will be in the second to last step of the proof, with (∃*x*)S*x* (EG, [insert the line number of Sf]) as the last step. (3) Can we get to Sf through the steps we already have? Well, all we need is (∃*x*)(P*x* · Q*x*), since that, combined via MP with 4, will get us Sf. So (∃*x*)(P*x* · Q*x*) is the next line up, and MP is the law listed in the Sf line. But how is (∃*x*)(P*x* · Q*x*) annotated? Remembering in Sq that (∃*x*)(P*x* · Q*x*) is the subaltern of premise 1, we annotate it (Sq, 1). And that connects the dots, giving us the sequence of steps below:

4. (∃*x*)(P*x* · Q*x*) → Sf (HS, 2, 3)
5. (∃*x*)(P*x* · Q*x*) (Sq, 1)
6. Sf (MP, 4, 5)
7. (∃*x*)S*x* (EG, 6)

You might be thinking at this point: Could I have done the proof another way and still gotten it right? The answer is yes—most proofs can be correctly done in more than one way. The only thing that counts in getting the proof right is for its steps to validly lead to the conclusion. Unless specified otherwise, do a proof in the way that is easiest for you.

Let's see a different way this same proof could have been written. In strategy (1), you could have immediately seen that (∃*x*)(P*x* · Q*x*) follows from 1 by Sq, that R follows from 2 and (∃*x*)(P*x* · Q*x*) by MP, and that Sf follows from 3 and R by MP. You could have also seen that (∃*x*)S*x*—the conclusion—follows from Sf by EG, which means you would be done before you even got to strategies (2) and (3). Accordingly, the proof would be written as follows:

4. (∃*x*)(P*x* · Q*x*) (Sq, 1)
5. R (MP, 2, 4)
6. Sf (MP, 3, 5)
7. (∃*x*)S*x* (EG, 6)

Pre-Homework Practice!

Now that we've walked through four proofs together, try to write two of them on your own. After writing each proof, check it against the answer(s) provided below it. Remember that even if your proof doesn't match the answer (or one of the answers), it could still be right. Just double-check that each step you used, terminating with the conclusion, follows logically in sequence.

Proof Prompt 1

1. P → (Q · ~R)
2. ~S → (Q → R)
3. ~S ∴ ~P

Solution 1

4. P → ~(Q → R) (NC, 1)
    a. Here we rewrote 1, replacing (Q · ~R) with the equivalent expression ~(Q → R) by NC. Remember that you can substitute equivalent expressions for one another in a line of a proof, just as long as it's rewritten and annotated.

5. ~S → ~P (RHS, 4, 2)
    a. This is a straightforward application of RHS—(1) A → B; (2) C → ~B; (3) ∴ C → ~A—using 4 and 2, where A is P, B is ~(Q → R), and C is ~S. You can see by DN that ~B is (Q → R). Again, DN occurs so frequently that it doesn't need to be cited.
6. ~P (MP, 5, 3)

Another Solution 1

4. Q → R (MP, 2, 3)
5. ~(Q · ~R) (NC, 4)
    a. Here we thought: by DN, Q → R ≡ ~(~(Q → R)). NC allows us to trade out the inner ~(Q → R) with Q · ~R, leaving us with ~(Q · ~R).
6. ~P (MT, 1, 5)

Proof Prompt 2

1. P ∨ Q
2. P → R
3. Q → S ∴ ~R → S

Solution 2

4. (P → R) · (Q → S) (Conj, 2, 3)
    a. If we conjoin 2 and 3, we'll have a nice little conditional dilemma on our hands!
5. R ∨ S (CD, 4, 1)
    a. Given 1, one of the consequents in 4 has to be true.
6. ~R → S (MI, 5)
    a. This is a clever application of DN where R ≡ ~(~R). So R ∨ S ≡ ~(~R) ∨ S. MI says that for any A and B, A → B ≡ ~A ∨ B. So let A be ~R and B be S, and then go from right to left on MI.

Homework Assignment 17

Write each of the following proofs.

Proof Prompt 1

1. P → (Q → R)
2. P
3. ~R
4. ~S → Q ∴ S

Proof Prompt 2

1. k = m
2. ~T → ~(*P*)(*P*k ↔ *P*m) ∴ T

Proof Prompt 3

1. S · (S ∨ T)
2. S → ~Uf ∴ ~Uf

18

Direct Proof (Part 2)

In this chapter we will continue working on proofs, getting up to normal-sized ones. You will use the same three strategies and three helpful tips you used to write shorter proofs in the last chapter. Any other proof you see in this course will not be significantly longer than the ones contained in this chapter. I think you're seeing how powerful having the laws of logic memorized can be. This makes writing proofs—a task which may have seemed intimidating at first—rather straightforward, once you combine the laws of logic with our strategies and tips. Before starting out, a word about the term *direct proof* is in order. What makes the proofs we did last chapter and we're doing this chapter "direct" is that they contain no assumptions, or things we suppose are true without knowing whether or not they actually are true. Rather, everything in a direct proof is an inference from a previous step or steps and therefore known to be true.

Four Proofs

Let's begin by working a short proof, whose prompt runs as follows:

1. ~(∃*x*)(P*x* · Q*x*)
2. Qa
3. Pa ∨ Ra ∴ Ra

Using strategy (1), we know from Sq that ~(∃*x*)(P*x* · Q*x*), i.e., the contradictory of (∃*x*)(P*x* · Q*x*), is (*x*)(P*x* → ~Q*x*). So this gives us our first step, comprising line 4. Moreover, we see that $(x)(\mathrm{P}x \rightarrow {\sim}\mathrm{Q}x)$ can be combined with 2 using UMT to yield ~Pa. This gives us our second step, comprising line 5. And we find that 3 can be combined with ~Pa using DS to give us Ra, which is the conclusion and final step (line 6). For this proof, we didn't even need strategies (2) and (3)! Hence the proof reads:

4. $(x)(\mathrm{P}x \rightarrow {\sim}\mathrm{Q}x)$ (Sq, 1)
5. ~Pa (UMT, 4, 2)
6. Ra (DS, 3, 5)

We move on to a longer proof, whose prompt goes like this:

1. $(\mathrm{P} \cdot \mathrm{Q}) \rightarrow \mathrm{R}$
2. $\mathrm{Q} \cdot {\sim}\mathrm{R}$ $\therefore ({\sim}\mathrm{P} \vee \mathrm{S}) \cdot (({\sim}\mathrm{P} \vee \mathrm{S}) \vee \mathrm{T})$

Let's apply our three strategies. (1) We know from Ex that 1 is equivalent to $\mathrm{P} \rightarrow (\mathrm{Q} \rightarrow \mathrm{R})$, which gives us line 3. We also know from NC that 2 is equivalent to ${\sim}(\mathrm{Q} \rightarrow \mathrm{R})$, thus providing line 4. And using MT on $\mathrm{P} \rightarrow (\mathrm{Q} \rightarrow \mathrm{R})$ and ${\sim}(\mathrm{Q} \rightarrow \mathrm{R})$, we get ~P, which is line 5. (2) Hopefully you recognize from Abs that the conclusion is equivalent to ${\sim}\mathrm{P} \vee \mathrm{S}$, such that Abs annotates the conclusion and ${\sim}\mathrm{P} \vee \mathrm{S}$ is the second to last line. But what annotates ${\sim}\mathrm{P} \vee \mathrm{S}$? (3) We can connect the dots from ~P to ${\sim}\mathrm{P} \vee \mathrm{S}$ by employing Add (to add S), so giving us the annotation of ${\sim}\mathrm{P} \vee \mathrm{S}$. With everything linked up, we write out the proof as follows:

3. $\mathrm{P} \rightarrow (\mathrm{Q} \rightarrow \mathrm{R})$ (Ex, 1)
4. ${\sim}(\mathrm{Q} \rightarrow \mathrm{R})$ (NC, 2)
5. ~P (MT, 3, 4)
6. ${\sim}\mathrm{P} \vee \mathrm{S}$ (Add, 5)
7. $({\sim}\mathrm{P} \vee \mathrm{S}) \cdot (({\sim}\mathrm{P} \vee \mathrm{S}) \vee \mathrm{T})$ (Abs, 6)

We are now ready to write a really long proof (for us, at least). But no need to worry, since we use exactly the same strategies and tips as before!

1. $\mathrm{a} \neq \mathrm{b}$
2. $(P)(P\mathrm{a} \leftrightarrow P\mathrm{b}) \leftrightarrow (\mathrm{Q} \vee (\mathrm{R} \cdot \mathrm{S}))$ $\therefore \mathrm{R} \rightarrow {\sim}\mathrm{S}$

Starting with strategy (1), we observe that 1 is equivalent to saying that ${\sim}(P)(P\mathrm{a} \leftrightarrow P\mathrm{b})$ by Id. This gives us the third line. We know from ME that 2 can be rewritten as the conjunction of both directions of the double-arrow, namely ((*P*)(*P*a ↔ *P*b) → (Q ∨ (R · S))) · ((Q ∨ (R · S)) → (*P*)(*P*a ↔ *P*b)). Long, but straightforward, thus giving us line 4. Now we can use Simp to pick off one of these two "if-then"s, but which one should we take? Well, the one that can be combined with ~(*P*)(*P*a ↔ *P*b), which is (Q ∨ (R · S)) → (*P*)(*P*a ↔ *P*b)). So we'll take this "if-then" as line 5 and combine it with ~(*P*)(*P*a ↔ *P*b) using MT in line 6, giving us ~(Q ∨ (R · S)).

Moving to strategy (2), we note that the conclusion, by MI, is equivalent to ~R ∨ ~S. So MI annotates the conclusion, with ~R ∨ ~S as the second to last line. Now to strategy (3)! Can we connect the dots and get from ~(Q ∨ (R · S)) to ~R ∨ ~S? In the first expression, let's distribute the ~ across the terms, per DeM, yielding ~Q · ~(R · S). This will be line 7. Now we can use DeM again to distribute the ~ across (R · S), giving us ~Q · (~R ∨ ~S) as line 8. Finally, we see how to get to ~R ∨ ~S: by using Simp to pick it off ~Q · (~R ∨ ~S)! So Simp annotates ~R ∨ ~S and completes the proof. Spelling out all our steps, we have:

3. ~(*P*)(*P*a ↔ *P*b) (Id, 1)
4. ((*P*)(*P*a ↔ *P*b) → (Q ∨ (R · S))) · (Q ∨ (R · S)) → (*P*)(*P*a ↔ *P*b)) (ME, 2)
5. (Q ∨ (R · S)) → (*P*)(*P*a ↔ *P*b)) (Simp, 4)
6. ~(Q ∨ (R · S)) (MT, 5, 3)
7. ~Q · ~(R · S) (DeM, 6)
8. ~Q · (~R ∨ ~S) (DeM, 7)
9. ~R ∨ ~S (Simp, 8)
10. R → ~S (MI, 9)

Let's write our last proof together before moving to the pre-homework practice. This one will be medium-long.

1. ~(∃*x*)(P*x* · Q*x*)
2. R → (*x*)(P*x* → Q*x*) ∴ ~S → ~R

Per strategy (1), we know from Sq that (∃*x*)(P*x* · Q*x*) and (∃*x*)(P*x* · ~Q*x*) are subcontraries. That means if one of them is false—and 1 tells us that (∃*x*)(P*x* · Q*x*) is—then the other one is true. So line 3 will read (∃*x*)(P*x* · ~Q*x*) (Sq, 1). Sq also tells us that (∃*x*)(P*x* · ~Q*x*) is the contradictory, or ~, of (*x*)(P*x* → Q*x*). So we can replace (∃*x*)(P*x* · ~Q*x*) with ~(*x*)(P*x* → Q*x*) in line 4. And ~(*x*)(P*x* → Q*x*), combined with 2, gives us ~R by MT, which is line 5. Using strategy (2), we see that the conclusion is equivalent to its contrapositive, namely R → S. So Cont annotates the conclusion and R → S constitutes the second to last line of the proof. So can we connect the dots from ~R to R → S? In strategy (3), we can add S to ~R by Add, thus giving us ~R ∨ S (Add, 5) for line 6. And this, per MI, is equivalent to R → S. Putting the pieces together, we arrive at our completed proof:

3. (∃*x*)(P*x* · ~Q*x*) (Sq, 1)
4. ~(*x*)(P*x* → Q*x*) (Sq, 1)
5. ~R (MT, 2, 4)
6. ~R ∨ S (Add, 5)
7. R → S (MI, 6)
8. ~S → ~R (Cont, 7)

Pre-Homework Practice!

Now try to write two normal-sized proofs on your own. After writing each proof, check it against the answer provided below it. How the answer proceeds from one step to the next should be clear in the annotations. Remember that even if your proof doesn't match the answer, it could still be right. Just double-check that each step you used, ending with the conclusion, follows logically in sequence.

Proof Prompt 1

1. P → ~Q
2. Q
3. ~P → ~(R ∨ S) ∴ ~S

Solution 1

4. Q → ~P (Cont, 1)
5. ~P (MP, 4, 2)
6. ~(R ∨ S) (MP, 5, 3)
7. ~R · ~S (DeM, 6)
8. ~S (Simp, 7)

Proof Prompt 2

1. Pc
2. R → ~(∃*x*)P*x*

3. ~R → S
4. ~T → ~S
5. U ∨ ~T ∴ U

Solution 2

6. (∃*x*)P*x* (EG, 1)
7. ~R (MT, 2, 6)
8. S (MP, 3, 7)
9. T (MT, 4, 8)
10. U (DS, 5, 9)

Homework Assignment 18

Write each of the following proofs.

Proof Prompt 1

1. (*P*)(*P*a ↔ *P*b)
2. R ↔ (a ≠ b) ∴ R → S

Proof Prompt 2

1. ~(∃*x*)(P*x* · Q*x*)
2. Pk
3. R → Qk
4. ~S ↔ R ∴ S

Proof Prompt 3

1. ~(*x*)(P*x* → ~Q*x*)
2. (∃*x*)(P*x* · Q*x*) → ((R · (R ∨ S)) ∨ T)
3. ~R
4. ~U → ~T ∴ U

19

Conditional Proof

SUPPOSE WE ARE GIVEN this to prove:

1. $\underline{P \cdot {\sim}Q \qquad \therefore P \rightarrow {\sim}Q}$

What happens if we use our three strategies? Via strategy (1), if we use NC on 1, we get ~(P → Q), which isn't the conclusion. Via strategy (2), if we reason backward from the conclusion using MI, we get ~P ∨ ~Q, which isn't the premise. Via strategy (3), there's no way to connect the dots between ~(P → Q) and ~P ∨ ~Q. So we clearly need to add a new strategy to complete this proof.

When we need to prove a conditional conclusion (an "if-then" conclusion) and the usual suspects (MI, NC, Ex) don't work, we use *conditional proof (CP)*. Conditional proof is a form of *indirect proof*. Unlike direct proof which makes no assumptions, indirect proof makes some assumptions. In conditional proof, we assume the if-clause (antecedent) we want to prove and, using this assumption and the premise(s), we deduce the then-clause (consequent) we want to prove. In other words, we show that if we start with the antecedent, then we end with the consequent. Thus antecedent → consequent.

How to Write a Conditional Proof

We indent all lines of a conditional proof to indicate that it is hypothetical in nature. The conditional proof begins with the antecedent we want to prove, annotated (Assume for CP), and ends with the consequent we want to prove. The following line (back to actual in nature) is not indented and deduces [first line of conditional proof] → [last line of conditional proof]. It is then annotated (CP, [first line of conditional proof]–[last line of conditional proof]).

So let's see how to complete the proof introduced above, where we'll rewrite the prompt for the sake of convenience.

1. P · ~Q ∴ P → ~Q
    2. P (Assume for CP)
    3. ~Q (Simp, 1)
4. P → ~Q (CP, 2–3)

Once we assume P in 2, then the only question is how to get ~Q. And this is straightforwardly obtained by Simp, as seen in 3. So we've shown that if P, then ~Q, which is precisely our conclusion, noted in 4.

Conditional proof can be a series of steps in a larger proof (if any part of a proof is indirect, the whole proof, by definition, is indirect because it makes at least one assumption). Let's see how we might use CP in helping to solve this proof.

1. ~V
2. ~D ∴ (V ∨ D) → G

It is useful to note that our strategies (formerly three, now four with CP) do not need to be used in order. We can "mix and match" strategies. Here we can start with strategy (2), in our mind's eye reasoning backwards from the conclusion to see that it by Cont is ~G → ~(V ∨ D) (the second to last step in the proof), which by DeM is ~G → (~V · ~D) (the third to last step in the proof). So we write the proof by getting ~G → (~V · ~D) from CP and then using "actual proof" for the rest, as just explained.

If we start the proof by assuming ~G for CP (line 3, indented), then the only question is how to get ~V · ~D. The answer is by using Conj on 1 and 2, which will be line 4, indented. So line 5 will be the unindented, "back to reality" ~G → (~V · ~D), annotated (CP, 3–4). The completed proof runs as follows:

    3. ~G (Assume for CP)
    4. ~V · ~D (Conj, 1, 2)
5. ~G → (~V · ~D) (CP, 3–4)

6. ~G → ~(V ∨ D) (DeM, 5)
7. (V ∨ D) → G (Cont, 6)

From this proof we learn another neat trick to put in our bag. If the conclusion is a conditional and the if-clause is a variable or an expression comprised of variables found nowhere in the premises, use conditional proof by assuming the if-clause. If the conclusion is a conditional and the then-clause is a variable or an expression comprised of variables found nowhere in the premises, then create the contrapositive of the conditional in your mind's eye and use conditional proof by assuming the if-clause of the contrapositive.

Let's now try to write together a proof with the following prompt:

1. ~(∃*x*)(P*x* · Q*x*) → R
2. U ∴ T → ((((∃*x*)(P*x* · Q*x*) ∨ R) ∨ S) · U)

Immediately CP suggests itself as the mode of proof we should employ, since the conclusion is a conditional and the antecedent T is a new variable found nowhere in the premises. Moreover, since T stands alone, we can't derive it by adding it through Add or Abs. So we should begin by assuming T, which will be the indented line 3. Using strategy (1), we detect that 1 can be rewritten as part of the consequent. By MI, ~(∃*x*)(P*x* · Q*x*) → R ≡ (∃*x*)(P*x* · Q*x*) ∨ R, giving us the indented line 4. We can now use Add to get the indented line 5, ((∃*x*)(P*x* · Q*x*) ∨ R) ∨ S, and we can employ Conj on 5 and 2 to get the entire consequent (line 6). Drawing the threads together, we can conclude in line 7 by CP that if antecedent, then consequent. Hence the proof is completed accordingly:

 3. T (Assume for CP)
 4. (∃*x*)(P*x* · Q*x*) ∨ R (MI, 1)
 5. ((∃*x*)(P*x* · Q*x*) ∨ R) ∨ S (Add, 4)
 6. (((∃*x*)(P*x* · Q*x*) ∨ R) ∨ S) · U (Conj, 5, 2)

7. T → ((((∃*x*)(P*x* · Q*x*) ∨ R) ∨ S) · U) (CP, 3–6)

Suppose we needed to write a proof with this prompt:

1. (~R → Q) → ~(*P*)(*P*a ↔ *P*b) ∴ (R · Q) → (a ≠ b)

We should be able to detect by now that the consequent of the conclusion, a ≠ b, is equivalent to the consequent of 1, ~(*P*)(*P*a ↔ *P*b), by Id. So can we get from the antecedent of 1, $\sim R \rightarrow Q$, to the antecedent of the conclusion, $R \cdot Q$? If we use MI, $\sim R \rightarrow Q \equiv R \vee Q$, which is clearly not the same as $R \cdot Q$. At this point we detect that CP is in order, where we will assume $R \cdot Q$ (the indented line 2) and try to get to $a \neq b$ (also indented; the second to last step in the proof overall). We already know the second to last step in the indented part of the proof (and the third to last step in the proof overall), which is $\sim(P)(Pa \leftrightarrow Pb)$. But we don't yet know its annotation.

So assuming $R \cdot Q$ and working forwards via strategy (1), we can begin to lay out a strategy. We should get from $R \cdot Q$ to $R \vee Q$, the latter of which we already know by MI is $\sim R \rightarrow Q$. That will allow us to use MP with 1 to get $\sim(P)(Pa \leftrightarrow Pb)$, and we know what to do from there. So to answer our earlier query, MP will be the annotation of the indented $\sim(P)(Pa \leftrightarrow Pb)$ line. Now let's carry out the strategy. We can deduce $R \vee Q$ from $R \cdot Q$ in two steps. First, use Simp to get R (or Q; the indented line 3), and use Add to get Q (or R; the indented line 4). Then the indented line 5 is our MI, the indented line 6 our $\sim(P)(Pa \leftrightarrow Pb)$, the indented line 7 our $a \neq b$, and the unindented line 8 our conclusion.

    2. $R \cdot Q$ (Assume for CP)
    3. R (Simp, 2)
    4. $R \vee Q$ (Add, 3)
    5. $\sim R \rightarrow Q$ (MI, 4)
    6. $\sim(P)(Pa \leftrightarrow Pb)$ (MP, 1, 5)
    7. $a \neq b$ (Id, 6)
8. $(R \cdot Q) \rightarrow (a \neq b)$ (CP, 2–7)

Pre-Homework Practice!

You're now ready to write two proofs, each using CP, on your own. After writing each proof, check it against the answer provided below it.

Proof Prompt 1

1. R $\therefore (a = b) \rightarrow ((S \rightarrow R) \vee T)$

Solution 1

2. a = b (Assume for CP)
    a. Since the antecedent of the conclusion is not 1 and cannot be derived from 1, we must get it as an assumption in CP.
3. R ∨ ~S (Add, 1)
    a. Our goal is to try to get from R to S → R. Knowing that S → R ≡ ~S ∨ R by MI, we can add the ~S in this step and then flip them in the next.
4. ~S ∨ R (Com, 3)
    a. This is the first time we've seen Com in a while! As suggested above, you can see in the next step how it pays off.
5. S → R (MI, 4)
6. (S → R) ∨ T (Add, 5)

7. (a = b) → ((S → R) ∨ T) (CP, 2–6)

Proof Prompt 2

1. (P → Q) · (R → S) ∴ ~(Q · S) → (~P ∨ ~R)

Solution 2

2. ~(Q · S) (Assume for CP)
    a. There's no obvious way to get from 1 to either the antecedent or the consequent of the conclusion. So we'll assume the antecedent for CP.
3. ~Q ∨ ~S (DeM, 2)
4. (~Q → ~P) · (~S → ~R) (Cont, 1)
    a. Here we simply replaced the components of 1 with their contrapositives. We did so to be able to use CD with 3. Accordingly:
5. ~P ∨ ~R (CD, 4, 3)

6. ~(Q · S) → (~P ∨ ~R) (CP, 2–5)

Homework Assignment 19

Write each of the following proofs using CP.

Proof Prompt 1

1. ~S
2. ~T → S ∴ P → (T ∨ (T · U))

Proof Prompt 2

1. Rd
2. (∃*x*)R*x* → (*x*)(S*x* → T*x*) ∴ (*x*)(U*x* · V*x*) → ((*x*)(S*x* → T*x*) ∨ (∃*x*)W*x*)

20

Reductio ad Absurdum

SUPPOSE YOU CAN'T SEE how to prove a conclusion directly or by conditional proof. You can then use another method of indirect proof, called *reductio ad absurdum* (*RAA*; Latin for "reducing to absurdity"). This is also called proof by contradiction. A contradiction states for some A that A · ~A. This statement is necessarily false—it is logically impossible for it to be true. The key to this method is that anything that implies a contradiction is false. Therefore, we can conclude that the negation of that thing is true. As we have already seen, many proofs can be done in multiple ways. Unless the method to use is specified, use whichever method is easiest. In this chapter, we will specify RAA as our method.

How RAA Works

In RAA, you prove the conclusion is true by proving that its negation leads to a contradiction. This shows that the negation of the negation of the conclusion is true, which by DN means that the conclusion is true. You indent all lines of RAA just like you do CP. Start by assuming for RAA the negation of the conclusion, annotating this line with (Assume for RAA). Then use it and the premises to deduce a contradiction. In the following line—which is unindented—you can deduce the conclusion, annotated by (RAA, [first step of RAA]–[last step of RAA]).

Let's write four proofs together using RAA, starting with this one.

1. P → (Q → R)
2. ~R ∴ ~P ∨ ~Q

We'll start by assuming the negation of the conclusion, which we will indent and mark like this:

3. ~(~P ∨ ~Q) (Assume for RAA)

Now we'll try to derive a contradiction—any contradiction—from it and the premises. So the appropriate strategy to employ at this point is our first one, namely, working forwards. The natural place to start is by distributing the ~ across all three terms:

4. P · Q (DeM, 3)

I think you may be able to see now how to get a contradiction. Recalling from Ex that P → (Q → R) ≡ (P · Q) → R, we have:

5. (P · Q) → R (Ex, 1)

At this point we can generate a contradiction in two ways, of which you can choose either. The first way is to use MP on 5 and 4 to get R (step 6), and then using Conj on 6 and 2 to get the contradiction R · ~R:

6. R (MP, 5, 4)
7. R · ~R (Conj, 6, 2)

The second way is to use MT on 5 and 2 to get ~(P · Q) (step 6), and then using Conj on 4 and 6 to get the contradiction (P · Q) · ~(P · Q):

6. ~(P · Q) (MT, 5, 2)
7. (P · Q) · ~(P · Q) (Conj, 4, 6)

Having derived a contradiction from the negation of the conclusion, we now conclude that the conclusion is in fact true in line 8, which is therefore unindented:

8. ~P ∨ ~Q (RAA, 3–7)

The second RAA proof we'll write together has the following prompt:

1. ~(∃*x*)(P*x* · ~Q*x*)
2. ~R → (*x*)(P*x* → ~Q*x*)
3. ~R ∨ H ∴ H

Like before, we'll start by assuming ~H (indented line 4) and working forwards. By DS on 3 and 4, we get ~R (indented line 5). Then by MP on 2 and 5, we get (*x*)(P*x* → ~Q*x*) (indented line 6). By Sq, (*x*)(P*x* → ~Q*x*) implies its subaltern (∃*x*)(P*x* · ~Q*x*) (indented line 7), which, with line 1, generates a contradiction (indented line 8). Hence H is true (unindented line 9), and our completed proof runs like this:

4. ~H (Assume for RAA)
5. ~R (DS, 4, 3)
6. (*x*)(P*x* → ~Q*x*) (MP, 2, 5)
7. (∃*x*)(P*x* · ~Q*x*) (Sq, 6)
8. (∃*x*)(P*x* · ~Q*x*) · ~(∃*x*)(P*x* · ~Q*x*) (Conj, 7, 1)

9. H (RAA, 4–8)

The prompt of the third RAA proof we will write together is as follows:

1. R · ~Q
2. ~(*P*)(*P*f ↔ *P*g) → Q ∴ f = g

We'll begin by assuming f ≠ g (indented line 3) and working forwards. By Id, f ≠ g is equivalent to ~(*P*)(*P*f ↔ *P*g) (indented line 4). Using MP with 2, we get Q (indented line 5). The contradiction should be evident by now. We can pick off ~Q from 1 (indented line 6) and then conjoin it with Q (indented line 7), giving us our contradiction. Consequently, f = g (unindented line 8).

3. f ≠ g (Assume for RAA)
4. ~(*P*)(*P*f ↔ *P*g) (Id, 3)
5. Q (MP, 2, 4)
6. ~Q (Simp, 1)
7. Q · ~Q (Conj, 5, 6)

8. f = g (RAA, 3–7)

One more RAA proof and you'll be ready to try one on your own! Consider the following:

1. ~(P · ~Q)
2. ~R ∨ S
3. P ∨ R ∴ ~(~Q · ~S)

We assume ~Q · ~S (indented line 4) and work forwards, trying to generate a contradiction. The obvious place to start is by picking ~S off ~Q · ~S (indented line 5) and then using DS on 2 and ~S to get ~R (indented line 6). Then we can use DS on 3 and ~R to get P (indented line 7). So how can we use P? Per DeM, we distribute the ~ across our three terms in 1 to get ~P ∨ Q (indented line 8) and apply DS with P to get Q (line 9). At this point we can pick off ~Q from ~Q · ~S (indented line 10), allowing us to generate the contradiction Q · ~Q (indented line 11). Since ~Q · ~S generates a contradiction, ~(~Q · ~S) is therefore true (unindented line 12).

4. ~Q · ~S (Assume for RAA)
5. ~S (Simp, 4)
6. ~R (DS, 2, 5)
7. P (DS, 3, 6)
8. ~P ∨ Q (DeM, 1)
9. Q (DS, 8, 7)
10. ~Q (Simp, 4)
11. Q · ~Q (Conj, 9, 10)

12. ~(~Q · ~S) (RAA, 4–11)

You may have seen a different way to complete the same proof using RAA. From indented step 4, you could have used DeM to get ~(Q ∨ S) as your indented step 5. Then you could use the indented step 8 above as your indented step 6. Afterward, you could employ a double application of MI, once on ~P ∨ Q to yield P → Q (indented step 7) and once on 2 to yield R → S (indented step 8). You could conjoin the two "if-then"s as your indented step 9 and then, with 3, used CD to get Q ∨ S as your indented step 10. But this contradicts ~(Q ∨ S), which you can spell out by Conj as your indented step 11. This also gets you to 12. Our alternate path runs like this:

4. ~Q · ~S (Assume for RAA)
5. ~(Q ∨ S) (DeM, 4)
6. ~P ∨ Q (DeM, 1)

7. P → Q (MI, 6)
8. R → S (MI, 2)
9. (P → Q) · (R → S) (Conj, 7, 8)
10. Q ∨ S (CD, 9, 3)
11. (Q ∨ S) · ~(Q ∨ S) (Conj, 10, 5)

12. ~(~Q · ~S) (RAA, 4–11)

Pre-Homework Practice!

You're now ready to write two proofs, each using RAA, on your own. After writing each proof, check it against the answer provided below it. Remember that there may be more than one way to write it. So if your answer does not match, just make sure to carefully check your sequence of steps to make sure you start with the contradiction of the conclusion, your second to last step is a contradiction, and your last step is the conclusion, with all steps following in logical sequence.

Proof Prompt 1

1. S · (S ∨ T)
2. S → Q ∴ Q

Solution 1

3. ~Q (Assume for RAA)
4. ~S (MT, 2, 3)
5. S (Simp, 1)
6. S · ~S (Conj, 5, 4)

7. Q (RAA, 3–6)

Proof Prompt 2

1. (*x*)(P*x* → Q*x*)
2. ~Qf
3. S → Pf ∴ ~S

Solution 2

4. S (Assume for RAA)
5. Pf (MP, 3, 4)
6. Qf (UMP, 1, 5)
7. Qf · ~Qf (Conj, 6, 2)

8. ~S (RAA, 4–7)

Homework Assignment 20

Write each of the following proofs using RAA.

Proof Prompt 1

1. k = m
2. ~T → ~(*P*)(*P*k ↔ *P*m)   ∴ T

Proof Prompt 2

1. P ∨ (Q · R)
2. P → ~Sf   ∴ ~Sf

21

Reviewing Methods of Proof

Over the last four chapters you have seen the power of knowing and applying the laws of logic in proving whether a purported conclusion follows validly from one or more premises. Learning how to prove things is an extremely important skill, which I applaud you for learning. But you may wonder why this skill is so important. The reason is that it enables you to test whether the conclusions or main points offered by people in all walks of life—from friends and family members to colleagues to television newscasters to lawyers to politicians—are actually supported by the evidence they give in support of those conclusions. To carry out this test, all you need to do is to symbolize each piece of their evidence—namely, their premises—and their conclusion, and then use either direct proof, conditional proof, or *reductio ad absurdum* to see if the conclusion can be properly drawn. If yes, the argument is valid, and you should now turn to the question of whether the premises are true. If no, the argument is invalid, and you shouldn't pay any more attention to it unless it seems that the conclusion follows probably, though not inescapably, from the premises.

For example, suppose a philosophy professor said to you, "Abstract objects are either thoughts in the mind of God or Platonic ideals. For abstract objects do not exist unless they are immaterial. And abstract objects aren't thoughts in the mind of God only if they are material. Of course, abstract objects exist." Is your professor making a valid argument? Recognizing that the word "for" is a premise indicator and that whatever sentiment precedes it is some sort of conclusion, we perceive that the first sentence is the conclusion and the last three sentences are premises. In the premise, "Abstract objects do not exist unless they are immaterial," we see our "not . . . unless . . ." double negative, which just means "If *a*bstract objects exist, then they are *i*mmaterial," symbolized A → I. Since the "only if" in the next premise means "then" and that the other clause is the if-clause, it can be rewritten, "If abstract objects aren't *t*houghts in the mind of God, then they are material." Now being material is, by DN, the same as not being immaterial. So this premise can be symbolized ~T → ~I. The last premise, "Abstract objects exist," is just A. And our conclusion, "Abstract objects are either *t*houghts in the mind of God or *P*latonic ideals," can be symbolized T ∨ P. All this gives us the following prompt for a proof.

1. A → I
2. ~T → ~I
3. A ∴ T ∨ P

If we can successfully complete this proof, the professor's argument is valid. (Now it may or may not be sound—this will depend on whether the premises are true.) If the proof can't be written, the professor's argument is invalid. So let's try writing it using our strategies. (1) Using MP, we can put 1 and 3 together to get I (line 4). And using MT, we can put 2 together with I to get T (line 5). Finally, we can use Add to tack P onto T (line 6), which is the conclusion. The completed proof appears as follows:

4. I (MP, 1, 3)
5. T (MT, 2, 4)
6. T ∨ P (Add, 5)

So we have proven the professor's argument to be valid! You can apply your proof-writing techniques to test the validity of any other argument you encounter in life.

Four Examples to Check Your Skills

Let's make sure you have the methods of proof under your belt by working four examples together. Consider first this proof prompt:

1. P · (Q ∨ R)
2. ((P · Q) ∨ (P · R)) → S
3. ~T → ~S ∴ T

What technique should we use? Well, we could use either direct proof or *reductio ad absurdum*, whichever you find easiest. We'll see how the proof can be written both ways.

We'll use direct proof first. Employing strategy (1), we find that 3 can be rewritten as its contrapositive, S → T (line 4). Then we can link up 2 with S → T via HS to yield ((P · Q) ∨ (P · R)) → T (line 5). So now all we need is ((P · Q) ∨ (P · R)) to get T. By Dist on 1, we get precisely this expression (line 6). Then we can use MP on 2 and ((P · Q) ∨ (P · R)) to reach our conclusion (line 7). Here we didn't need strategies (2) and (3). (There are other ways, using direct proof, we could have reached the same conclusion; you may see one of them.) Our direct proof is completed like this:

4. S → T (Cont, 3)
5. ((P · Q) ∨ (P · R)) → T (HS, 2, 4)
6. (P · Q) ∨ (P · R) (Dist, 1)
7. T (MP, 5, 6)

Now we'll turn to RAA. We'll assume ~T, the negation of the conclusion, and try to derive a contradiction (indented line 4). Combining 3 with ~T by MP gives ~S (indented line 5). And combining 2 with ~S by MT yields ~((P · Q) ∨ (P · R)) (indented line 6). Then we can use Dist on 1 to obtain (P · Q) ∨ (P · R) (indented line 7). Conjoining lines 7 and 6 produces a contradiction (indented line 8), such that T logically follows from our RAA (unindented line 9).

    4. ~T (Assume for RAA)
    5. ~S (MP, 3, 4)
    6. ~((P · Q) ∨ (P · R)) (MT, 2, 5)
    7. (P · Q) ∨ (P · R) (Dist, 1)
    8. ((P · Q) ∨ (P · R)) · ~((P · Q) ∨ (P · R)) (Conj, 7, 6)

9. T (RAA, 4–8)

We now turn to our second proof prompt:

1. $(x)(Px \rightarrow {\sim}Qx)$
2. Qf
3. $\underline{{\sim}R \rightarrow Pf \qquad\qquad \therefore (\exists x)(Tx \cdot {\sim}Ux) \rightarrow (R \cdot (R \vee S))}$

Here we immediately see a conditional conclusion, where the antecedent contains elements nowhere found in nor derivable from our premises. This scenario therefore demands CP, where we'll assume the antecedent in the indented step 4. We should also notice, per strategy (2), that the consequent of the conclusion is, by Abs, equivalent to R. Remember that it's fine to employ whatever strategies we need in whatever order we prefer. So our goal is to use the three premises to derive R. We next turn to strategy (1). Using UMT on 1 and 2, we obtain ~Pf (indented line 5). Using MT on 3 and ~Pf, we obtain R (indented line 6). Then the indented line 7 uses Abs to get (R ∨ S), allowing us to draw our conclusion in the unindented line 8. The full proof therefore reads as follows:

   4. $(\exists x)(Tx \cdot {\sim}Ux)$ (Assume for CP)
   5. ~Pf (UMT, 1, 2)
   6. R (MT, 3, 5)
   7. $R \cdot (R \vee S)$ (Abs, 6)
8. $(\exists x)(Tx \cdot {\sim}Ux) \rightarrow (R \cdot (R \vee S))$ (CP, 4–7)

Our third proof has this prompt:

1. ${\sim}T \rightarrow ({\sim}V \vee S)$
2. ${\sim}T \vee P$
3. $\underline{V \cdot {\sim}S \qquad\qquad \therefore P \vee (P \cdot Q)}$

Since the conclusion is not a conditional, we have direct proof and RAA at our disposal as the methods we can use. Let's use each in turn.

In direct proof, the first thing to notice, per strategy (2), is that the conclusion is equivalent to P by Abs. So the conclusion, annotated Abs, will be the proof's last line, and P will be our second to last line. But we don't yet know its annotation. Still working backwards, we query: How could we get P? Well, if we knew T, then P would follow by DS from 2 and T. So the annotation of the P line will include DS, and the third to last line will be T. We'll now use strategy (1) to obtain T. Recall that one of our neat tricks—always encouraged—is cleverly employing DN. We can think in our mind's eye that 3 is, by DN, equivalent to ~(~(V · ~S)). Then we can distribute the inner ~ across the terms to get ~(~V ∨ S) by DeM, which will be line 4. This we can combine with 1 via MT to get T (line 5). So the complete proof runs accordingly:

4. ~(~V ∨ S) (DeM, 3)
5. T (MT, 1, 4)
6. P (DS, 2, 5)
7. P ∨ (P · Q) (Abs, 6)

Now we'll use RAA to solve the proof. We first assume ~(P ∨ (P · Q)):

    4. ~(P ∨ (P · Q)) (Assume for RAA)

Then we use Abs to convert the expression inside the first set of parentheses to P:

    5. ~P (Abs, 4)

Finally, we duplicate steps 4 through 6 in the direct proof as our indented steps 6 through 8:

    6. ~(~V ∨ S) (DeM, 3)
    7. T (MT, 1, 6)
    8. P (DS, 2, 7)

Now we conjoin 8 and 5 to yield our contradiction:

    9. P · ~P (Conj, 8, 5)

Finally, we draw our unindented conclusion:

10. P ∨ (P · Q) (RAA, 4–9)[1]

1. Another way of completing the proof using RAA runs like this:

    4. ~(P ∨ (P · Q)) (Assume for RAA)
    5. ~P (Abs, 4)
    6. ~T (DS, 2, 5)
    7. ~V ∨ S (MP, 1, 6)
    8. V → S (MI, 7)
    9. ~(V → S) (NC, 3)
    10. (V → S) · ~(V → S) (Conj, 8, 9)

11. P ∨ (P · Q) (RAA, 4–10)

Let's move to our final proof prompt before the pre-homework practice:

1. (*x*)(P*x* → Q*x*)
2. (*x*)(Q*x* → R*x*)
3. (*x*)(R*x* → ~S*x*)
4. ~Te → Se
5. Pe ∴ (∃*x*)T*x*

At first glance, direct proof looks easiest because we see, via UHS, that 1–3 can be combined into (*x*)(P*x* → ~S*x*) (line 6). Q*x* and R*x* constitute our two links in the chain. Working forwards per strategy (1), we then use UMP on (*x*)(P*x* → ~S*x*) and 5 to get ~Se (line 7). And this can be combined with 4 using MT to obtain Te (line 8). From that our conclusion follows by EG (line 9).

6. (*x*)(P*x* → ~S*x*) (UHS, 1–3)
7. ~Se (UMP, 6, 5)
8. Te (MT, 4, 7)
9. (∃*x*)T*x* (EG, 8)

Pre-Homework Practice!

Here are three proofs for you to write on your own, doing so in whatever way works best for you. A possible solution is given below each one for you to check your answer.

Proof Prompt 1

1. (*x*)(R*x* → ~Q*x*)
2. (a = b) → ~(∃*x*)(R*x* · ~Q*x*) ∴ Y → ~(*P*)(*P*a ↔ *P*b)

Solution 1

3. Y (Assume for CP)
    a. Since our conclusion is a conditional and Y appears nowhere in the premises, CP is required for this proof.

4. $(\exists x)(Rx \cdot \sim Qx)$ (Sq, 1)
    a. This is the subaltern of 1.
5. $a \neq b$ (MT, 2, 4)
6. $\sim(P)(Pa \leftrightarrow Pb)$ (Id, 5)

7. $Y \rightarrow \sim(P)(Pa \leftrightarrow Pb)$ (CP, 3–6)

Proof Prompt 2

1. $\sim P \rightarrow (U \cdot V)$
2. $\sim U$ $\therefore (P \cdot (P \vee R)) \vee (\exists x)(Sx \cdot Tx)$

Solution 2

3. $\sim U \vee \sim V$ (Add, 2)
    a. In this step and the next one, we're trying to get something we can use via MT with 1.
4. $\sim(U \cdot V)$ (DeM, 3)
5. P (MT, 1, 4)
6. $P \cdot (P \vee R)$ (Abs, 5)
7. $(P \cdot (P \vee R)) \vee (\exists x)(Sx \cdot Tx)$ (Add, 6)
    a. This is the beauty of Add—you can literally tack on anything, no matter how crazy-looking!

Proof Prompt 3

1. $P \rightarrow (Q \rightarrow R)$
2. $(\sim P \rightarrow (e = f)) \cdot (Z \rightarrow Q)$
3. $\sim R$ $\therefore (e = f) \vee \sim Z$

Solution 3

4. $(P \cdot Q) \rightarrow R$ (Ex, 1)
5. $\sim(P \cdot Q)$ (MT, 4, 3)
6. $\sim P \vee \sim Q$ (DeM, 5)

7. (~P → (e = f)) · (~Q → ~Z) (Cont, 2)

    a. Here we need, in 2, to replace Z → Q with its contrapositive in order to use CD with 6 in the next step.

8. (e = f) ∨ ~Z (CD, 7, 6)

Homework Assignment 21

Write each of the following proofs.

Proof Prompt 1

1. (~Pc · Rc) → Qc
2. ~(Rc → Qc)
3. Pc ↔ (S ∨ T)   ∴ ~S → T

Proof Prompt 2

1. (*P*)(*P*a ↔ *P*b)
2. ~(U ∨ V) → (a ≠ b)
3. (~W → ~U) · (V → (*x*)(R*x* → ~S*x*))   ∴ W ∨ ~(∃*x*)(R*x* · S*x*)

22

Illustrating Validity and Invalidity with Ellipse Diagrams

Let's begin this chapter by talking about when ellipse diagrams are useful. Suppose you don't need to prove that an argument featuring "all," "no," "some," and/or "some . . . not" is valid but want to quickly find out whether it is valid. Note that an ellipse diagram is not a proof, since it doesn't lay out the logical steps needed to get from the premises to the conclusion. So if you're asked to prove something, it's incorrect to use an ellipse diagram. Two conditions are needed for the ellipse diagram method to work. First, the argument is quantified, namely, featuring "all," "no," "some," and/or "some . . . not." Second, the conclusion is definite. In other words, the conclusion states what is, as opposed to what is probable, possible, impossible, rational, etc. In sum, if you're simply asked the question of a quantified argument with a definite conclusion, "Is it valid?," then it's perfectly appropriate to figure out the answer with an ellipse diagram.

Drawing Quantified Statements

All A are B ≡ $(x)(Ax \rightarrow Bx)$ looks like this:

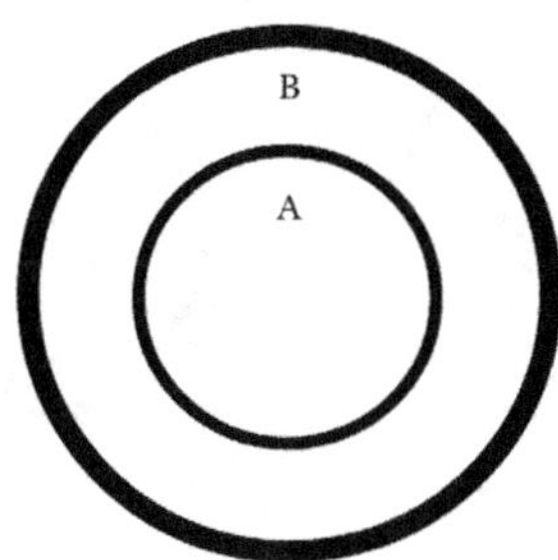

No A are B ≡ $(x)(Ax \rightarrow \sim Bx)$ looks like this:

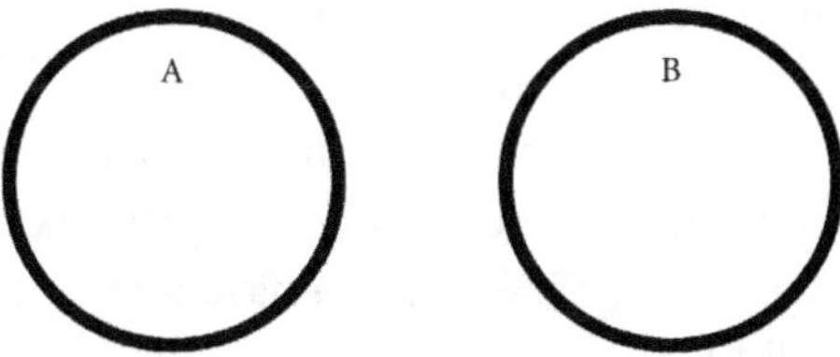

Some A are B ≡ $(\exists x)(Ax \cdot Bx)$ looks like this:

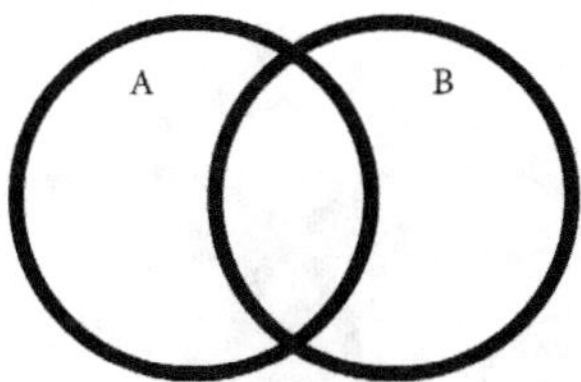

It is ambiguous how to draw "Some A are not B" ≡ $(\exists x)(Ax \cdot \sim Bx)$, since we don't know how many A aren't B. So we err on the side of caution and draw it like "All A are not B," namely, "No A are B."

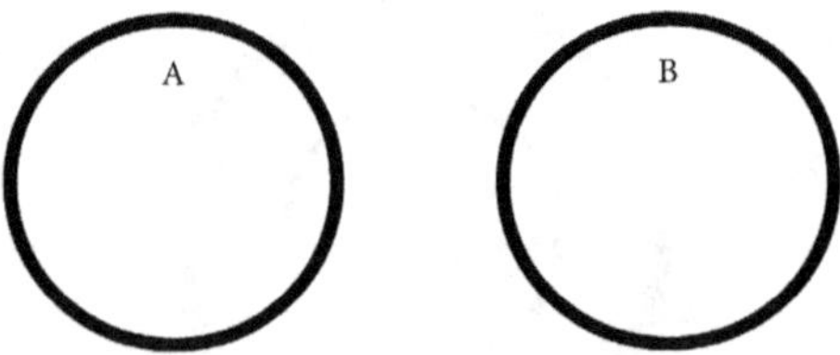

Guilty Unless It Must Be Drawn Innocent

Key to the ellipse diagram method is that we draw the pictures assuming the conclusion does not follow from the premises (i.e., assuming invalidity). To use courtroom language, we assume that the argument is guilty (i.e., invalid) unless it must be drawn innocent (i.e., valid). If we can draw the pictures such that the argument looks invalid, it is invalid. If the argument can only be drawn in such a way that it looks valid, it is valid. So only overlap circles if (1) you have to or (2) doing so makes the argument invalid.

Let's employ our method to see whether this argument is valid: "Every stupid cat is an epistemological sewer. Some epistemological sewers run for public office. So some runners for public office are stupid cats." Let's abbreviate stupid cats as SC, epistemological sewers as ES, and runners for public office as R.

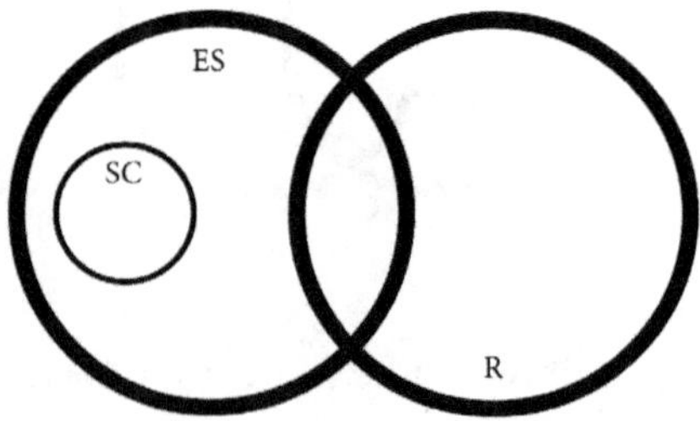

The argument can be drawn such that no runners for public office are stupid cats. So it is invalid.

At this juncture an important observation about drawing individual members of a group (e.g., a particular stupid cat named Agi) is in order. Individual members of a group can only be put in one place.

Keeping with the "guilty unless it must be drawn innocent" motto, put individual members of a group in only that group unless putting it in multiple groups makes the argument invalid. Let's use this advice in checking whether another argument is valid: "Only organisms are trees. No organism is a DVD. So the pink DVD isn't a tree." Remember that "only organisms are trees" means "all trees are organisms." We abbreviate trees as T, organisms as O, DVDs as D, and the pink DVD as p (lowercase since it's an individual member of a group).

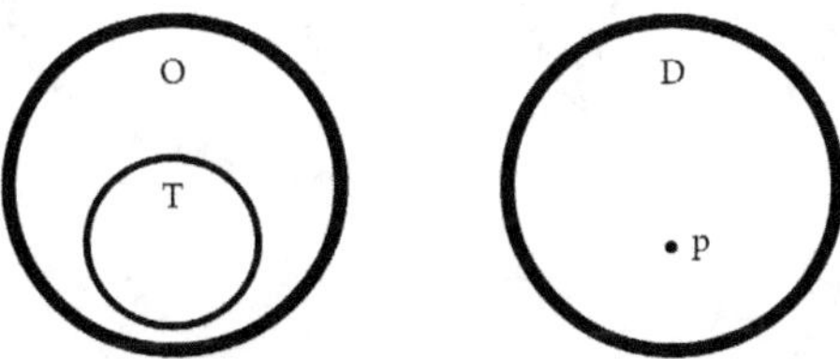

There's no way to draw this such that the pink DVD is a tree. So the argument is valid.

Now consider this argument: "All cats breathe. No cat is a lobster. So the lobster crawling around on my kitchen counter doesn't breathe." We abbreviate cats as C, breathers as B, lobsters as L, and the lobster crawling around on my kitchen counter as l. How are we going to draw the lobster group? So as to make the argument invalid if possible! In other words, we'll intersect the lobster group with the breather group. Where are we going to put the lobster crawling around on my kitchen counter? So as to make the argument invalid if possible! Thus we'll place this lobster in the section of lobsters that are breathers.

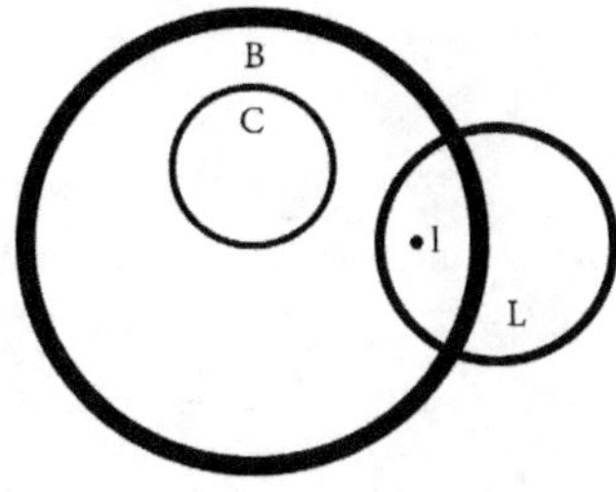

As our drawing illustrates, the argument is invalid.

Let's determine whether this argument is valid using the diagram method: "Some yellow shoes are comfortable. All comfortable things are attractive. For these reasons, some attractive things are yellow shoes." We abbreviate yellow shoes as YS, comfortable things as C, and attractive things as A.

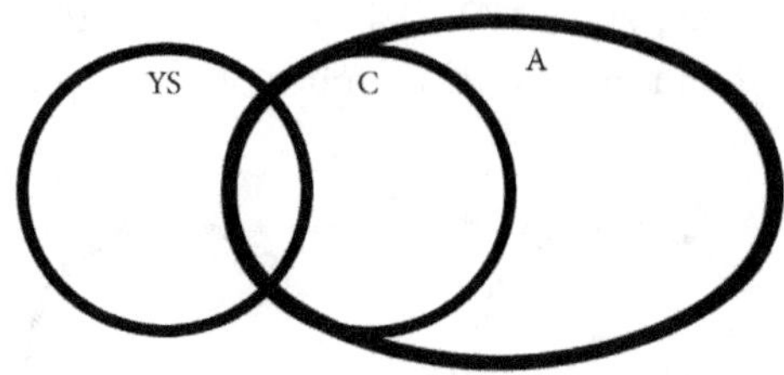

So this argument is valid.

Here's a tricky argument to test for validity: "All humans eat pizza. All pizzas eat hair dryers. All hair dryers eat spiders. So all humans eat spiders." This looks like UHS but isn't. Why not? Recall that we must rewrite quantified statements with the copula (is/are) as the verb. When we do this, we see that the argument means "All humans are pizza eaters. All pizzas are hair dryer eaters. All hair dryers are spider eaters. So all humans are spider eaters." Obviously, pizza eaters aren't necessarily pizzas and hair dryer eaters aren't necessarily hair dryers. There's no reason at all to think that the group of pizza eaters overlaps with the group of pizzas or that the group of hair dryer eaters overlaps with the group of hair dryers. Hence there are no links in the chain and so no chain! Abbreviating humans as H, pizza eaters as PE, pizzas as P, hair dryer eaters as HDE, hair dryers as HD, and spider eaters as SE, our drawing proceeds like this:

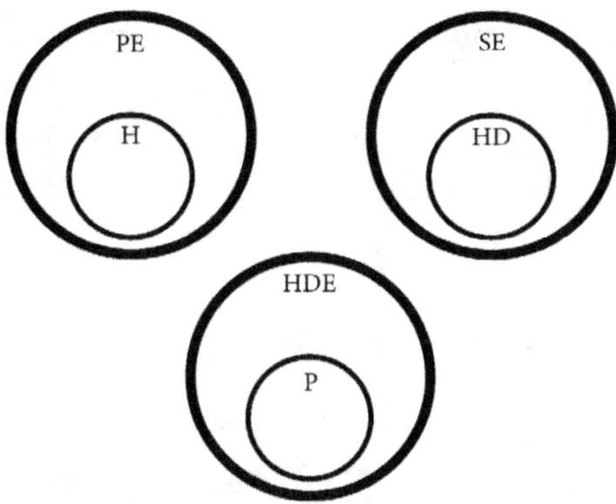

This argument is invalid.

Pre-Homework Practice!

Now try drawing two arguments on your own using the ellipse diagram method to see whether they are valid. Afterwards, check your drawing with the drawing below each argument.

1. Some delicious things are apples. Some apples are red. All red things exemplify the abstract object of redness. So some things that exemplify the abstract object of redness are delicious.
   a. Abbreviating delicious things as D, apples as A, red things as R, and redness exemplifiers as RE, the drawing appears as follows.

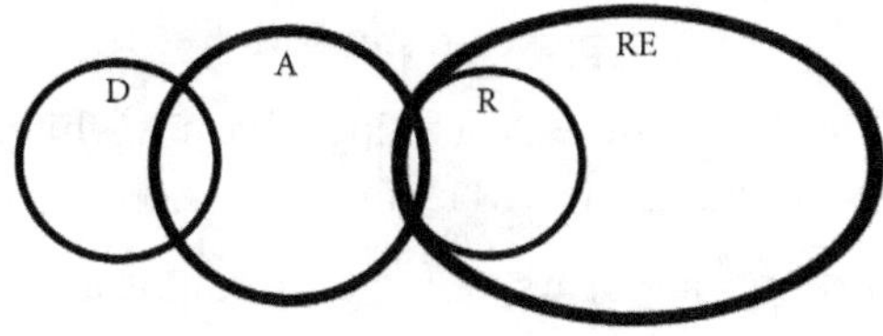

This argument is invalid.

2. Only dogs growl. Every dog chases mail carriers. Only logic textbooks are mail carrier chasers. Annie is a growler. So Annie is a logic textbook!

a. Remember that "only dogs growl" means "all growlers are dogs." Likewise, remember that "only logic textbooks are mail carrier chasers" means "All mail carrier chasers are logic textbooks." Abbreviating growlers as G, dogs as D, mail carrier chasers as MCC, logic textbooks as LT, and Annie as a, the drawing appears as follows:

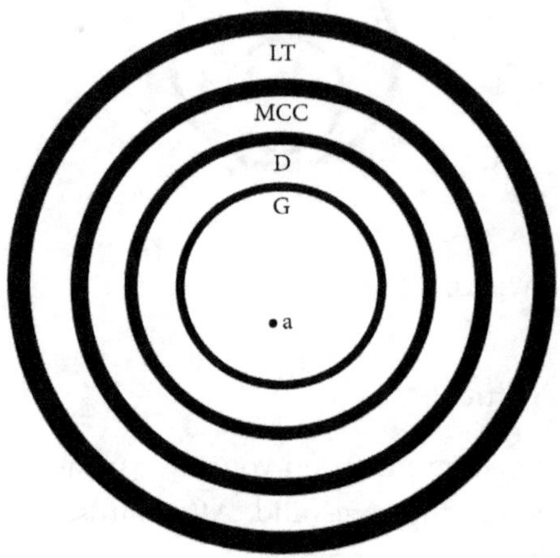

This argument is valid.

Homework Assignment 22

Use ellipse diagrams to figure out if each argument is valid or invalid.

1. Every ear of corn is healthy. Some things that taste bad are healthy. So the ear of corn I just picked tastes bad.
2. All cirrus clouds are white. Not a single barn is white. So there does not exist a barn that is a cirrus cloud.
3. Only mean things are bears. Some traffic signs are bears. So every traffic sign is mean.

23

Fallacies (Part 1)

Fallacies are extremely frequent in today's culture. Every day, politicians, pundits, newscasters, lawyers, advertisements, and people on social media commit fallacies. Scarcely a day will go by in your life where you will not hear at least one fallacy. So what are fallacies? Fallacies are ways an argument can be weak and therefore bad. Pointing out a fallacy or explaining why, in plain English, something is a fallacy exposes where the argument is most susceptible to attack. There are two broad types of fallacies: *formal* and *informal*. Formal means something is wrong with the argument's structure, such that the argument is structured so poorly that even if all its premises are true, its conclusion still does not follow. Informal means something is wrong with the argument's content, such that the content of one or more of the premises makes it impossible to infer the conclusion from the truth of the premises. To be a good critical thinker, it is extremely important for you to be able to recognize fallacies right away and dismiss them right away as bad arguments that aren't worth your attention. Unless you know your fallacies and can spot them immediately, you potentially fall prey to being duped by them.

We will spend the next three chapters learning the various fallacies and why they are fallacies. You will probably find these chapters to be the most practically relevant of all those in this textbook. Upon studying them, you'll start recognizing fallacies instantly. From two decades of teaching experience, my students frequently comment after learning this material that they are amazed at how many fallacies they encounter on a daily basis and now know why not to believe them. Moreover, they—and you—can explain to friends and family why various arguments are fallacies and why they should not believe these arguments.

Formal Fallacies

Let's start by reviewing various formal fallacies you have already encountered in this book, grouped according to the mistake they commit. The fallacy of affirming the consequent looks like this:

1. $A \rightarrow B$	1. If I'm in my basement, then I'm enjoying myself.
2. B	2. I'm enjoying myself.
3. $\therefore$ A	3. Therefore, I'm in my basement.

Similarly, the fallacy known as the converse error wrongly infers from $A \rightarrow B$ that $\therefore$ $B \rightarrow A$. We can illustrate the converse error using the propositions above: "If I'm in my basement, then I'm enjoying myself. Therefore, if I'm enjoying myself, then I'm in my basement." The fallacy of universal affirming the consequent is the quantified version of affirming the consequent and looks like this:

1. $(x)(Ax \rightarrow Bx)$	1. All even numbers are pleasant to me.
2. Bc	2. My blue hair dryer is pleasant to me.
3. $\therefore$ Ac	3. Therefore, my blue hair dryer is an even number.

The fallacy known as the universal converse error—the quantified version of the converse error—wrongly infers from $(x)(Ax \rightarrow Bx)$ that $\therefore$ $(x)(Bx \rightarrow Ax)$. The universal converse error can be illustrated as follows: "All even numbers are pleasant to me. Therefore, all things that are pleasant to me are even numbers." So what is the common mistake these four fallacies—affirming the consequent, the converse error, universal affirming the consequent, and the universal converse error—commit? In plain English, these are fallacies because they confuse a necessary condition for a sufficient condition.

Our next group of fallacies also contains four members. The fallacy of denying the antecedent runs as follows:

1. $A \rightarrow B$	1. If I'm in my basement, then I'm enjoying myself.
2. $\sim A$	2. I'm not in my basement.
3. $\therefore \sim B$	3. Therefore, I'm not enjoying myself.

Likewise, the fallacy known as the inverse error wrongly infers from $A \rightarrow B$ that $\therefore \sim A \rightarrow \sim B$. Using the most recent propositions, an example of the inverse error would be "If I'm in my basement, then I'm enjoying myself. Therefore, if I'm not in my basement, then I'm not enjoying myself." Both of these fallacies also have quantified versions. The fallacy of universal denying the antecedent incorrectly reasons:

1. $(x)(Ax \rightarrow Bx)$	1. All even numbers are pleasant to me.
2. $\sim Ac$	2. My blue hair dryer is not an even number.
3. $\therefore \sim Bc$	3. Therefore, my blue hair dryer is not pleasant to me.

The fallacy known as the universal inverse error wrongly infers from $(x)(Ax \rightarrow Bx)$ that $\therefore (x)(\sim Ax \rightarrow \sim Bx)$. The universal inverse error can be illustrated as follows: "All even numbers are pleasant to me. Therefore, all non-even numbers are not pleasant to me." So what is the common mistake these four fallacies—denying the antecedent, the inverse error, universal denying the antecedent, and the universal inverse error—commit? In plain English, these are fallacies because they confuse a sufficient condition for a necessary condition.

The fallacy of confusing inclusive or for exclusive or reasons from (1) $A \vee B$ and (2) A that (3) $\therefore \sim B$, or it reasons from (1) $A \vee B$ and (2) B that (3) $\sim A$. To illustrate, "I'll eat lunch at either McDonald's or Burger King. I eat lunch at McDonald's. Therefore, I didn't eat lunch at Burger King." Or again, "I'll eat lunch at either McDonald's or Burger King. I eat lunch at Burger King. Therefore, I didn't eat lunch at McDonald's." In plain English, this is a fallacy because saying that it's one or the other doesn't mean it can't be both.

A formal fallacy you haven't yet encountered is *counterfeit universal hypothetical syllogism*. Here an argument appears to be UHS but the premises are something other than "all" statements, such as "almost all" statements, "most" statements, "many" statements, etc., or a combination thereof. For example:

1. Virtually all trumpets are made from brass.
2. Virtually everything made from brass is unable to be played.
3. Therefore, virtually all trumpets are unable to be played.

This is a fallacy because of shrinking probabilities, as the structural probability of the premises must be multiplied together to learn the structural probability of the conclusion. "Virtually all" only guarantees 95 percent. So 95 percent times 95 percent is something less than 95 percent, making the argument weak and therefore bad.

Informal Fallacies

We now turn to informal fallacies. The first category of informal fallacies we will consider is the *ad hominem* (Latin for "against the person") category. *Ad hominem* fallacies incorrectly attack the person(s) holding a position instead of the position itself. There are three kinds of *ad hominem* fallacies. The *abusive* kind incorrectly reasons like this: the person holding a position has a character defect (e.g., they lie on a regular basis, they cheat, they steal, they're bigoted, etc.) Therefore, the position is false. Here's an example of *ad hominem* abusive that you might see in a court of law: "You lied repeatedly to the police. You lied in your affidavit. So your testimony to this court is obviously false." (A classic lawyer's trick!)

The *circumstantial* kind incorrectly reasons like this: The circumstances of the person holding a position give them motive to consciously or unconsciously skew the truth about the position. In other words, their circumstances make them biased. Therefore, their position is false. Let's return to the courtroom setting for this example of *ad hominem* circumstantial: "In exchange for your testimony against my client, you will receive immunity from the prosecutor. So your testimony is obviously false." (Another classic lawyer's trick!)

The *hypocritical* kind (also known as *tu quoque*, Latin for "you too") incorrectly reasons like this: The person holding a position is a hypocrite. They don't believe part or all of their own position. Therefore, the position is false. Here's an illustration of *ad hominem* hypocritical: "You say we should oppose climate change. But you buy plastic all the time at the store! So we shouldn't oppose climate change."

Ad hominem arguments of all kinds are fallacies because positions stand or fall on their own merits, independently of anything about who holds them. Repeated liars, biased people, hypocrites, and so forth can all hold true positions! So pointing out a problem with those advocating a position does nothing to refute the position.

The next fallacy we will examine is called the *genetic fallacy*. The genetic fallacy incorrectly attacks a position based on how that position originated. A skeptic of God's existence might commit the genetic fallacy as follows: "Belief in God came from our pre-scientific, illiterate, barbaric, primal ancestors trying to feel safe in a chaotic world. So God doesn't exist."[1] Genetic fallacy arguments are all fallacies because positions stand or fall on their own merits, independently of how they originated. Genetic fallacy arguments overlook the possibility that evidence may actually prove the truth of positions that arose in suspicious circumstances.

The *straw man* fallacy takes its name from farming. Imagine that, when you were growing up, there was a bully who tormented you in school. Suppose you really wanted to beat up the bully, but you didn't have the physical or self-defense skills to do it. So instead, you went out to a farmer friend's field and set up a scarecrow—a straw man—which you dressed up to make look like the bully, and you beat up the scarecrow instead, knocking it down instantly. Then suppose you showed the knocked-down scarecrow to your friends and bragged, "Ha, ha! I beat up the bully!" Maybe a few of your more naïve friends will believe you, thinking, "Well, it sure looks like the bully. So it must be him." But have you in fact done anything to the actual bully? Of course not! In precisely the same way, a straw man fallacy, instead of refuting a position, refutes a caricature of that position that's easy to knock down, just like a scarecrow in a field. Here's an example: "Paul Tillich believed in religious socialism. But religious socialism is just Stalinist communism, disproven once and for all by the fall of the Soviet Union. So religious socialism is false."[2] Straw men are fallacies because they do nothing to refute the actual position in question. They're just rhetorical bait-and-switches by the arguer, hoping the listener doesn't notice that they're being duped!

Our next fallacy is called *ad baculum vel metum* (Latin for "appeal to force or fear"). This fallacy incorrectly reasons as follows: Something bad is going to happen to you if you hold that position, so the position is false. An angry student-athlete with connections to organized crime

1. In point of fact, the historical and anthropological evidence that belief in God originated in this way is virtually nil. A much more plausible account is furnished by Otto, *Idea of the Holy*.

2. That religious socialism is not at all the same as Stalinist communism should be evident from MacGregor, *Tillich and Religious Socialism*.

might threaten me with this *ad baculum vel metum* argument: "You say I earned a D rather than a C in Modern Logic. People who make me athletically ineligible tend to disappear, never to be seen from or heard from again. Understand? So I earned a C in Modern Logic."[3] *Ad baculum vel metum* is a fallacy because the truth of a position has nothing to do with the consequences of holding it.

The last fallacy we will consider in this chapter is *equivocation of terms*. Equivocation of terms is the fallacy of meaning one thing by a term in one part of an argument and meaning something else by the term in another part of the argument to make the argument appear valid. We illustrate this fallacy as follows: "That concert was gold! Gold conducts electricity. So that concert conducts electricity." Equivocation of terms is a fallacy because the different meanings prohibit any chain of reasoning from forming.

Pre-Homework Practice!

Now try to name the fallacy committed by each of the following arguments. Then check your answer against the one provided below each argument.

1. Most Republicans are against gun control. Virtually everyone who is against gun control hasn't been the victim of a violent crime. So most Republicans haven't been victims of violent crimes.
   a. *Counterfeit universal hypothetical syllogism*
2. Nancy is pro-choice. But the pro-choice position is nothing more than hatred of babies. Clearly the pro-choice position is wrong.
   a. *Straw man*
3. You claim the Bible is divinely inspired. But you're a Christian! So we can dismiss your claim about the Bible being divinely inspired.
   a. *Ad hominem circumstantial*
4. Dwiane started believing he should be a Youtuber because a pink elephant told him this in a dream. So Dwiane shouldn't be a Youtuber.
   a. *Genetic fallacy*

3. This example is purely fictional.

Homework Assignment 23

Name the fallacy committed by each argument below.

1. Hitler said that cats are evil. But come on, he's Hitler! Therefore, cats are not evil.
2. Some books by Joseph Campbell are outdated. Some outdated books are enjoyed by cats. Therefore, some books by Joseph Campbell are enjoyed by cats.
3. You came to believe in Hinduism because you were born and raised in India. So you shouldn't believe in Hinduism.
4. Bob just gave that *modus ponens* argument. Let's reconstruct Bob's argument as follows: (1) If A, then B. (2) B. (3) Therefore, A. This commits the fallacy of affirming the consequent. So Bob's argument is bad.

24

Fallacies (Part 2)

In this chapter we will consider ten more informal fallacies. Doubtless you have already begun to recognize other people commit the fallacies discussed in the last chapter. Sadly, the fallacies in this chapter are likewise all too common. The good news is that you're immunizing yourself from being persuaded by these fallacies by learning about them!

Ten More Informal Fallacies

The fallacy of *ad populum* (Latin for "[appeal] to the people") assumes two forms. First, it incorrectly reasons that if everyone else in question believes something or does something, then you should too. Think of a high school student who says to his mom, "All my friends smoke weed. So I should smoke weed." Second, it incorrectly reasons that if you want to be part of or accepted by a group that believes something, the thing in question is true. Imagine a conservative Christian who says to a fellow church member who is skeptical of an eternal hell, "All real Christians believe in an eternal hell. Don't you go to church every week? So the doctrine of an eternal hell is true." *Ad populum* is a fallacy because it provides no rational basis for one's believing or doing the thing in question. For it gives no evidence that the position is true!

The fallacy of *ad verecundiam* (Latin for "[appeal] to illegitimate authority") incorrectly reasons that since an authority in an irrelevant field or a biased authority in the relevant field says something, it is true. Regarding an authority in an irrelevant field, consider this example:

"LeBron James says drinking Gatorade is good for you. So drinking Gatorade is good for you." (A classic advertiser's trick!) The problem is obvious: LeBron James is a reliable authority on basketball, not on beverages. If LeBron James tells you how to shoot a three-pointer, you should believe him! But he has no more authority to speak about Gatorade than any other non-expert on beverages. Regarding a biased authority in a relevant field, take this illustration: "The chemist employed by the pharmaceutical company says their drug is safe. So their drug is safe." The chemist's bias makes them an unreliable authority on the drug. However, be careful at this point! We cannot conclude that the drug is not safe, since this would be *ad hominem* circumstantial against the chemist. We can only conclude there's no legitimate evidence for its safety.

The fallacy of *ad ignorantiam* (Latin for "[argument] from ignorance") occurs when the absence of evidence for or against something is wrongfully taken as evidence that the thing is respectively false or true. To illustrate, suppose two archaeologists excavated the city of Jericho. The first archaeologist was a militant atheist who wanted to refute as much of the Bible as he could. He went on the dig in hopes of proving that the biblical account of the battle of Jericho was unhistorical. The second archaeologist was an ardent Christian who wanted to verify as much of the Bible as he could. He went on the dig in hopes of proving that the biblical account of the battle of Jericho was historical. The excavation turned out to be inconclusive, providing evidence neither for nor against the historicity of the battle of Jericho. However, when interviewed by the media about the dig, both archaeologists seized the opportunity to spin things to their own advantage. The first archaeologist said, "I am pleased to report from my dig at Jericho that there is not a shred of evidence that the battle of Jericho happened. Therefore, the battle of Jericho never happened." But the second archaeologist said, "I am pleased to report from my dig at Jericho that there is not a shred of evidence that the battle of Jericho didn't happen. Therefore, the battle of Jericho happened." Both archaeologists are committing the fallacy of *ad ignorantiam*. Just because there's not a shred of evidence that the battle of Jericho happened doesn't mean it didn't happen, and just because there's not a shred of evidence that the battle of Jericho didn't happen doesn't mean it happened! *Ad ignorantiam* is a fallacy because it fails to consider that we shouldn't necessarily expect to find evidence for something when it's true and we shouldn't necessarily expect to find evidence against something when it's false. Absence of evidence is clearly not the presence of evidence for anything!

The fallacy of *ad misericordiam* (Latin for "[appeal] to pity") claims that because you feel sorry for a person, you should believe or do something. For example, suppose a student said to me, "If you don't change my grade in Modern Logic from a C to a B, I'll lose my academic scholarship for next year! So you should change my grade to a B." This is a fallacy because it provides no rational basis for your believing or doing anything. In this case, we have no evidence that the student really earned a B!

The fallacy of *ignorantio elenchi* (red herring) occurs when a position is allegedly refuted by distracting premises that have nothing to do with that position! Consider this example: "You claim that your shoes are comfortable. But your shoes were made by a multinational corporation that uses slave labor in developing countries. This corporation has been condemned by ethicists. So your shoes aren't comfortable." This is a fallacy because the premises do nothing to show the position—that my shoes are comfortable—is false. In this case, brazenly unethical companies can make comfortable shoes!

The fallacy of *petitio principii* (Latin for "begging the question") occurs when a conclusion is allegedly—but not actually—proven by sneaking the conclusion into at least one of the premises. This is also known as assuming what you're trying to prove or circular reasoning. Suppose a Jōdō Buddhist gave this argument: "The *Kyōgyōshinshō* was divinely inspired by Amida Buddha. The *Kyōgyōshinshō* says that Amida Buddha is a god. So Amida Buddha is a god." Notice that the first premise, "The *Kyōgyōshinshō* was divinely inspired by Amida Buddha," is a tricky way of stating, "Amida Buddha is a god, and he inspired the *Kyōgyōshinshō*." For the claim that someone divinely inspired something entails that the one doing the inspiring is a god. So in order to allegedly prove that Amida Buddha is a god, the arguer assumes that he is a god in the first premise. In sum, *petitio principii* is a fallacy because you can't prove a position by assuming its truth before you even consider the evidence!

The fallacy of *appeal to the past* occurs when a person incorrectly reasons, "This is the way it was in the past. Therefore, it's still this way." As a Tiger Woods fan, I might be tempted to appeal to the past as follows: "Tiger Woods was the best golfer in the world for many years. So he's still the best golfer in the world." This fallacy fails to consider that things have changed in the present. In Tiger's case, his 2021 car crash left him with a series of injuries from which he has not fully recovered to date.

The *fallacy of composition* incorrectly reasons that because all the parts of something have a property, the whole thing has that property.

Suppose I argued, "Every musician in the orchestra is first-rate. Therefore, the orchestra is first-rate." But they could all be first-rate trumpet players, leaving you with a lousy orchestra! In short, the fallacy of composition goes wrong in assuming that properties necessarily transfer over from parts to the whole. Now let's consider another fallacy which is the mirror converse of this fallacy.

The *fallacy of division* incorrectly reasons that because something has a property, every part of the thing has that property. We illustrate as follows: "This brick is heavy. So every subatomic particle in this brick is heavy." The fallacy of division goes wrong in assuming that properties necessarily transfer over from the whole to its parts.

The fallacy of *confusing correlation with causation* incorrectly reasons that because two things happen together (i.e., they are correlated), one of the two things causes the other thing. For example, suppose I commented, "Every time my mutual fund increases in value, the S&P 500 goes up. So the growth of my mutual fund causes the S&P 500 to go up." Confusing correlation with causation is a fallacy because it fails to consider three alternate explanations. First, it may be that the two things in question have nothing to do with each other. That one happens when the other does would then be purely coincidental. Second, it may be that there is a cause-and-effect relationship between the two items, but it is reversed. Third, it may be that a third factor or set of factors causes both things in question, each of which is causally unrelated to the other.

Pre-Homework Practice!

Try to identify the fallacy committed in each of the following examples. Then check your identification against the solution provided below each one.

1. For each of the last five years, our football team has been the best in the nation. So anyone can see that our football team is the best in the nation.
    a. *Appeal to the past* (maybe there are no longer any star players on the team, and the team is in a rebuilding phase).

2. My biology professor says that Confucius never existed. That proves it: Confucius never existed!
   a. *Ad verecundiam* (your biology professor is an authority on biology, not on history).
3. Whenever a crowd comes out to the pavilion, the band performs. Hence the crowd's coming out makes the band perform.
   a. *Confusing correlation with causation*
4. Real Americans stand for the national anthem. You love our country, don't you? Therefore, you should stand for the national anthem.
   a. *Ad populum*
5. For hundreds of years, people have tried to disprove the existence of space aliens, with no success. I told you so: space aliens are real!
   a. *Ad ignorantiam*

Homework Assignment 24

Name the fallacy committed by each argument below.

1. Prosecutor: Notice how the defense attorney has not proven that the defendant is innocent. So the defendant is as guilty as sin, and you must convict.
2. That cat was shivering so much on the ASPCA commercial. And I felt so sorry for the abuse suffered by that dog on the commercial. Therefore, we should give a donation to the ASPCA to save those animals.
3. Whenever I play my trumpet, the earth rotates on its axis. Wow, my trumpet playing is so powerful that it makes the earth rotate!
4. Everyone I know drinks at least one glass of wine a night. Therefore, I should drink at least one glass of wine at night.
5. My house was designed by an architect. So every molecule making up my house was designed by an architect.
6. You say you got a great high school education? The teachers at that high school are underpaid and unrepresented by a union. Those teachers aren't allowed to speak on controversial views. Therefore, your high school education stunk.

25

Fallacies (Part 3)

We conclude our study of fallacies in this chapter by focusing on informal fallacies that exhibit confusion. Remember that any argument committing a fallacy is weak and therefore bad. So make sure to avoid these and other fallacies in your own thinking as well as detecting them in the thinking of others.

Informal Fallacies that Exhibit Confusion

The fallacy of *confusing correlation with identity* incorrectly reasons that because two things are correlated, they're really just the same thing. A neuroscientist might commit this fallacy by arguing, "Every time there is a mental event, there is a brain event, and vice versa. So the mind just is the brain." This is a fallacy because correlation of two things does nothing to prove that, for any property, it is possessed by the first thing iff it is possessed by the second thing, which is required by Id. In other words, it fails to consider whether there may be something true of one thing and false of the other thing, which disproves identity.

The fallacy of *confusing possibility with probability or certainty* incorrectly reasons that because something is possible, it's probably true or just plain true. For example, someone appearing on a television program designed to provoke controversy about the Bible might allege, "It's possible that Judas wrote the Gospel of Judas. So this is likely to be the case."[1]

1. To my knowledge, no professional biblical scholar believes either that Judas wrote the Gospel of Judas or that it is likely that Judas wrote the Gospel of Judas.

This is a fallacy because possibilities come cheap—anything is possible so long as it doesn't violate the laws of logic. But this gives no reason to believe the thing is probably true, much less definitely true!

The *post hoc ergo propter hoc* (Latin for "after this; therefore, because of this") fallacy incorrectly reasons that because thing 2 happened after thing 1, thing 1 caused thing 2. This is also known as the *false cause* fallacy. To illustrate, imagine that a superstitious student claimed, "Every MWF, Prof. X shows up in room 202 at 8:50, and Prof. Y shows up in room 204 at 8:55. So Prof. X causes Prof. Y to show up." This is a fallacy because it fails to consider that the two things may be completely unrelated to each other (as is clearly true in our example).

The fallacy of *confusing percentages with amounts* incorrectly draws a conclusion about an amount from a percentage without regard to the number that it's a percentage of. Politicians often commit this fallacy. Suppose a mayoral candidate in a tiny Kansas town said, "90 percent of students entering kindergarten this year at school X are illiterate. Clearly a huge number of pre-K children can't read." But suppose only 10 students entered kindergarten this year at school X. 9 illiterate students isn't a huge number. By contrast, suppose a mayoral candidate in Los Angeles said, "Only 10 percent of students at schools in this city are bullied. So bullying doesn't affect many students here." But suppose there are two million students at schools in Los Angeles. That's two hundred thousand bullied students, which is a huge number. The lesson to be learned from this fallacy is that a high percentage doesn't necessarily mean a high amount, and a low percentage doesn't necessarily mean a low amount.

The fallacy of *reasoning about a population from an unrepresentative sample* occurs when someone draws a conclusion about a whole group—a *population*—from a subset of that group—a *sample*—that is either too small, too biased, or improperly studied. Such a problematic sample is called *unrepresentative*, as it does not sufficiently mirror the population. By contrast, *representative samples* sufficiently mirror the population. Let's give three examples of this fallacy, also known as the fallacy of *hasty generalization*. First, take this example: "Of a random sample of ten people in Kansas, nine are Republicans. So approximately 90 percent of Kansans are Republicans." It's an unbiased sample, but there aren't enough people. Nor do we know how the sample was studied. Second, consider this illustration: "75 percent of 1800 people who attended a Christian camp in Colorado opposed premarital sex. So approximately 75 percent of people in Colorado oppose premarital sex." There are enough people, but it's a biased sample. Moreover, we have no idea how the sample was studied. Finally, consider this example: "A group that knows nothing about probability and statistics took a random sample of 847 Kansans, and they concluded that 26 percent of these Kansans oppose Trump's tariffs. So about 26 percent of Kansans oppose Trump's tariffs." There are enough people and an unbiased sample, but we can repose no confidence in the group's ability to draw conclusions from that sample.

The fallacy of *bad analogy* incorrectly reasons that since two things are alike in some respects, they are alike in the relevant respect. We illustrate this fallacy as follows: "Both dogs and humans are mammals, breathe, drink water, and reproduce. So chocolate is safe for both dogs and humans to eat." But chocolate is poisonous for dogs![2] Bad analogy is a fallacy because to show that two things are alike in the relevant respect, you need good evidence regarding that particular respect, and none is provided.

The fallacy of *appeal to guilt* incorrectly reasons that someone else should believe or do something because "they owe you." Imagine a dad telling his son who just graduated from high school, "I'm your father! I've fed you and put a roof over your head for the last eighteen years. Therefore, you must go to college at Oklahoma State University, my alma mater." The appeal to guilt is a fallacy because it provides no evidence that the person should believe or do the thing in question.

The *line-drawing fallacy* incorrectly reasons for some position A that since we cannot stipulate exactly when A stops being true and ~A starts being true, there's no actual distinction between A and ~A.[3] Suppose a motoring enthusiast who enjoys fast driving argued like this: "In 1996, Montana interstates contained speed limit signs telling drivers during daylight hours to drive 'reasonable and prudent' speeds. But what exactly counts as an unreasonable or imprudent speed? Is it eighty? Eighty-one? Eighty-two? Eighty-three? Therefore, in 1996 there could not be any violations of the speed limit on Montana interstates." This is a fallacy because it violates the law of noncontradiction; for any A, either A or ~A is true under each set of circumstances, even if we don't know which one is true.

Related to the line-drawing fallacy is the *relativist fallacy*. This fallacy incorrectly reasons that since many people disagree over whether A or ~A is true, neither of them is objectively true; the truth-value of

2. This illustration is inspired by Epstein, *Critical Thinking*, 253.

3. I am indebted to Epstein, *Critical Thinking*, 14–15 for calling my attention to this fallacy.

each is subjective.[4] For example, imagine that a religious pluralist alleged, "Many people disagree about whether Muhammad was called to be a prophet by God. So there is no objective truth about the matter." This is a fallacy because objectivity depends strictly on reality, not on perception. Even if we disagree over whether A or ~A is true, the law of noncontradiction mandates that, under any given set of circumstances, one is objectively true (i.e., true independently of how we feel, what we believe, etc.) and the other is objectively false.

We now come to our final fallacy. The fallacy of *deriving an ought from an is* incorrectly draws a prescriptive conclusion (i.e., a conclusion about what ought to be) from purely descriptive premises (i.e., premises about what actually is the case). Here is an example of deriving an ought from an is: "Birch trees are beautiful. They produce oxygen. They increase your property value. Therefore, you should plant a birch tree in your yard." This is a fallacy because a prescriptive conclusion can only be derived from an argument containing at least one prescriptive premise. In this case, the needed prescriptive premise would be, "If a tree is beautiful, produces oxygen, and increases your property value, then you should plant it in your yard." Were this premise part of the argument, it would be valid. But without this premise, the argument is fallacious. A special case of deriving an ought from an is worth highlighting is arguing *ad antiquatatem* (Latin for "[appeal] to tradition"). This appeal mistakenly reasons that because something has always been done a certain way, it should keep being done in that way. To illustrate this case, imagine someone from Cambodia insisted, "Our people have eaten dogs for the past two thousand years. They're delicious! Therefore, those animal rights people are full of it; we should keep eating dogs." *Ad antiquatatem* has been—and tragically still is—used by people to justify all sorts of prejudices and other moral travesties.

Pre-Homework Practice!

Now it's your turn to attempt identifying the fallacy committed in each of the following examples. Then check your identification against the solution provided below each one.

1. People disagree over whether Jesus resurrected from the dead. Therefore, the truth about this matter is subjective.

4. I am indebted to Epstein, *Critical Thinking*, 20–21 for calling my attention to this fallacy.

   a. *Relativist fallacy* (as a matter of history, either Jesus resurrected from the dead or he didn't! It's objectively one or the other.)

2. A whopping 83 percent of Alaskans subscribe to Inuit religion. So Inuit religion is believed by millions of people.
   a. *Confusing percentages with amounts* (less than a million people live in Alaska).
3. The vast majority of Kansans I've met are friendly people. So the vast majority of Kansans are friendly people.
   a. *Reasoning about a population from an unrepresentative sample*
4. It's possible that the ark of the covenant produced electricity. Hence the ark was most likely an ancient generator.
   a. *Confusing possibility with probability*
5. Both guinea pigs and humans have a central nervous system. Eating Timothy hay is the most healthy diet for guinea pigs. So eating Timothy hay is the most healthy diet for humans.
   a. *Bad analogy*

Homework Assignment 25

Name the fallacy committed by each argument below.

1. You say there's a distinction between people who are rich and people who aren't. But what's the cut-off point between the two? $100,000? $150,000? $249,998? $249,999? $250,000? You can't tell me! So the difference between the rich and the non-rich is an illusion.
2. I've done great work in all your classes. I never missed a single session. I even came over to your house for dinner! So you need to write me a letter of recommendation to medical school.
3. Every time you're happy, you possess well-being. And every time you possess well-being, you're happy. So well-being is happiness.
4. I got a haircut and then my mood improved. So my haircut caused my mood to improve.
5. Since the seventh century, nearly all Christians have regarded monothelitism as a heresy. Therefore, Christians should not embrace monothelitism.

26

Finding the Sufficient Assumption (Part 1)

YOUR PROOF-WRITING SKILLS WILL come in extremely handy in the next six chapters. Chapters 26–29 utilize your ability to connect the dots. Let's explain how. Many invalid arguments are only one premise away from being valid. That premise may or may not be true, of course. In the case of an argument exhibiting a fallacy, the missing premise will typically be false. But if we find that premise and add it, the argument will be valid. Adding it is enough to make the argument valid. In other words, the premise is sufficient for the argument's validity. It connects the dots of the argument. Anyone who thinks the argument works without it must be assuming this premise. Hence it is known as a *sufficient assumption*. A sufficient assumption logically permits us to draw the conclusion.

So how do we find the sufficient assumption? We use our knowledge of the laws of logic—particularly MP, UMP, MT, UMT, DS, DDS, HS, UHS, RHS, URHS, and CD. All these laws (and others) furnish forms or patterns valid arguments can take. Accordingly, we ask: what premise is missing from the argument that, if added, would make it exhibit one of these forms?

One Premise Away from Validity

Let's start out with an argument we've seen before (and which commits the fallacy of *ad ignorantiam*): "I am pleased to report from my dig at

Jericho that there is not a shred of *e*vidence that the battle of Jericho happened. Therefore, the *b*attle of Jericho never happened." We would symbolize this argument as ~E; ∴ ~B. Notice that the premise is unrelated to the conclusion. Here's a neat trick: *whenever we have a premise and an unrelated conclusion, the missing premise will always be [premise] → [conclusion] or (by Cont) [not conclusion] → [not premise]*. So here it's ~E → ~B, which we (by Cont) could equivalently write as B → E. If we add it as ~E → ~B ("If there's no evidence for the battle of Jericho, then there was no battle of Jericho"), the argument becomes MP and therefore valid. If we add it as B → E ("if there was a battle of Jericho, then there's evidence for the battle of Jericho"), the argument becomes MT and therefore valid. (Whichever way we want to add it, the missing premise here is false, as is unsurprising for the sufficient assumption of a fallacy.)

Here's a new argument that works the same way: "You like cooking shows. Therefore, you watch the Food Network." Again, the premise is unrelated to the conclusion. Using our neat trick, adding the premise "If you like cooking shows, then you watch the Food Network" makes the argument MP and is therefore the sufficient assumption. We could also write the sufficient assumption as the generality "Everyone who likes cooking shows watches the Food Network," which makes the argument UMP.

Now consider this argument: "If I went to the store, then I bought a blank CD. So I bought a blank CD." Here the premise and the conclusion are not totally unrelated, as the consequent of the premise is the conclusion. So we think, "Is there a form with a conditional, something else (which will be the missing premise), and then a conclusion affirming the conditional's consequent?" and we arrive at MP. Adding the premise "I went to the store"—the antecedent of the conditional—makes the argument MP and is therefore the sufficient assumption.

On a related note, take this argument: "If I'm rich, then I own 183 custom-made suits. So I'm not rich." The premise and the conclusion are related, as the conclusion is the negation of the conditional premise's antecedent. So we ask ourselves, "Is there a form with a conditional, something else, and a conclusion denying the conditional's antecedent?" and we arrive at MT. Adding the premise "I don't own 183 custom-made suits"—the negation of the conditional's consequent—makes the argument MT and is therefore the sufficient assumption. Let's review your knowledge of premise indicators with this example: "Thundersnow is awesome because trees are pretty." "Because" here is the premise indicator, such that the argument means: "Trees are pretty. Therefore, thundersnow is awesome." Since the premise and conclusion are completely unrelated, we use our neat trick. By MP, the sufficient assumption is, "If trees are pretty, then thundersnow is awesome."

Conditional Premises and a Conditional Conclusion

Suppose you're trying to find the sufficient assumption of an argument with conditional premises and a conditional conclusion. In this scenario, the obvious choices are HS, UHS, RHS, and URHS. You'll be asking, "What premise completes the chain?" Consider this argument: "If I'm *r*ich, then I own 183 custom-made *s*uits. So if I won the *l*ottery, then I own 183 custom-made suits." In symbolic form, this argument is R → S; ∴ L → S. Note well the identical consequents of the premise and the conclusion. *Whenever this happens, it shows you that the given premise is the final premise of a HS, namely, the premise immediately before the conclusion. It also shows you that the missing premise is the initial premise of that HS.* So what first premise would provide the link necessary to complete the chain? It is L → R ("If I won the lottery, then I'm rich"). Adding it makes R the link in the chain of HS, rendering "If I won the lottery, then I'm rich" the sufficient assumption.

Let's try a related argument: "If I'm *r*ich, then I own 183 custom-made *s*uits. So if I'm rich, then I own five hundred hand-painted silk *t*ies." In symbolic form, this argument is R → S; ∴ R → T. Note well the identical antecedents of the premise and the conclusion. *Whenever this happens, it shows you that the given premise is the initial premise of a HS. It also shows you that the missing premise is the final premise of that HS, namely, the premise immediately before the conclusion.* So we need to find this missing premise, which connects the first premise to the conclusion. By HS, the missing premise (sufficient assumption) is S → T ("If I own 183 custom-made suits, then I own five hundred hand-painted silk ties"), because this premise makes S the link in the chain.

Now consider an argument that employs the skills learned in both of the previous two examples: "If I'm *r*ich, then I own 183 custom-made *s*uits. If I invest in *g*old, then I will *m*ake more money. So if I'm rich, then I will make more money." In symbolic form, this argument is R → S; G → M; ∴ R → M. The identical antecedents of the first premise and the conclusion show you that the first premise is the initial premise of a HS. The identical consequents of the second premise and the conclusion show you that the second premise is the final premise of that HS, namely, the premise immediately before the conclusion. So we're looking for the conditional premise between the initial and final premises, one that provides both links in the chain. *That missing premise will have the consequent of the initial premise as its if-clause and the antecedent of the final premise as its then-clause.* So it is S → G ("If I own 183 custom-made suits, then I invest in gold").

Pre-Homework Practice!

We'll put all the skills we learned in this chapter together in your pre-homework practice. Using these skills, try to find the sufficient assumption of each of the following arguments. Then check your answer against the solution provided below it.

1. I don't like red shoes since I haven't mown my lawn.
   a. *If I haven't mown my lawn, then I don't like red shoes.* (This is the initial premise of MP.)
2. If Al Gore had been president, the United States would not have invaded Iraq. So Al Gore wasn't president.
   a. *The United States invaded Iraq.* (This is the final premise of MT.)
3. I didn't wash my hair. For I didn't wash my hair on the condition that I didn't have shampoo.
   a. *I didn't have shampoo.* (This is the final premise of MP.)
4. If Hubmaier was burned at the stake, then he died in 1528. So if Hubmaier was an Anabaptist, then he died in 1528.
   a. *If Hubmaier was an Anabaptist, then he was burned at the stake.* (This is the initial premise of HS.)
5. If Anselm wrote *Cur Deus Homo*, then Anselm devised the satisfaction model of the atonement. If Aquinas wrote *Summa Theologiae*, then Aquinas was the greatest Catholic philosopher ever. So if Anselm wrote *Cur Deus Homo*, Aquinas was the greatest Catholic philosopher ever.
   a. *If Anselm devised the satisfaction model of the atonement, then Aquinas wrote* Summa Theologiae. (This is the premise between the initial and final premises of HS.)

Homework Assignment 26

What is the sufficient assumption of each argument?

1. If Kierkegaard thought faith and reason were opposed, then he developed the concept of the leap of faith. If God is infinite and humans are finite, then Kierkegaard regarded Jesus as a paradoxical figure. So if Kierkegaard thought faith and reason were opposed, then he regarded Jesus as a paradoxical figure.
2. If there are 5,812 ancient Greek manuscripts of the New Testament, then we can accurately reconstruct the original New Testament documents. It follows that we can accurately reconstruct the original New Testament documents.
3. Melissa never dated a guy with red hair. For pillows are soft.
4. If Molina died in 1587, then he never would have finished writing the *Concordia*. So Molina didn't die in 1587.
5. If I take out the trash on Friday, I'll go to Olive Garden on Saturday. So if I'm not too tired on Thursday night, I'll go to Olive Garden on Saturday.

27

Finding the Sufficient Assumption (Part 2)

IN THIS CHAPTER WE will complete our discussion of sufficient assumptions. Once you find the sufficient assumption of an argument, you know that adding it makes the argument valid. So suppose you know the sufficient assumption of an argument. What if you don't need to make the argument valid but to just make it stronger than it is? Or what if you want to make the argument weaker than it is? We'll learn a method for performing each of these tasks—strengthening an argument and weakening an argument—based on the sufficient assumption you've already detected.

Seeing "Or" in an Invalid Argument

Whenever you see the logical connector "or" in a premise—and only the premise—of an invalid argument, you should immediately think of DS and DDS as the forms you should use to find the sufficient assumption. But whenever you see "or" in the conclusion of an invalid argument (regardless of whether it also occurs in a premise), you should immediately think of CD as the form you should use to find the sufficient assumption.

Consider this example: "I'm reading the newspaper or the phone book. So I'm reading the newspaper." Since "or" occurs only in the premise and the premise isn't quantified, we know DS is the form to utilize. In particular, we're looking for the final premise that eliminates the phone book as a possible option. As a result, our sufficient assumption is "I'm not reading the phone book"; adding this to the argument completes DS.

Similarly, take this illustration: "Since all trumpet players in the orchestra play on a Bach mouthpiece or a Schilke mouthpiece, the principal trumpet player of the orchestra plays on a Schilke mouthpiece." "Since" is our premise indicator, meaning that the first clause of the sentence is the premise and the second clause is the conclusion. "Or" only occurs in the premise, and the premise is quantified, talking about all the trumpet players in the orchestra. So we know DDS is the form we need. In particular, we're looking for the final premise that eliminates the principal trumpet player's playing on a Bach mouthpiece as a possible option. Accordingly, our sufficient assumption is "The principal trumpet player of the orchestra doesn't play on a Bach mouthpiece." Adding this to the argument completes DDS.

Now let's look at an argument where "or" occurs only in the conclusion: "If Peter wrote 2 Peter, then 2 Peter was written no later than 64 CE; and if my watch is working, then it doesn't need a new battery. So either 2 Peter was written no later than 64 CE or my watch doesn't need a new battery." Thus our first inclination is CD. *Since our premise has two "if-then"s, we know the missing premise is the second (final) premise in CD.* That second premise affirms one or the other if-clauses in the first premise. Consequently, the sufficient assumption reads, "Either Peter wrote 2 Peter or my watch is working." This premise completes CD.

Finally, let's examine an argument where "or" occurs in both the conclusion and the premise: "Arby's sells roast beef sandwiches or Burger King sells paint. So I'll eat at Arby's or I'll paint my house." That "or" occurs in the conclusion signals CD as the form we need. *Since our premise has an "or," we know the missing premise is the first (initial) premise in CD.* That premise contains the two "if-then"s. The if-clause of premise 1's first conditional is the first option in the given premise, and the then-clause of the first conditional is the first option in the conclusion. The if-clause of premise 1's second conditional is the second option in the given premise, and the then-clause of the second conditional is the second option in the conclusion. So the sufficient assumption is "If Arby's sells roast beef sandwiches, then I'll eat at Arby's; and if Burger King sells paint, then I'll paint my house." Adding this to the argument completes CD.

Strengthening an Argument: Method 1

Once you find the sufficient assumption of an argument, you can strengthen the argument by either stating it outright or stating something else that increases the sufficient assumption's probability. Stating it outright would make the argument valid. Here's an argument we saw in the last chapter: "If Hubmaier was burned at the stake, then he died in 1528. So if Hubmaier was an Anabaptist, then he died in 1528." As you already discovered, the sufficient assumption is "If Hubmaier was an Anabaptist, then he was burned at the stake." However, what if we don't need to make the argument valid but simply to make it stronger than it was before? Then we strengthen the argument by stating something else that increases the probability that the sufficient assumption is true. There's no one right answer; just use your imagination! Every argument has multiple possible strengtheners. As long as your proposed strengthener provides even a little bit of evidence for the truth of the sufficient assumption, it is correct. So what could make it more probable that if Hubmaier was an Anabaptist, then he died in 1528? Here's one possible right answer: "Over ten thousand Anabaptists were burned at the stake in the sixteenth century." This strengthens the argument without going so far as to make it valid.

Let's now test two skills at once by trying to find the sufficient assumption and a strengthener other than the sufficient assumption. The argument under consideration runs as follows: "Either you love me or you hate me. So you love me." Here the "or" occurs only in the premise, which means we need the final premise of DS. Hence the sufficient assumption is "You don't hate me." Now what would increase the probability that you don't hate me? Many things would do the trick; here's one: "I've always treated you very kindly." Another is "You've always treated me very kindly." Either one strengthens the argument. Now let's do the same thing with this argument: "I pulled weeds in my flower bed. So my finger is cut badly." The fact that the conclusion is not related to the premise (and the fact that there are no "or"s) means MP. Here the sufficient assumption would be "If I pulled weeds in my flower bed, then my finger is cut badly." As for the strengthener, what would increase the probability that if I pulled weeds in my flower bed, then my finger is cut badly? One possible right answer is "The weeds in my flower bed are tall and prickly." Indeed if I pulled them, my finger has a good chance of getting cut badly!

Weakening an Argument: Method 1

Upon finding an argument's sufficient assumption, you can weaken the argument by either stating its contradictory or stating something else that decreases the sufficient assumption's probability (another way of saying this is that it increases the contradictory's probability). Adding to an argument the contradictory of its sufficient assumption weakens the argument. Furthermore, we can weaken the argument by finding anything else that makes the sufficient assumption less likely (and the contradictory of the sufficient assumption more likely). Let's try these skills out on a previous example: "I am pleased to report from my dig at Jericho that there is not a shred of evidence that the battle of Jericho happened. Therefore, the battle of Jericho never happened." We know that the sufficient assumption is "If there's no evidence for the battle of Jericho, then there was no battle of Jericho." We could weaken this argument by stating the contradictory of the sufficient assumption. (Remember, per NC, that the contradictory, or ~ ("not"), of A → B is A · ~B. In other words, the contradictory of "if A, then B" is "A and not B.") So the contradictory of the sufficient assumption is "There's no evidence for the battle of Jericho and there was a battle of Jericho." Now if we want the argument to be weaker without using the contradictory of the sufficient assumption, we ask ourselves the question, "What constitutes evidence against the sufficient assumption (or evidence for its contradictory)?" Just use your imagination; anything that answers this question is correct. Here's a possible right answer: "A tremendous amount of water and wind erosion occurred at Jericho since 1200 BCE, potentially annihilating any ancient remains there." This is a successful weakener, because it entails that we shouldn't expect to find any evidence for the battle of Jericho even if it did happen.

Now let's test three skills at once by finding the sufficient assumption, its contradictory, and a weakener other than the contradictory of the sufficient assumption for a pair of arguments. First consider this argument: "If Law and Order was on TV yesterday, then I made a reference to it in my Philosophy of Law class today. So Law and Order wasn't on TV yesterday." Here we think, "What form has a conditional premise, another premise, and a conclusion denying the conditional premise's antecedent?" The answer is MT. So the missing premise, or sufficient assumption, is "I didn't make a reference to Law and Order in my Philosophy of Law class today." The contradictory of the sufficient assumption is

"I did make a reference to Law and Order in my Philosophy of Law class today." Regarding the weakener, what would count as evidence against the sufficient assumption (and evidence for its contradictory)? One possible right answer, among many, is "Several of my Philosophy of Law students discussed Law and Order in the dining hall just after class." This indeed makes it more likely that I referred to Law and Order in class.

Second, take this argument: "If I'm going to the movie, then Dwiane is going to the movie. If I see an animated movie, then it'll be a Pixar production. So if I'm going to the movie, it'll be a Pixar production." As we learned in the last chapter, the identical antecedents of the first premise and the conclusion show you that the first given premise is the initial premise of a HS. The identical consequents of the second premise and the conclusion show you that the second given premise is the final premise of that HS. So the sufficient assumption is the conditional premise between the initial and final premises, one that provides both links in the chain. This is "If Dwiane is going to the movie, then I see an animated movie," which completes HS. Its contradictory is "Dwiane is going to the movie and I don't see an animated movie." Concerning the weakener, one state of affairs, among many, that would count as evidence against the sufficient assumption (and evidence for its contradictory) is "Dwiane really wants to see a documentary at the movies."

Pre-Homework Practice!

Before doing the homework, let's put all four skills together. For each argument below, try to find its sufficient assumption, its contradictory, a strengthener other than the sufficient assumption, and a weakener other than the contradictory of the sufficient assumption. While there's only one right answer for the sufficient assumption and contradictory questions (as provided below), there are many possible right answers for the strengthener and weakener questions. Even if your strengthener and/or weakener don't match mine, they're fine as long as they make the sufficient assumption, respectively, more and less probable.

1. Djokovic or Sabalenka is playing at Wimbledon. So Djokovic will win the men's singles title or Sabalenka will win the women's singles title.
   a. *Sufficient assumption:* "If Djokovic is playing at Wimbledon, then Djokovic will win the *men*'s singles title; and if Sabalenka

is playing at Wimbledon, then Sabalenka will win the *women's* singles title." (The "or" in the conclusion suggests CD, and the "or" in the premise shows that the sufficient assumption is the initial premise of CD. My italicization is for the sake of explaining its contradictory.)

b. *Contradictory:* "Djokovic is playing at Wimbledon and won't win the men's singles title, or Sabalenka is playing at Wimbledon and won't win the women's singles title." (This is a tricky one because you've got to be patient in applying the "not" across everything. In other words, $\sim((D \rightarrow M) \cdot (S \rightarrow W)) \equiv \sim(D \rightarrow M) \vee \sim(S \rightarrow W) \equiv (D \cdot \sim M) \vee (S \cdot \sim W)$.)

c. *Strengthener:* "Djokovic and Sabalenka have each won multiple major championships." (This makes it more likely that both will succeed, per the sufficient assumption.)

d. *Weakener:* "Both Djokovic and Sabalenka are injured." (This makes it less likely that both will succeed, per the sufficient assumption, and more likely that at least one of them will fail, per its contradictory.)

2. If Laozi was a historical figure, then he met with Confucius. So Laozi wasn't a historical figure.

   a. *Sufficient assumption:* "Laozi didn't meet with Confucius." (This is the final premise of MT.)

   b. *Contradictory:* "Laozi met with Confucius."

   c. *Strengthener:* "No credible ancient source reports that Laozi and Confucius met." (This increases the probability that the sufficient assumption is true.)

   d. *Weakener:* "A credible ancient source reports that Laozi and Confucius met." (This decreases the probability that the sufficient assumption is true and increases the probability that its contradictory is true.)

Homework Assignment 27

Find the sufficient assumption of each argument and its contradictory. Then state a strengthener other than the sufficient assumption. Then state a weakener other than the contradictory of the sufficient assumption.

1. Barth is not my favorite twentieth-century theologian. So Tillich is my favorite twentieth-century theologian.
2. If Dole had been elected president, the president would not have been impeached in 1998. So if Dole had been elected president, the Senate wouldn't have held an impeachment trial in 1999.

28

Finding a Necessary Assumption

THIS CHAPTER WILL FOCUS on finding a *necessary assumption* of an invalid argument. At this point you may wonder: how is a necessary assumption different from the sufficient assumption? Let's assume for the sake of argument that all the premises of an invalid argument are true. If the sufficient assumption is true, it guarantees that the conclusion is true. This is why it's called sufficient; if the sufficient assumption, then the conclusion. But if the sufficient assumption is false, the conclusion could still be true. The situation would just make the conclusion's truth less likely. A necessary assumption is the opposite. If a necessary assumption is false, it guarantees that the conclusion is false. This is why it's called necessary; if not the necessary assumption, then not the conclusion. But if a necessary assumption is true, the conclusion could still be false. The situation would just make the conclusion's truth more likely.

Find the Negation of a Destructor

Unlike the sufficient assumption of an invalid argument (there's only one, although it may be phrased in different ways), most invalid arguments have several necessary assumptions. All you need to do is find one. It may take you too long to use the laws of logic to find a necessary assumption. But it can be done. However, the better way is to use common sense coupled with your knowledge of fallacies. Just ask yourself, "What is consistent with the truth of the premises and would destroy the conclusion?" Or to put the same question another way, "What is consistent with the truth of the premises and would guarantee the truth of the contradictory of the conclusion?" Here I define a *destructor* as a proposition that is consistent with the truth of the premises of an argument and would make the argument's conclusion necessarily false (thereby making the contradictory of the conclusion necessarily true). Once you've found a destructor (and most invalid arguments have multiple destructors), all you need to do to get a necessary assumption is to negate the destructor. *The negation of a destructor of any argument is a necessary assumption of that argument.* I call this the "find the negation of a destructor" method. It works every time!

If the argument commits a fallacy, then the most important necessary assumption will be the unwarranted one made by the fallacy. For example, the fallacy of confusing percentages with amounts unjustifiably assumes that a high (or low) percentage at least sometimes means a high (or low) amount. If you use the "find a negation of a destructor" method on an argument committing this fallacy, the destructor will be something like "A high (or low) percentage never means a high (or low) amount." Using Sq, the negation of this destructor is "A high (or low) percentage sometimes means a high (or low) amount," which is the necessary assumption alluded to previously.

This reveals an important principle that we can apply to many invalid arguments. *Be on the lookout for places where the premises are about one thing and the conclusion is about something related but slightly different. The most important necessary assumption will be that these two things are linked.* Take this example: "Whenever Joe reads books, he reads Christian books from his library. Today Joe is reading a book. So Joe is probably reading a Christian book published by True Light." Here the premises are about Christian books from Joe's library, and the conclusion is about Joe's reading a Christian book published by True Light. Using our "find the negation of a destructor" method, what thing consistent with both premises would destroy the conclusion? That no Christian book in Joe's library is published by True Light! If this destructor is true, the conclusion becomes impossible. Accordingly, a necessary assumption is the negation of this destructor, namely, that some Christian books from Joe's library are published by True Light. Again, we use Sq to see that the negation of a "no" claim is a "some" claim. Notice how, as predicted, the necessary assumption we found links Christian books from Joe's library with Joe's reading a Christian book published by True Light.

Now consider this example: "Brandy was the best debater in the state for the past eight years. So Brandy is clearly the best debater in the state." Let's use the "find the negation of a destructor" method to get a necessary assumption of this argument. Employing your imagination, can we find a proposition consistent with Brandy's being the best debater in the state for the past eight years and which would destroy the conclusion that Brandy is now the best debater in the state? One possible proposition is "No one can be the best debater in the state for nine straight years." Negating this destructor via Sq, a necessary assumption is "A person can be the best debater in the state for nine straight years." Another possible destructor is "Brandy died yesterday." Accordingly, another necessary assumption is "Brandy didn't die yesterday." Hopefully you recognize that this example commits the fallacy of appeal to the past. That fallacy assumes, without justification, that what's true of the past is still true now. Both necessary assumptions we found makes this notion more likely in the case of Brandy.

Here's an example a conservative politician might give: "Americans predominantly watch TV shows containing what almost everyone—regardless of religion or politics—would regard as immoral sexual acts, like rape. These same kinds of acts are tragically prevalent in America. Therefore, TV shows are to blame for immoral sexual acts in America." Let's get a necessary assumption by our "find the negation of a destructor" method. So, using your imagination, can we find a proposition consistent with the two premises which would destroy the conclusion? Here's one possible destructor: "Americans never make their choices about sexual behavior based on what they see on TV shows." If that's true, the conclusion must be false! Accordingly, a necessary assumption is "Americans sometimes make their choices about sexual behavior based on what they see on TV shows." Again, we used Sq to negate the destructor. The conservative politician here is committing the fallacy of confusing correlation with causation. For saying "TV shows are to blame for immoral sexual acts in America" means that TV shows cause these immoral acts. The fallacy assumes, without justification, that just because two things occur together, that one is the cause of the other. Notice that our necessary assumption makes this notion more likely in the case of TV shows and sexual behavior.

Let's now try to find a necessary assumption of this argument: "The foundational documents of the United States give the president broad discretionary powers. Accordingly, any action of a president is probably immune from criminal prosecution after they leave office." First we find a destructor, something consistent with the president's broad discretionary powers and which destroys the conclusion that any action of a president is likely immune from prosecution upon leaving office. Here's a possible destructor: "All presidents can be criminally prosecuted for actions clearly falling outside their broad discretionary powers after they leave office." If this is true, the conclusion cannot be true. So negating our destructor via Sq, a necessary assumption is "Some presidents cannot be criminally prosecuted for actions clearly falling outside their broad discretionary powers after they leave office." The argument needs this assumption in order to have any hope of being true. Another possible destructor is "The broad discretionary powers of a president do not make probable that any action of a president is immune from criminal prosecution after they leave office." Negating this destructor, another necessary assumption is "The broad discretionary powers of a president make probable that any action of a president is immune from criminal prosecution after they leave office." The argument also needs this assumption to be true to have any hope of survival. Notice how the argument links two unrelated things: a president's broad discretionary powers and any of the president's actions being immune from future prosecution. The second necessary assumption we found makes this link more likely.

Consider this argument a contemporary philosopher inspired by the famous early modern philosopher René Descartes might make: "Knowing something is true entails having certainty of its truth. So knowing something is true likely entails that its truth is necessary."[1] This argument assumes that two unrelated things are linked: certainty and necessity. Accordingly, a possible destructor of this argument would be "Certainty of something's truth always entails that its truth is not necessary." If the destructor is right, the conclusion cannot possibly be true. The trick in this argument is negating the destructor, which requires a good knowledge of Sq. Recall that the negation of an "all" statement ("always" is a temporal stylistic variant of "all") is a "some . . . not" statement (where "sometimes . . . not" is a temporal stylistic variant of "some . . . not"). So our necessary assumption is "Certainty of something's truth sometimes entails that its truth is not not (a double negation) necessary," namely, "Certainty of

1. Descartes's first meditation in *Meditations on First Philosophy* assumes that knowledge entails certainty (13–17). Most contemporary epistemologists, or theorists of knowledge, disagree with this claim.

something's truth sometimes entails that its truth is necessary." The argument requires this assumption to even get off the ground.

Let's work one more example together before your pre-homework practice. We turn to finding a necessary assumption of this argument: "Every element making up this compound is poisonous to humans. So the compound is probably poisonous to humans." Hopefully you realize that this argument commits the fallacy of composition. That fallacy assumes, without justification, that properties possessed by every part of something are also possessed by the whole thing. So a possible destructor of the argument is "No properties of individual elements making up a compound are shared by the entire compound." If this is right, the compound in question cannot be poisonous to humans. Using Sq to negate the destructor, a necessary assumption is "Some properties of individual elements making up a compound are shared by the entire compound."

Pre-Homework Practice!

You're now ready to find a destructor and a necessary assumption to various invalid arguments on your own. Here are three to try. Afterwards, check your answers against the possible answers suggested. Remember that your answers don't have to match; most invalid arguments you encounter have many destructors and so many necessary assumptions. As long as your destructor is consistent with the truth of the premises and renders impossible the conclusion, it is correct. And your necessary assumption is correct if it properly negates a correct destructor.

1. I like most dogs. So most dogs are probably friendly.
    a. *Destructor*: "Every dog I like is unfriendly," which is logically equivalent to "No dog I like is friendly."
    b. *Necessary assumption*: "Some dogs I like are friendly."
2. Most rich people are likely to spend too much money on luxurious items. For rich people tend to enjoy luxurious items.
    a. *Destructor*: "No rich person tends to enjoy items on which they spend too much money." (Keep in mind that the premise of this argument is the second sentence.)
    b. *Necessary assumption:* "Some rich people tend to enjoy items on which they spend too much money."

3. Gender discrimination is pervasive in many Middle Eastern countries. These countries export large amounts of oil to many African countries that could not otherwise obtain oil. So any gender discrimination in these African countries likely results from their dependence on Middle Eastern oil.
    a. *Destructor:* "A nation's dependence upon a foreign power for a resource never leads the nation to emulate the foreign power's gender policies." (In other words, correlation does not indicate causation in this case.)
    b. *Necessary assumption:* "A nation's dependence upon a foreign power for a resource sometimes leads the nation to emulate the foreign power's gender policies." (In other words, correlation might indicate causation in this case.)

Homework Assignment 28

Find a destructor of each argument. Then use it to find a necessary assumption of each argument.

1. Trumpet mouthpiece manufacturers recognize that above high D, the note sounded by the trumpet is a reflection of the note sounded by the mouthpiece if buzzed without insertion into the trumpet. Trumpet mouthpiece manufacturers make only mouthpieces playable by most trumpet players. Most trumpet players strongly desire to play above high D. So most trumpet mouthpieces are manufactured with the capacity to independently buzz notes above high D.
2. Our high school has held a month-long band camp before school starts for the past forty years. During that time, we have consistently received superior ratings at state band competitions and been invited to perform in nationally televised parades. So our high school should keep holding a month-long band camp before school starts.
3. Triple-brownie ice cream tastes wonderful. So triple-brownie ice cream is widely sold by ice cream companies.

29

Using Necessary Assumptions and Resolving Problems

In this chapter we will learn how to use necessary assumptions in order to strengthen and weaken arguments. We will also learn two helpful techniques in resolving problems. One is finding the point of contention between two parties who disagree with each other. Another is resolving a seemingly paradoxical situation through our ability to connect the dots in that situation.

Strengthening/Weakening an Argument: Method 2

Once you find a necessary assumption of an argument, you can strengthen the argument by either stating the necessary assumption outright or stating something else that increases the necessary assumption's probability. Likewise, you can weaken the argument by either stating a destructor outright or stating something else that decreases the necessary assumption's probability (and thus increases the destructor's probability). Recall from the last chapter this argument: "Whenever Joe reads books, he reads Christian books from his library. Today Joe is reading a book. So Joe is probably reading a Christian book published by True Light." We saw that a necessary assumption of the argument is that some Christian books from Joe's library are published by True Light. This assumption strengthens the argument. But let's use our imagination to find another strengthener, which will be anything that makes the necessary assumption more likely. Here's one: "Joe thinks True Light is a great publisher." We also saw in the last chapter that a destructor of the argument is that no Christian book in Joe's library is published by True Light. The destructor weakens the argument (indeed, weakens it to the point of destruction). But if we want to weaken the argument without destroying it, we can state anything that makes the necessary assumption less likely (and makes the destructor more likely). One such weakener is this: "Joe thinks True Light is a lousy publisher."

Let's strengthen and weaken the following argument using our second method: "Divine omniscience holds that God knows only and all true propositions. Open theism denies that God has knowledge of future contingents but maintains that God knows all truths. Yet in the end, open theism denies divine omniscience." Before finding a strengthener and a weakener, we need to locate a destructor and then negate the destructor to derive a necessary assumption. Remember that a destructor is a proposition consistent with the premises that destroys the conclusion, namely, that guarantees that the negation of the conclusion is true. The conclusion of this argument is "Open theism denies divine omniscience," as "in the end" is a synonym of "therefore." Accordingly, the negation of the conclusion is "Open theism does not deny divine omniscience." Now if, per premise 1, divine omniscience means God's knowledge of all true propositions and if, per premise 2, open theism denies God's knowledge of future contingents, the only way the conclusion's negation can be true is if future contingents are not true propositions. Then God would still be omniscient even without knowing future contingents. So the destructor is "No future contingents can be true." By negating our destructor, a necessary assumption is "Some future contingents can be true." So let's strengthen the argument by using our imagination: what would make it more likely that some future contingents can be true? Because I'm currently hungry as I write this chapter, my imagination leads me to this strengthener: "It seems to me that the proposition 'I will freely eat at Burger King tomorrow' is true." Indeed this increases the probability that some future contingents can be true. Now let's weaken the argument by asking what would make it less likely that some future contingents can be true (and more likely that no future contingents can be true)? Here's a possible weakener: "It is highly unlikely that statements about things that do not yet exist, like things in the future, can be true."

Now consider this argument: "Those who believe in the doctrine of karma have a fatalistic outlook on life. So the doctrine of karma entails fatalism." Before finding a strengthener and a weakener using our second method, we need to locate a destructor and a necessary assumption. The argument links the outlook of believers in karma with an entailment of karma. To break this link, we could use the following destructor: "Everyone who holds a fatalistic outlook on life does so in contradiction to the entailments of the doctrines they believe." If this is true, it would be impossible for karma to entail fatalism. Employing Sq to negate the destructor, a necessary assumption would be "Some people who hold a fatalistic outlook on life don't do so in contradiction to the entailments of the doctrines they believe." This must be true in order for the argument to have any hope of success. Regarding a strengthener, can we imagine a statement that increases the probability of the necessary assumption? Here's one: "Some staunch Calvinists have a fatalistic outlook on life, which seems consistent with the Calvinist doctrine of divine sovereignty." Of course, there are numerous others you can use, but hopefully you get the point. Regarding a weakener, can we imagine a statement that decreases the probability of the necessary assumption (and increases the probability of the destructor)? This statement will do the trick: "My friend Bob holds a fatalistic outlook on life but affirms the doctrine of libertarian human freedom." (The doctrine of libertarian human freedom holds that, for some thoughts and actions, humans can choose between the alternatives of thinking the thought/doing the action or not thinking the thought/not doing the action.) Again, numerous other statements will also work.

Point of Contention

When trying to resolve a dispute between two people, one first needs to find out exactly where they disagree. In other words, one needs to find the place where both people have a belief and where those two beliefs contradict each other. This is known as the *point of contention* or the point at issue. The point of contention cannot be something about which one of the people lacks a belief. For example, person 1 believes such-and-such about X and person 2 doesn't have any belief about X. That's not a point of contention. But where person 1 believes such-and-such about X and person 2 believes the contradictory of such-and-such about X, that's the point of contention.

Consider the following conversation between myself (Kirk) and Doug:

> Kirk: Ric Flair is the greatest professional wrestler of all time. His interview skills have never been surpassed. His trilogy of matches with Ricky Steamboat in 1989 was the greatest trilogy of matches ever. He won sixteen world championships from 1981 to 2000.
>
> Doug: Eddie Gilbert is the most underrated professional wrestler of all time. He wrestled some classic matches with Sam Houston in 1987. And the skills he showed in one of his 1989 interviews are the best the world has ever seen.

So what is the point of contention between myself and Doug? Whether Eddie Gilbert once surpassed Ric Flair's interview skills in 1989. I believe Flair's interview skills have never been surpassed, while Doug believes that Eddie Gilbert in a 1989 interview showed the world's best interview skills (which means they were better than Flair's). On everything else, only one of us has an opinion.

Now take this conversation between Jennifer and Kate. Try to find the point of contention. This example is tricky, since they seem to disagree on multiple issues but in reality only disagree on one.

> Jennifer: *Beverly Hills Cop* was the best movie Eddie Murphy starred in. For in that film, the performances of Gil Hill, Judge Reinhold, John Ashton, and Ronny Cox perfectly supplemented Murphy's humor and sense of timing. These two skills constitute Murphy's most valuable acting talents.
>
> Kate: Eddie Murphy's greatest cinematic performance occurred in *Coming to America*. For he played many different roles in that movie, which cannot be said for *Beverly Hills Cop*. Moreover, John Ashton's punching Murphy in the stomach in *Beverly Hills Cop* failed to resonate with Murphy's timing.

The point of contention is whether, in *Beverly Hills Cop*, John Ashton perfectly supplemented Murphy's sense of timing. Jennifer says yes, and Kate says no. Now you might think Jennifer and Kate disagree on the best movie Murphy starred in. But take a closer look! While Jennifer thinks this movie is *Beverly Hills Cop*, Kate never expresses a viewpoint on this topic but discusses the different issue of the movie in which Murphy's greatest cinematic performance occurred. It's entirely possible for *Beverly Hills Cop* to be the better movie and for Murphy's greatest movie performance to have transpired in *Coming to America*. Maybe *Beverly Hills Cop* grossed more money at the box office! Likewise, Jennifer and Kate do not disagree on whether Murphy's greatest movie performance transpired in *Coming to America*, as Jennifer never weighs in on that topic. You might also think Jennifer and Kate disagree over what constitutes Murphy's most valuable acting talents. Again, not so fast! Only Jennifer expresses an opinion on this. In addition, Kate never says that Murphy did not show humor or timing skills in *Coming to America*.

Resolving a Seemingly Paradoxical Situation

Sometimes you will encounter situations that appear paradoxical. However, none of the premises describing the scenario contradict each other. So how might you resolve the situation? To do this, find a proposition that: (1) is consistent with every premise (detail) of the situation; and (2) shows how the seemingly paradoxical situation actually makes sense. In other words, connect the dots by finding a proposition that makes the premises consistent with each other. Let's take this situation: "Dwiane spilled red Gatorade on the living room carpet. Kirk worked very hard in trying to clean up the stain. Now the carpet is as clean as it has ever been. And yet the stain is worse." Here the seeming paradox is this: how can the carpet be cleaner and yet the stain be worse? So we use our imagination to find a proposition consistent with both of these details and the other details of the scenario. One possible resolution runs as follows: "Kirk used a diluted bleach solution on a tan carpet to clean the red stain, which turned the stain white and even more noticeable." Bleach could easily make the carpet cleaner and at the same time make the stain worse. Many other resolutions are also possible.

Now consider this situation: "It is possible that the earliest extant manuscripts of the Septuagint, the Greek translation of the Hebrew Bible, contain the original name Yahweh for God instead of translating it as *Kyrios*. Yet many textual critics believe that the Septuagint never originally contained the name Yahweh but consistently translated it as *Kyrios*." Here there are many ways to resolve the seeming paradox. Let me offer two. First: "Whenever the early manuscripts in question of the Septuagint have the name Yahweh, extra space occurs after the name, where the space taken by Yahweh plus the extra space is equal to the space that it takes to spell *Kyrios*." This scenario indicates that the earliest extant manuscripts copied from even earlier—though nonextant (non-available)—manuscripts of the Septuagint containing *Kyrios*, deleted it, and filled in the blank space with the shorter word Yahweh. This would explain the view attributed to the textual critics above. Here's a second possible resolution: "Carbon-dating has called into question the notion that the manuscripts in question are the earliest extant manuscripts of the Septuagint, and potentially earlier extant manuscripts contain *Kyrios* instead of Yahweh." This makes sense because the possibility of being the earliest is not the same as probably, much less actually, being the earliest.

Pre-Homework Practice!

Let's practice each of the three skills learned in this chapter. First, recall the argument in the last chapter: "Most rich people are likely to spend too much money on luxurious items. For rich people tend to enjoy luxurious items." We saw that a destructor was "No rich person tends to enjoy items on which they spend too much money." Likewise, we saw that a necessary assumption (the contradictory of the destructor) was "Some rich people tend to enjoy items on which they spend too much money." Now using the second method, what is a strengthener of this argument other than the necessary assumption and a weakener of this argument other than the destructor? Try to come up with an answer before looking at my suggestions below.

- *Strengthener:* "Joelle's rich uncle loves food and spends $10,000 a week on food."
- *Weakener:* "Joelle's rich uncle enjoys basketball but spends no money on it."

Now try to find the point of contention between Aimee and Brandy in the following conversation. Afterwards, check the answer below.

> Aimee: The American government is the greatest one on earth. It gives everyone an equal opportunity at life, liberty, and the pursuit of happiness. It surpasses monarchy in every respect.
>
> Brandy: But think about the failures of the American government. There are occasions where democratic socialism is better than democracy by itself. And Breonna Taylor, a Black American, certainly wasn't given the opportunity to live that white Americans enjoy.

The point of contention is *whether the American government gives everyone an equal opportunity at life.* On everything else, only one of the two speakers expresses an opinion. Now you might think, "Don't they disagree over whether the American government is the greatest one on earth?" Well, no! Aimee affirms this, and Brandy's claims that the American government has failed and that democratic socialism is sometimes better than democracy *per se* are perfectly consistent with Aimee's affirmation. For suppose that Brandy thinks every other government on earth has failed worse than the American government and that there is no democratic socialist nation on earth. The fact that Brandy could very well think this shows that Aimee and Brandy don't actually disagree about the greatness of the American government. On everything besides the point of contention, then, only one of the two speakers has an opinion.

Finally, attempt to find a scenario that resolves this seemingly paradoxical situation. Then check your answer with the possible resolution below the situation.

> Situation: Jill's vocal range is better than it has ever been. She can now sing four octaves. And yet she can't sing second space C in the bass clef.
>
> *Possible resolution:* Jill's vocal range goes from third-line D in the bass clef to the D above the D two ledger lines above the staff in the treble clef. (That's four octaves, and her range starts one whole step higher than second space C in the bass clef.)

Homework Assignment 29

Find a destructor and a necessary assumption of this argument. Then find a strengthener other than the necessary assumption and a weakener other than the destructor.

1. Some people believe that art exhibits only intrinsic beauty. Other people believe that art exhibits only extrinsic beauty. And still other people believe that art exhibits no beauty at all. For these reasons, there cannot be any good definition of art.

Find the point of contention.

2. Joelle: If God exists, then objective moral values exist. And God certainly exists. So the objectivity of moral values is secure, grounded in the perfectly good nature of God. God also provides us with the best foundation for objective moral duties and accountability.

Courtney: But objective moral values exist even if God does not exist. For regardless of the existence or nonexistence of God, objective moral values find their ground in abstract objects that exist independently of God. Human beings have a duty to love each other.

Find a scenario that resolves this seemingly paradoxical situation.

3. Guido believes in the infallibility of the Bible. Yet he believes that the Bible contains statements that are not factually correct. For example, he believes that Matthew's report of the guard posted at Jesus' tomb is a legend constructed by the Christian community a generation after Jesus' crucifixion.

30

Diagramming Arguments

When confronted with arguments in English, it is often very helpful to diagram them. A diagram illustrates the logical sequence of an argument, from top to bottom. It furnishes a kind of flowchart of the argument which reveals the role that each statement in the argument plays. Two things should be kept in mind when diagramming an argument. First, the goal is not to determine if the argument is valid. For example, suppose a statement in an argument is used as a premise for a subconclusion. Then draw the two statements in question as premise and subconclusion, even if the subconclusion does not validly follow from the premise. Second, often speakers add a premise to an argument even after drawing a subconclusion and then put the subconclusion together with the new premise to draw a further conclusion, either subconclusion or main conclusion. In this case, locate the new premise together with—and so on the same line as—the subconclusion with which it teams up in the argument. Here, a general rule may be stated: *Always put statements on the same line as other statements with which they team up.* So if three premises team up to draw a (sub)conclusion, the three premises would go on one line and the (sub) conclusion would go on the line just below it.

How to Diagram Arguments

The first step in diagramming an argument is to sort out, using your knowledge of the laws of logic (especially forms), what is background information, a premise, a subconclusion, and the conclusion. In doing so, remember the different ways "if-then" and "and" statements can be phrased. Moreover, remember that different propositions can be contained in the same sentence. This reminder is especially useful in two cases. First, you may see that part of a compound proposition containing "and" or one of its synonyms (e.g., a conjunction)—but not the entire thing—supports a (sub)conclusion. In this case, treat the simple propositions making up the conjunction as separate premises. Second, if the argument supports only part of the conclusion and the conclusion is a conjunction, treat the parts as separate propositions. Otherwise, do not split up compound propositions into simple propositions. In the text of the argument, bracket each proposition and number it sequentially, keeping the two aforementioned rules in mind.

So what goes where in the diagram? Suppose the argument contains background information. Then put the numbers of statements constituting background information on the top line. Connect these numbers to nothing. These numbers alone must be placed on the top line. Only if the argument contains no background information will one or more premises be on the top line. When just one proposition directly supports another, put it on a line and draw a downward arrow from that proposition to the supported proposition on the following line. When multiple propositions join forces (as in a logical form) to directly support another, put them on the same line, bracket them, and draw a downward arrow from them to the supported proposition on the following line. The conclusion (and any proposition conjoined to it) will always go on the bottom line. If the conclusion has a proposition conjoined to it (e.g., connected to it with "and" or one of its synonyms), link the conclusion and the connected proposition with a horizontal dash on the bottom line. The connected proposition is termed *consistent with the conclusion*. After following these steps for the entire argument, the last step of the diagram is to label each proposition as background information, premise, subconclusion, conclusion, or consistent with the conclusion.

Let's now work four examples together. Consider the following argument:

> Kansas produces a fair amount of oil each year. There are several oil wells around McPherson. All oil from the McPherson wells is sold at various Kansas gas stations. So some oil from the McPherson wells is sold at various Kansas gas stations. Either no oil from the McPherson wells is sold at various Kansas

gas stations or $2 + 2 \neq 8$. Consequently, $2 + 2 \neq 8$, even though we already knew that.

We begin by sorting out what is background information, a premise, a subconclusion, and the conclusion. On a first read-through, we see that the first two sentences contribute nothing to the argument. So they are background information. We also notice the indicator word "so" in the fourth sentence and the synonymous "consequently" in the last sentence. Accordingly, the fourth and last sentences—in whole or in part—must each be conclusions of some type, either subconclusion or main conclusion. The third sentence appears to be a premise supporting the fourth sentence, an appearance confirmed by our knowledge of Sq. From "All oil from the McPherson wells is sold at various Kansas gas stations," we can infer as a subaltern that "Some oil from the McPherson wells is sold at various Kansas gas stations." Further, we detect that sentences four and five join forces in DS to support the first clause of the final sentence, a conjunction employing "even though" as a synonym of "and." Hence sentence four is a subconclusion, and sentence five is a premise. The first clause of the final sentence is the conclusion, and the second clause is consistent with the conclusion. Now we bracket each proposition in the argument and number it sequentially:

> [1][Kansas produces a fair amount of oil each year.] [2][There are several oil wells around McPherson.] [3][All oil from the McPherson wells is sold at various Kansas gas stations.] [4][So some oil from the McPherson wells is sold at various Kansas gas stations.] [5][Either no oil from the McPherson wells is sold at various Kansas gas stations or $2 + 2 \neq 8$.] [6][Consequently, $2 + 2 \neq 8$,] [7][even though we already knew that.]

In our diagram, numbers 1 and 2 will go on the top line by themselves. 3 will go on the next line. On the line below it, we place number 4, drawing a downward arrow from 3 to 4. Since 5 teams up with 4, we put 5 on the same line as 4 and bracket them. On the final line we put 6 and 7, drawing a downward arrow from the bracket to 6 and drawing a horizontal dash between 6 and 7. Then we label 1 and 2 as background information, 3 as a premise, 4 as a subconclusion, 5 as a premise, 6 as the conclusion, and 7 as consistent with the conclusion.

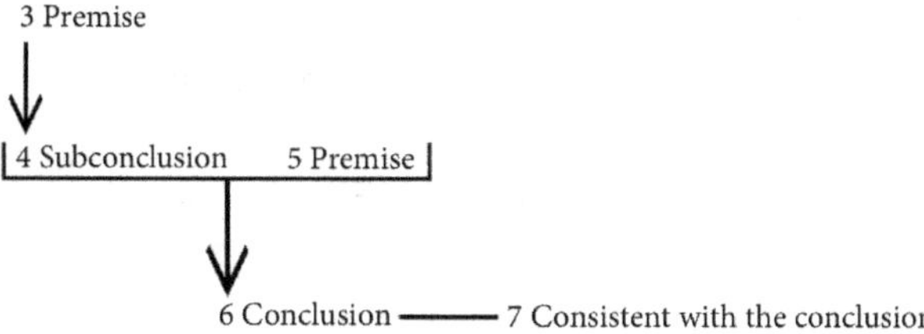

Now let's diagram a second argument:

> Gray clouds are in the air, and rain is coming soon. So it's going to rain. I really don't like rain! It's not going to rain unless one of my colleagues lives in a brick house. That means one of my colleagues lives in a brick house. For this reason, a colleague of mine living in a brick house exists. This situation may remind us of existentialism.

On an initial read-through of the argument, we notice that the second sentence logically follows by Simp from the first sentence, a fact confirmed by the indicator word "so" at the start of the second sentence. The third sentence plays no role in the argument and is therefore background information. We detect that the fourth sentence contains the double-negative "not . . . unless . . . ," a tricky way of saying "if . . . , then . . ." We also see that the fourth and second sentences join forces in MP to give us the fifth sentence. Moreover, the fifth sentence, by EG, gives us the sixth sentence. The final sentence contributes nothing to the argument, making it background information. Accordingly, the first sentence is a premise, and the second sentence is the resulting subconclusion. The fourth sentence is a premise which teams up with the second sentence, with the fifth sentence as a subconclusion derived from sentences two and four. The sixth sentence is the conclusion, derived from the fifth sentence. We then bracket and number each proposition in the argument:

> [1][Gray clouds are in the air, and rain is coming soon.] [2][So it's going to rain.] [3][I really don't like rain!] [4][It's not going to rain unless one of my colleagues lives in a brick house.] [5][That means one of my colleagues lives in a brick house.] [6][For this reason, a colleague of mine living in a brick house exists.] [7][This situation may remind us of existentialism.]

In our diagram, 3 and 7 will occupy the top line. 1 occupies the next line, with 2 on the line immediately below. We draw a downward arrow from 1 to 2. 4 is placed on the same line as 2 and bracketed with it. The following line contains 5, with a downward arrow from the bracket to 5. The final line contains 6, with a downward arrow from 5 to 6.

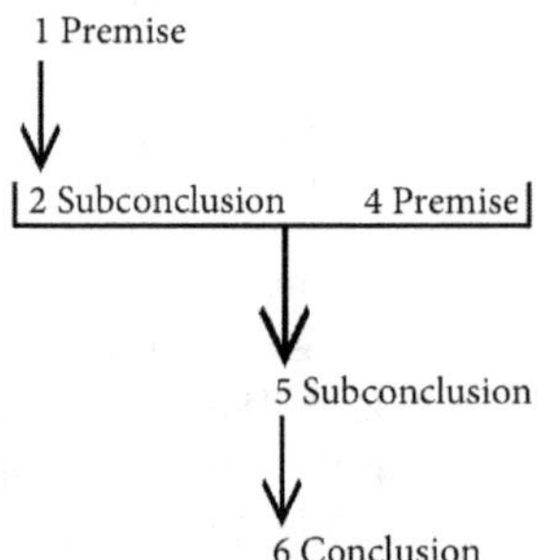

Our third example clearly reveals how valuable a diagram can be. For this argument is crazy but makes good sense once it is diagrammed. The crazier the argument, the more valuable a diagram of that argument is.

> Just because we don't know why something exists does nothing to show that it does not exist. I don't know exactly why my car exists! Given that my car is parked beside a tan car, my car needs an oil change. Now my car doesn't need an oil change. That's good news because the person who changed my oil last charged me too much. Indeed my car isn't parked beside a tan car or the Chiefs have their stadium in Kansas, despite that the Chiefs are great. For my car isn't parked beside a tan car.

When beginning our read-through of the argument, we see the word "because" in the first sentence. But be careful! Immediately before "because" is the word "just," which means "only." While "because" by itself would be a premise indicator and "only (if)" by itself would indicate the consequent of a conditional, the combined "just because" isn't an indicator of anything! This is evident by the fact that the first sentence could be rewritten, "Not knowing why something doesn't exist is by itself no evidence that it doesn't exist," which contains nothing that even looks like an indicator. As we continue to read, we detect that the first sentence plays no role in the argument. Neither does the second sentence, rendering both the first and second sentences background information. In the third sentence, "given that" means "if," making the first clause the antecedent and the second clause the consequent. The fourth sentence joins forces with the third sentence in MT to give us the last sentence. The word "for" beginning the last sentence shows us that it serves as evidence for at least part of the previous (sixth) sentence. While "for" is a premise indicator, note that a subconclusion serves as both a conclusion in itself and a premise for a further conclusion. So "for" may be used to indicate a subconclusion. By Add, we detect that it serves as evidence for the clause "my car isn't parked beside a tan car or the Chiefs have their stadium in Kansas" but not the conjoined clause "despite that (i.e., and) the Chiefs are great." That leaves only the fifth sentence, which contributes nothing to the argument and so is background information. The argument, bracketed and numbered, looks like this:

> [1][Just because we don't know why something exists does nothing to show that it does not exist.] [2][I don't know exactly why my car exists!] [3][Given that my car is parked beside a tan car, my car needs an oil change.] [4][Now my car doesn't need an oil change.] [5][That's good news because the person who changed my oil last charged me too much.] [6][Indeed my car isn't parked beside a tan car or the Chiefs have their stadium in Kansas,] [7][despite that the Chiefs are great.] [8][For my car isn't parked beside a tan car.]

In our diagram, 1, 2, and 5 go on the top line. 3 and 4 occupy the next line and are bracketed together. 8 occupies the subsequent line, with a downward arrow from the bracket to 8. The last line is occupied by 6 and 7, with these two numbers connected with a horizontal dash and an arrow pointing from 8 to 6. Finally, we label 1, 2, and 5 as background information, 3 and 4 as premises, 8 as the subconclusion, 6 as the conclusion, and 7 as consistent with the conclusion.

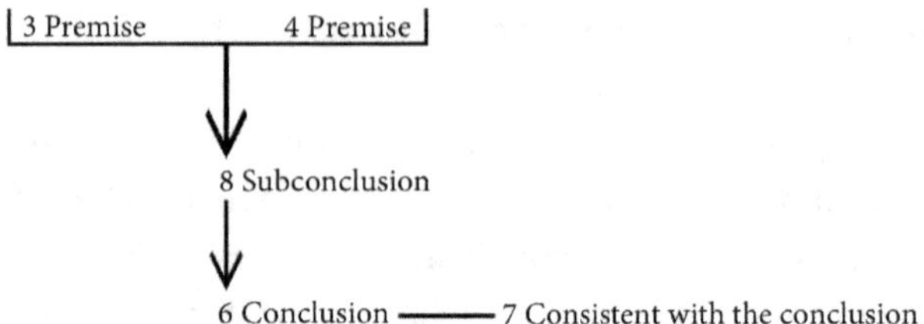

Our last argument before the pre-homework practice reads as follows:

> Physical therapy is very helpful for people recovering from car accidents. While the physical therapy center closest to my house shares a building with a kinesiology center, every car accident victim I know goes there. For Picasso's art is beautiful only if every car accident victim I know goes to the aforementioned physical therapy center. And Picasso's art is beautiful.

Reading through the argument, we see that the first sentence is background information, playing no role in the argument. The second sentence contains the term "while," a synonym of "and." So the question becomes whether we should split this into two propositions or keep this as a single compound proposition. The indicator word "for" beginning the third sentence shows that the third sentence is a premise and that at least part of the second sentence is the conclusion. "Only if" signals the consequent of an if-then statement. The last sentence joins forces with the third sentence in MP to yield the second clause of the second sentence. So we should split the second sentence into two propositions. Accordingly, the third and fourth sentences are premises, and the second clause of the second sentence is the conclusion. The first clause of the second sentence is consistent with the conclusion.

Bracketing and numbering the propositions, we have:

> [1][Physical therapy is very helpful for people recovering from car accidents.] [2][While the physical therapy center closest to my house shares a building with a kinesiology center,] [3][every car accident victim I know goes there.] [4][For Picasso's art is beautiful only if every car accident victim I know goes to the

aforementioned physical therapy center.] [5][And Picasso's art is beautiful.]

The top line is occupied by 1. The second line is occupied by 4 and 5 which are bracketed together. The bottom line contains 3 and 2, with an arrow from the bracket to 3 and a horizontal dash from 3 to 2. We already know the role each proposition plays and label them as seen in the diagram below.

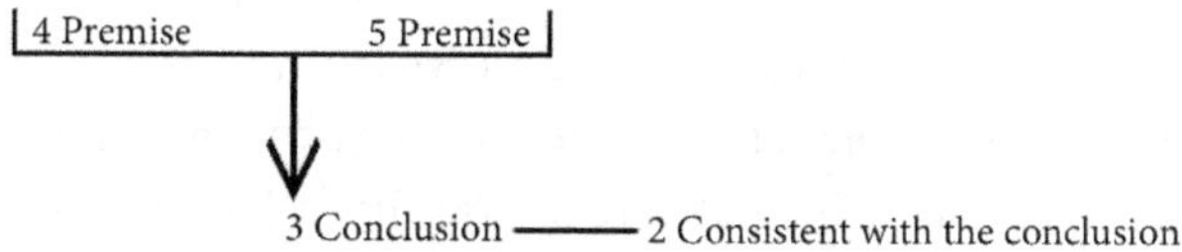

Pre-Homework Practice!

Try to bracket and number the propositions in and then diagram each of the following arguments. Only after doing so should you look at the bracketed and numbered argument as well as the diagram in the solution.

Argument 1

The doctrine of original sin troubles many people. Notwithstanding its unfairness, this doctrine was formulated by Augustine. For I don't have a stuffed tabby cat unless Augustine formulated the doctrine of original sin. Indeed I have a stuffed tabby cat. His name is Guido. He's a replica cat of the cat from the opening scene of the Godfather.

Solution 1

[1][The doctrine of original sin troubles many people.] [2][Notwithstanding its unfairness,] [3][this doctrine was formulated by Augustine.] [4][For I don't have a stuffed tabby cat unless Augustine formulated the doctrine of original sin.] [5][Indeed I have a stuffed tabby cat.] [6][His name is Guido.] [7][He's a replica cat of the cat from the opening scene of the Godfather.]

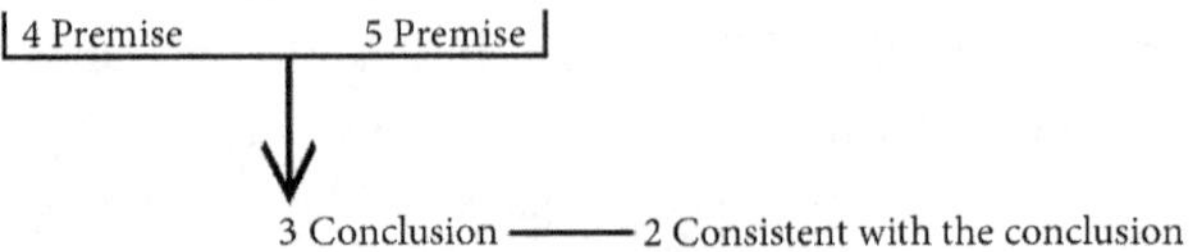

Argument 2

Whenever the speed limit is 20 mph, police officers are out in full force to pull people over for speeding. This follows from the fact that the city needs more revenue. Indeed, the city needs more revenue and the speed limit is 20 mph only if police officers are out in full force to pull people over for speeding. Therefore, if the city needs more revenue, then if the speed limit is 20 mph, police officers are out in full force to pull people over for speeding. I sure hope I don't get a ticket on my street, where the speed limit is 20 mph.

Solution 2

[1][Whenever the speed limit is 20 mph, police officers are out in full force to pull people over for speeding.] [2][This follows from the fact that the city needs more revenue.] [3][Indeed, the city needs more revenue and the speed limit is 20 mph only if police officers are out in full force to pull people over for speeding.] [4][Therefore, if the city needs more revenue, then if the speed limit is 20 mph, police officers are out in full force to pull people over for speeding.] [5][I sure hope I don't get a ticket on my street, where the speed limit is 20 mph.]

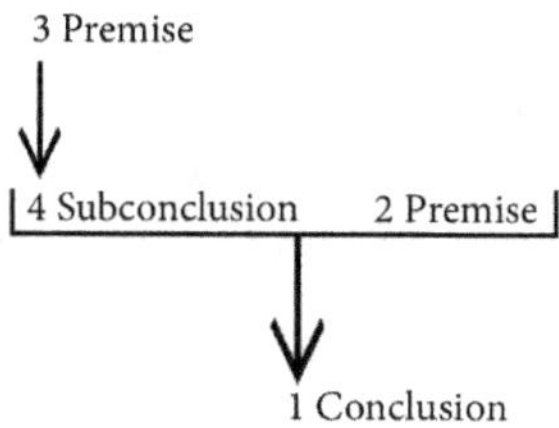

Homework Assignment 30

Bracket and number the propositions in and then diagram each of the following arguments.

Argument 1

Many people consider the doctrine of the Trinity a mystery at best or a logical contradiction at worst. They ask, "How could three be one or one be three?" Yet contemporary philosophers have developed plausible models of the Trinity. These models focus on either the unity or the plurality. But if a model focuses on the unity, it must be careful to avoid positing a single person with multiple aspects; and if a model focuses on the plurality, it must be careful to avoid positing three gods. So contemporary models must be careful to avoid either positing a single person with multiple aspects or positing three gods, notwithstanding the fact that both of these challenges can be met.

Argument 2

Tomorrow Jill is going to the doctor because she's worried about her health. Her family has a history of heart attacks, strokes, and cancer. But if Jill eats at Pizza Hut tomorrow, she will not go to the doctor tomorrow. Therefore, Jill won't eat at Pizza Hut tomorrow. It is the case, then, that Jill won't eat at Pizza Hut tomorrow, and either Jill won't eat at Pizza Hut tomorrow or she'll miss church this Sunday.

31

Drawing the Conclusion

You can use your proof skills to draw conclusions from facts every day in the real world. Indeed, drawing conclusions is just doing proofs without prior knowledge of what you're proving (and translating each step of the proof into English). Lawyers, historians, doctors, scientists, psychiatrists, and people in a host of other professions are confronted daily with various pieces of evidence and need to draw the appropriate conclusions from that evidence. People with proof skills possess a decided advantage in all of these professions, as they can draw conclusions more quickly and more accurately than people without proof skills.

So how do you know when you've found the thing you're proving? Suppose you're presented with an assortment of pieces of evidence related to a topic. Treat each of these pieces of evidence as a premise, and then express it in symbolic form. You need to use all your premises in the proof. If you haven't used one of your premises to draw an inference, you're not done. Once you've used all your premises, you're either done or one step away from being done. If the last line in your proof is clear when translated into English, you're done. If the last line of your proof is unclear when translated into English and it's logically equivalent to something clear, use one more step to apply the logical equivalence and you're done. Essentially, you're using the proof strategy of working forwards until you've both used all your premises in the proof and ensured that the last line of the proof is clear. The last line of the proof is the conclusion. The other lines of the proof are subconclusions. Both the conclusion and the subconclusions follow from the premises.

Using Your Proof Skills in Real Life

Let's consider the following example: "If *M*olina had never lived, *o*pen theism would be the prevalent view among Christian philosophers today. Yet open theism is not the prevalent view among Christian philosophers today. Either Molina never lived or *e*ssence precedes existence. Now essence does not precede existence unless everything true of *T*ully is also true of *C*icero and vice versa." We begin by symbolizing and numbering each of the premises, underlining the last one. The first three sentences are easy to symbolize. The final sentence employs "not . . . unless . . . ," which means "if . . . , then . . ." In the consequent, you hopefully recall that "everything true of Tully is also true of Cicero and vice versa" means that for every property *P*, Tully has the property iff Cicero has the property. Accordingly, the premises, symbolized and numbered, run as follows.

1. ~M → O
2. ~O
3. ~M ∨ E
4. <u>E → (*P*)(*P*t ↔ *P*c)</u>

Now we start drawing inferences in the proof (i.e., working forwards), afterwards translating each inference into English.

5. M (MT, 1, 2)	Molina lived.
6. E (DS, 3, 5)	Essence precedes existence.
7. (*P*)(*P*t ↔ *P*c) (MP, 4, 6)	Everything true of Tully is also true of Cicero and vice versa.

At this point we've used all our premises in the proof. However, there's a much clearer way to express 7, namely,

8. t = c (Id, 7)	Tully is Cicero.

Now we're done! "Tully is Cicero" is the conclusion; "Molina lived," "Essence precedes existence," and "Everything true of Tully is also true of Cicero and vice versa" are subconclusions.

Let's draw the conclusion (and the subconclusions along the way) from the following statements: "If no *c*ockroaches *d*eserve to live, then all *s*tuffed animals are *p*lush. It's false that all stuffed animals are plush unless Pol Pot was *e*vil. Either Pol Pot was not evil or I have a *b*rown chair in my living room. It's not the case that some cockroaches deserve to live." The first statement is a conditional made up of two quantified parts, a "no" antecedent and an "all" consequent. The second statement contains the tricky "it's false . . . unless . . . ," which just means "if . . . , then . . ." The third and fourth statements are straightforward to symbolize. Keeping these observations in mind, we symbolize and number our premises:

1. $(x)(Cx \rightarrow {\sim}Dx) \rightarrow (x)(Sx \rightarrow Px)$
2. $(x)(Sx \rightarrow Px) \rightarrow E$
3. ${\sim}E \vee B$
4. $\underline{{\sim}(\exists x)(Cx \cdot Dx)}$

There are at least two ways to proceed in drawing our conclusion. One way is to notice by Sq that ${\sim}(\exists x)(Cx \cdot Dx)$—the contradictory of $(\exists x)(Cx \cdot Dx)$—is $(x)(Cx \rightarrow {\sim}Dx)$. From there the rest of the proof is fairly straightforward.

5. $(x)(Cx \rightarrow {\sim}Dx)$ (Sq, 4)	No cockroaches deserve to live.
6. $(x)(Sx \rightarrow Px)$ (MP, 1, 5)	All stuffed animals are plush.
7. E (MP, 2, 6)	Pol Pot was evil.
8. B (DS, 3, 7)	I have a brown chair in my living room.

Since we've used all our premises, the proof is complete, with the conclusion being "I have a brown chair in my living room." "No cockroaches deserve to live," "All stuffed animals are plush," and "Pol Pot is evil," constitute subconclusions. Another way to proceed in drawing the same conclusion modifies steps 6 and 7. In 6, we could combine 1 and 2 by HS as follows:

6. $(x)(Cx \rightarrow {\sim}Dx) \rightarrow E$ (HS, 1, 2)	If no cockroaches deserve to live, then Pol Pot was evil.

Then 7 would read like this:

7. E (MP, 6, 5)	Pol Pot was evil.

So "If no cockroaches deserve to live, then Pol Pot was evil" is an additional subconclusion we can draw from the statements provided.

The following example throws the proverbial kitchen sink at you to make sure you remember how to symbolize very complex and trickily worded statements: "All *b*ooks written by me are *r*eadable. *L*ara or *D*wiane likes gardening. *U*nderstanding Stochastic Processes is readable only if it is false that it's *s*nowing on the condition that it's not *n*ight. Lara doesn't like gardening unless it's night, and Dwiane likes gardening only if it's snowing." The first two statements are straightforward:

1. $(x)(\mathrm{B}x \rightarrow \mathrm{R}x)$
2. L ∨ D

However, the third statement needs significant clarification. We begin by noticing the "only if," which means "then" and that the first clause is the if-clause. The phrase "it is false" after "only if" means "not" with everything after it in parentheses. Within the parentheses we have a further if-then, indicated by the phrase "on the condition that," a synonym of "if." Putting this all together, the third statement can be rewritten, "If *Understanding Stochastic Processes* is readable, then it is not the case that if it's not night, then it's snowing," which is symbolized:

3. Ru → ~(~N → S)

The fourth statement is easier, with two conditionals conjoined together. In the first clause we notice the "doesn't . . . unless . . ." (i.e., "if . . . , then . . ."), and in the second clause we notice the "only if" (i.e., "then").

4. (L → N) · (D → S)

We're now ready to start our proof. We begin by detecting that 4 and 2 can be combined by CD to yield:

5. N ∨ S (CD, 4, 2) It's night or it's snowing.

With premises 2 and 4 out of the way, we still need to use premises 1 and 3. But how? Well, 5 contains the same variables as the consequent of 3. So we ask: is there a clever way, using a logical law, to rewrite N ∨ S so as to use it with 3? What gets us from an "or" to an "if-then"? The answer is MI! MI teaches that for any A and B, A → B ≡ ~A ∨ B. Now N ∨ S ≡ ~(~N) ∨ S (recall that DN often comes in handy!), which by MI is logically equivalent to ~N → S.

6. ~N → S (MI, 5) If it's not night, then it's snowing.

This can be combined with 3 using MT, which enables us to complete the rest of the proof.

7. ~Ru (MT, 3, 6) *Understanding Stochastic Processes* isn't readable.
8. ~Bu (UMT, 1, 7) *Understanding Stochastic Processes* isn't a book written by me.

Accordingly, "*Understanding Stochastic Processes* isn't a book written by me" is the conclusion, and "It's night or it's snowing," "If it's not night, then it's snowing," and "*Understanding Stochastic Processes* isn't readable" constitute subconclusions reached along the way.

Our final example before the pre-homework practice is easier than the last one but demands that you remember your synonyms: "That *y*ogurt shakes taste good requires that *t*iramisu is my favorite dessert. If *j*azz music isn't easy to play or yogurt shakes don't taste good, then it's false that only *w*olves *h*owl. Jazz music is easy to play only if tiramisu isn't my favorite dessert." We first recall that, for any X and Y, "X requires Y" means "if X, then Y." We then remember that "only wolves howl" means "all howlers are wolves." All the other tricks in this example should be fairly easy to sort out. Consequently, our premises are symbolized as follows:

1. Y → T
2. (~J ∨ ~Y) → ~(*x*)(H*x* → W*x*)
3. <u>J → ~T</u>

The key to using all our premises is seeing that 1 and 3 can be combined using RHS. In light of this, steps 4 through 6 should be easy to follow.

4. J → ~Y (RHS, 1, 3) If jazz music is easy to play, then yogurt shakes don't taste good.
5. ~J ∨ ~Y (MI, 4) Jazz music isn't easy to play or yogurt shakes don't taste good.
6. ~(*x*)(H*x* → W*x*) (MP, 2, 5) It's false that all howlers are wolves.

Even though we've used the premises, 6 is unclear. We can use Sq to make it clear and so arrive at our conclusion.

7. (∃x)(Hx · ~Wx) (Sq, 6) Some howlers aren't wolves.

In summary, "Some howlers aren't wolves" is the conclusion, and "If jazz music is easy to play, then yogurt shakes don't taste good," "Jazz music isn't easy to play or yogurt shakes don't taste good," and "It's false that all howlers are wolves" represent subconclusions.

Pre-Homework Practice!

You are now ready to try drawing the conclusion and all subconclusions along the way from sets of statements. For each set of statements below, use the proof method explained in this chapter to perform these tasks. Check your answer against the solution.

Statement Set 1

The mind is the soul. Jane doesn't run track only if it's false that everything true of the mind is true of the soul and vice versa.

Solution 1

1. m = s
2. ~J → ~(*P*)(*P*m ↔ *P*s)
3. (*P*)(*P*m ↔ *P*s) (Id, 1) Everything true of the mind is true of the soul and vice versa.
4. J (MT, 2, 3) Jane runs track.

"Jane runs track" is the conclusion. "Everything true of the mind is true of the soul and vice versa" is a subconclusion.

Statement Set 2

Only things that run on batteries are graphing calculators. Everything that runs on batteries is electrical. Richard is a graphing calculator and either Richard is a graphing calculator or Richard runs on batteries. Richard isn't electrical unless leaves fall from trees in the autumn.

Solution 2

1. $(x)(Gx \rightarrow Bx)$
2. $(x)(Bx \rightarrow Ex)$
3. $Gr \cdot (Gr \vee Br)$
4. $\underline{Er \rightarrow L}$
5. $(x)(Gx \rightarrow Ex)$ (UHS, 1, 2) All graphing calculators are electrical.
6. Gr (Abs, 3) Richard is a graphing calculator.
7. Er (UMP, 5, 6) Richard is electrical.
8. L (MP, 4, 7) Leaves fall from trees in autumn.

"Leaves fall from trees in autumn" is the conclusion. "All graphing calculators are electrical," "Richard is a graphing calculator," and "Richard is electrical" are subconclusions.

Homework Assignment 31

Draw the conclusion and all subconclusions along the way using the proof method.

Statement Set 1

Some diet pop is caffeinated. If some gold rings aren't books, then truth is the same as fact. If all gold rings are books, then no diet pop is caffeinated.

Statement Set 2

My remote control isn't reliable only if I washed my car. My remote control isn't reliable unless the red pillow is soft, and I washed my car only if fireworks are loud. If thundersnow isn't awesome, then fireworks aren't loud. And the red pillow isn't soft.

32

Principles and Modal Logic

CONGRATULATIONS ON REACHING THE final chapter of *Exploring Modern Logic!* I applaud you for all your hard work and persistence in learning how to symbolize English sentences, the laws of logic, how to write proofs, how to recognize and avoid fallacies, how to find sufficient and necessary assumptions, how to strengthen and weaken arguments, and how to draw conclusions from data sets. These skills put your critical thinking abilities head and shoulders above those of most people in Western society and will serve you very well throughout your life in whatever career you embrace. To round out your study of modern logic, this chapter will consider principles and modal logic.

Principles

A special kind of conclusion is known as a *principle*. Principles are drawn in a wide variety of real-life situations, from figuring out how to run a social club to formulating law. Every rule is a principle, but not vice versa. A principle does two things. First, it logically links the facts of the case to the resolution of the case. Second, it generalizes this linkage so that it applies to any other case like it. So in finding a principle, employ your imagination in carrying out these two tasks. Often multiple principles can govern the same case. However, any principle that successfully carries out these two tasks is correct. Frequently lawyers will argue before judges that a previous case (or a set of related previous cases) represents a principle or stands for a principle, such that the principle should be applied to the present, similar case. If more than one principle can govern the previous case (or set of related previous cases), a lawyer will argue for the principle that, if applied to the present case, will give the lawyer the resolution they want.

Consider this case: "Mary planted a tree five inches away from the property line she shares with her neighbor. When the tree grew, its branches extended into the neighbor's property. The neighbor sued Mary in civil court. The judge ordered Mary to remove the tree immediately or be liable to the neighbor for payment of damages." In finding a principle, we use our imagination. Can we craft a rule that logically links the case's facts to its resolution and then generalizes the linkage so that it applies to future, similar cases? Here's one possibility that does the trick: "Anyone who plants anything on their property that intrudes on their neighbor's property will be subject to immediate removal of the plant or payment of damages to the neighbor."

Principles are used in sports as well as in the law. Let's try to find a principle that covers this scenario in college athletics: "Marvin is a college football player. He wants to compete this fall. In the previous fall, he earned twelve credit hours. In the previous spring, he earned eight credit hours. The coach told him he was ineligible to compete this fall. Then Marvin earned four credit hours during the summer. The coach told him he was now eligible to compete this fall." Our principle should explain both Marvin's previously ineligible state and his current eligible state, but in a general way so as to apply to other student-athletes. This principle would constitute such an explanation: "To be eligible for competition in any fall or spring term, any student-athlete must earn at least twenty-four credit hours since the term occurring at the same time last year." Of course, other principles are possible as well.

Let's return to the law—specifically the traffic court—for a final illustration: "Karen was driving 80 mph in a residential area, where the speed limit is 35 mph. The police officer charged her with reckless driving, a more severe offense than speeding. The trial judge agreed that she was guilty of reckless driving since she greatly endangered the lives of minors living in that area." What principle could this case stand for that could be applied to future cases like it? To answer this question, all we need to do is connect the facts and resolution of the case in a general way. This principle would suffice: "Anyone who drives a vehicle in a residential area housing any minors at over twice the posted speed limit commits reckless driving."

Modal Logic

Modal logic (in proofs, write *ML*) concerns what is *necessary*, *possible*, and *contingent*. Anything necessarily true could not be false under any circumstances. "Necessarily" is denoted by □. You can infer from something's being necessarily true that it's just plain old true. So we can reason: 1. □A; 2. ∴ A (ML, 1). Anything possibly true is true under some circumstances and false under other circumstances. "Possibly" is denoted by ◊. Anything that is true and is merely possibly true (i.e., could have been false) is contingently true (or contingent).

Let's now consider six equivalences in modal logic, all of which we will abbreviate ML. First, if something is not possibly true, it is necessarily false. This equivalence is symbolized ~◊A ≡ □~A (ML). Second, if something is not necessarily true, it is possibly false. This equivalence is symbolized ~□A ≡ ◊~A (ML). Third, if something is not possibly false, it is necessarily true. This equivalence is symbolized ~◊~A ≡ □A (ML). Fourth, if something is not necessarily false, it is possibly true. This equivalence is symbolized ~□~A ≡ ◊A (ML).[1] Fifth, necessarily, if A then B means if necessarily A, then necessarily B. This equivalence is symbolized □(A → B) ≡ □A → □B (ML). Sixth, possibly, if A then B means if possibly A, then possibly B. This equivalence is symbolized ◊(A → B) ≡ ◊A → ◊B (ML). These last two equivalences show that □ and ◊ distribute across "if-then" (and "iff") statements. Failure to keep this in mind results in modal logical fallacies. However, when □ and ◊ distribute to an arrow, it just stays an arrow. But now an important warning is in order: □ and ◊ *do not* distribute across "and" and "or" statements. Failure to keep this in mind results in modal logical fallacies. Accordingly, think of modal logical operators as the reverse of the ~ operator (DeM), which distributes across "and" and "or" statements but not "if-then" (and not "iff") statements.

With these equivalences and the aforementioned warning in mind, we can use our proof skills to evaluate whether various modal logical arguments are valid or fallacious. Take this argument:

1. □(A → B)
2. □A ∴ □B

1. I am indebted to Moreland and Craig, *Philosophical Foundations*, 44 for these first four equivalences.

This argument is valid and easy to prove. All we need to do is to distribute □ across the if-then in 1 and then use MP to get our conclusion.

3. □A → □B (ML, 1)
4. □B (MP, 4, 2)

Now let's consider if this argument is valid or fallacious.

1. □(A → B)
2. A ∴ □B

This argument is fallacious, since 2 does not distribute □ to A. In fact, this constitutes the most common modal logical fallacy. It is called *confusing the necessity of the consequence with the necessity of the consequent.* In other words, it confuses the fact that, necessarily, B is the consequence of A with necessarily B (the consequent of the if-then).[2]

Take this next argument. Is it valid or fallacious?

1. ◊(A → B)
2. ~◊B ∴ ~◊A

This argument is valid and easy to prove. All we need to do is to distribute ◊ across the if-then in 1 and then use MT to get our conclusion.

3. ◊A →◊ B (ML, 1)
4. ~◊A (MT, 4, 2)

Finally, let's evaluate whether this argument is valid or fallacious.

1. □(A ∨ B) ∴ □A ∨ □B

This argument is fallacious, since modal logical operators (□ and ◊) do not distribute across or-statements (disjunctions) and and-statements (conjunctions). In fact, the argument in question constitutes perhaps the second most common modal logical fallacy. It is *confusing the necessity of the disjunction* (the "or" statement as a whole) *with the necessity of the disjuncts* (the parts making up the "or" statement).

2. Moreland and Craig, *Philosophical Foundations*, 46.

Pre-Homework Practice!

Before completing your last homework assignment, let's practice your ability to formulate a principle and to evaluate an argument through modal logic. Upon answering each of the following two questions, compare your answer against the solution below. Remember that, on the principle question, your principle does not need to match mine. It only needs to link the facts and the resolution of the case in a general way to be correct.

What principle applies to this situation?

> My son Dwiane cleans up after the guinea pigs every day and takes in the trash cans after the garbage collector empties them each week. As a result, I give him a $20 weekly allowance.
>
> a. *Principle:* Parents financially reward their children for regularly doing household chores.

Symbolize this argument. Is it valid or fallacious? Why?

> Necessarily, if God foreknows that I will go to Olive Garden tomorrow, I will go to Olive Garden tomorrow. God foreknows that I will go to Olive Garden tomorrow. Therefore, I will necessarily go to Olive Garden tomorrow.
>
> 1. $\Box(F \rightarrow O)$ (F ≡ "God foreknows that I will go to Olive Garden tomorrow"; O ≡ "I will go to Olive Garden tomorrow")
> 2. F ______________ $\therefore \Box O$

This argument commits the fallacy of confusing the necessity of the consequence with the necessity of the consequent.

Homework Assignment 32

What principle applies to this situation?

1. It's true that my hair either comes down over my ears or hits my shirt collar in the back or comes down into my eyes. So I'm going to get a haircut.

Symbolize each argument below. Is it valid or fallacious? If it's valid, prove it. If it's fallacious, name the fallacy.

2. Necessarily, if 2 + 2 = 8, 3 + 3 = 9. Not necessarily, 3 + 3 = 9. So not necessarily, 2 + 2 = 8.
3. Necessarily, Joe is telling the truth or Joe is lying. So Joe is necessarily telling the truth or Joe is necessarily lying.

Solutions to Homework Assignments

Homework Assignment 1

NOTE: You can use different letters than I do. My letter explanations are italicized.

1. *Let L ≡ "Laozi composed the Daodejing" and C ≡ "An anonymous community composed the Daodejing."* L ∨ C
2. *Let K ≡ "I know something" and "B" ≡ "I have justified true belief in that thing."* K ↔ B
3. *Let L ≡ "Luther opposed the Roman Catholic Church" and C ≡ "Calvin opposed the Roman Catholic Church."* L · C
4. *Let S ≡ "Two-liters of caffeine-free Diet Coke are on sale for $1 each" and B ≡ "I'll buy eight two-liters of caffeine-free Diet Coke."* S → B
5. *Let E ≡ "I am eating at Olive Garden tomorrow."* ~E

Homework Assignment 2

NOTE: You can use different letters than I do. My letter explanations are italicized.

1. *Let C ≡ "I will wear a color of sneakers" and Y ≡ "The color is yellow."* C → Y
2. *Let E ≡ "Agi was entertaining" and D ≡ "Agi was dumber than a freaking brick."* E · D
3. *Let R ≡ "My research is sound" and "E" ≡ "Hubmaier proposed a free state church ecclesiology."* R → E

4. *Let P ≡ "I'll practice my trumpet tonight" and T ≡ "I'm extremely tired."* P · T
5. *Let K ≡ "God could have middle knowledge" and I ≡ "God relies on God's intuition."* K → I
6. *Let C ≡ "A person can think critically" and L ≡ "A person can reason logically."* C → L
7. *Let B ≡ "Beethoven was the greatest classical musician of all time" and M ≡ "Mozart died before he turned forty years old."* B → M
8. *Let R ≡ "Anselm was a realist" and C ≡ "Aquinas was a conceptualist."* R ∨ C

Homework Assignment 3

NOTE: You can use different letters than I do. What they stand for should be self-explanatory through my italicizing letters in the statements.

1. My earning *a*ll-state honors in trumpet is necessary for my invitation to perform in the *U*nited States Collegiate Wind Band. ~A → ~U
2. *T*illich's being an outspoken religious socialist was sufficient for *H*itler to want him dead. T → H
3. Two things are *s*ymmetric to each other precisely when they geometrically *m*irror one another. S ↔ M
4. The article's passing *d*ouble-blind peer review requires its *p*ublication in the journal. D → P
5. Your wearing *c*lothes must be true for you to eat in that *r*estaurant. ~C → ~R
6. No; converse error
7. Yes; Com

Homework Assignment 4

NOTE: You can use different letters than I do. What they stand for should be self-explanatory through my italicizing letters in the statements.

1. Something's being *t*rue ensures its being a *f*act, assuming *W*ittgenstein was wrong. ~W → (T → F)

2. *B*ernard of Clairvaux and *M*olina correctly analyzed counterfactuals only if the *g*rounding objection fails. $(B \cdot M) \rightarrow \sim G$

3. Given that *o*pen theism entails God's not having exhaustive *f*oreknowledge, my car is *w*hite only if it's not *g*reen. $(O \rightarrow \sim F) \rightarrow (W \rightarrow \sim G)$

4. If *C*alvinism is true and *A*rminianism is false, *l*ibertarian human freedom does not exist. $(C \cdot \sim A) \rightarrow \sim L$

5. Either the church has a *p*resbyterian style of government or *W*ynton Marsalis and someone other than *D*izzy Gillespie professionally recorded *Autumn Leaves*. $P \vee (W \cdot \sim D)$

Homework Assignment 5

NOTE: You can use different letters than I do. What they stand for should be self-explanatory through my italicizing letters in the statements.

1. It's not true that I wear *p*urple sneakers or I drive a *F*errari. $\sim(P \vee F) \equiv \sim P \cdot \sim F \equiv$ I don't wear purple sneakers and I don't drive a Ferrari.

2. It's a lie that if I go to *S*ubway, I won't buy a *F*ootlong. $\sim(S \rightarrow \sim F) \equiv S \cdot F \equiv$ I go to Subway and I buy a Footlong.

3. The contradictory of the statement that *M*adonna or someone besides *P*rince recorded *Purple Rain* is true. $\sim(M \vee \sim P) \equiv \sim M \cdot P \equiv$ Madonna didn't record *Purple Rain* and Prince recorded *Purple Rain*.

4. It is not the case that I'm sitting on my couch and I'm in my office. $\sim(C \cdot O) \equiv \sim C \vee \sim O \equiv$ I'm not sitting on my couch or I'm not in my office.

5. It's false that if Hans Küng didn't *w*rite *Christ and the Modern Mind*, then Küng was an *a*gnostic. $\sim(\sim W \rightarrow A) \equiv \sim W \cdot \sim A \equiv$ Hans Küng didn't write *Christ and the Modern Mind* and Küng was not an agnostic.

Homework Assignment 6

1. Yes; Abs

2. No; $\vee$ and $\cdot$ cannot be interchanged

3. Yes; Dist

4. Yes; Abs
5. Yes; Dist

Homework Assignment 7

NOTE: My letter choices are italicized.

1. Some *s*tatistical generalizations are not *a*ccurate. (∃*x*)(S*x* · ~A*x*)
2. All *o*bjective moral duties possess a *m*etaphysical ground. (*x*)(O*x* → M*x*)
3. *L*ove is an *o*bjective moral duty. Ol
4. No *l*aptops have *s*ouls. (*x*)(L*x* → ~S*x*)
5. Some *t*rees are *p*etrified. (∃*x*)(T*x* · P*x*)

Homework Assignment 8

NOTE: My letter choices are italicized.

1. Not every *k*eyboard is *m*ade by Yamaha. (∃*x*)(K*x* · ~M*x*)
2. Only some *B*ibles are *t*ranslated from Latin. (∃*x*)(∃*y*)((B*x* · T*x*) · (B*y* · ~T*y*))
3. Only *s*tringed instruments are *v*iolins. (x)(Vx → Sx)
4. Not a single *j*ar of peanut butter tastes like *S*prite. (*x*)(J*x* → ~S*x*)
5. There exists a *l*iving *f*alcon. (∃*x*)(F*x* · L*x*)

Homework Assignment 9

1. All people are ultimately going to heaven.
2. No people are ultimately going to heaven.
3. Some people aren't ultimately going to heaven.
4. Some people are ultimately going to heaven.
5. Yes. The two statements are subcontraries.
6. Yes. The two statements are contraries.

Homework Assignment 10

1. Valid
2. Weak (converse error)
3. Valid
4. Strong
5. Strong
6. Weak (violates Sq)

Homework Assignment 11

NOTE: To help you see things more clearly, I put background information in brackets—this must be disregarded as not part of the argument. The logical order of steps are numbered (1), (2), etc.

1. [Is it better for God to love everyone or to love only good people?] [According to some Muslims, it's better for God not to love people like Adolf Hitler.] (1) If the *Q*uran literally states "God loves the evildoers," then *s*now is not white. (3) Clearly the Quran doesn't literally state "God loves the evildoers," (2) for snow is white. [And thundersnow is freaking awesome!] (1) Q → S; (2) ~S; (3) ∴ ~Q. Valid. MT.
2. (3) That it's terrible to be body-slammed on brass tacks stands to reason. [I've seen the bloody impact this makes on pro wrestlers.] [Brass tacks are so sharp!] (2) Indeed, pro wrestling is very dangerous. (1) And if it's *t*errible to be body-slammed on brass tacks, *p*ro wrestling is very dangerous. (1) T → P; (2) P; (3) ∴ T. Weak and therefore bad. Affirming the consequent.
3. (1) Each witness who *t*estified at the trial lied *u*nder oath. [Sadly, this led to an innocent man getting a life sentence.] (2) But *L*ara didn't testify at the trial! (3) So Lara didn't lie under oath. [This makes sense in light of Lara's virtuous character.] (1) (*x*)(T*x* → U*x*); (2) ~Tl; (3) ∴ ~Ul. Weak and therefore bad. Universal denying the antecedent.
4. (1) Everyone who *s*hoots an associate of the Corleone family in the head just to watch him die *w*orks for Barzini. (3) We all know that Francisco works for Barzini. (2) After all, *F*rancisco shot an associate

of the Corleone family in the head just to watch him die. [We've already seen that Francisco is a despicable scumbag.] [Maybe Michael Corleone will seek retribution for the shooting.] (1) $(x)(Sx \rightarrow Wx)$; (2) Sf; (3) ∴ Wf. Valid. UMP.

Homework Assignment 12

NOTE: To help you see things more clearly, I put background information in brackets—this must be disregarded as not part of the argument. The logical order of steps are numbered (1), (2), etc.

1. (1) I am not *d*riving to Lindsborg without my *m*usic. [I'm performing at a gig in Lindsborg.] (2) I'll *p*lay *Lean on Me* at the gig on the condition that I have my *m*usic. [*Lean on Me* is a great Bill Withers song.] (3) Accordingly, if I drive to Lindsborg, I'll play *Lean on Me* at the gig. [In any case, the jazz band will be grooving.] (1) D → M; (2) M → P; (3) ∴ D → P. Valid. HS.
2. [Eddie Murphy movies are so funny!] (1) Eddie Murphy starred in either B*everly Hills Cop* or D*irty Rotten Scoundrels*. [Whichever one it is, I'm looking forward to watching both movies.] (2) But it's false that Eddie Murphy starred in *Dirty Rotten Scoundrels*. [Nevertheless, the twist at the end of that movie is hilarious.] (3) So Eddie Murphy starred in *Beverly Hills Cop*. (1) B ∨ D; (2) ~D; (3) ∴ B. Valid. DS.
3. [Ever since its condemnation by the Christian church in the fourth century CE, Arianism has continued to rear its ugly head at various points throughout church history.] (2) Everyone who *h*olds that Jesus is Michael the Archangel *m*aintains that Jesus died exclusively for Adam's sin. [That notion is patently unbiblical.] (1) Only people who hold that Jesus is Michael the Archangel are Jehovah's *W*itnesses. (3) So all Jehovah's Witnesses maintain that Jesus died exclusively for Adam's sin. [How do they think their own sins will be forgiven by God?] (1) $(x)(Wx \rightarrow Hx)$; (2) $(x)(Hx \rightarrow Mx)$; (3) ∴ $(x)(Wx \rightarrow Mx)$. Valid. UHS.
4. (1) Everyone *c*ompeting in the US Open is a *p*rofessional golfer or an exceptionally talented *a*mateur golfer. [It doesn't look like any amateur golfers will make the thirty-six-hole cut this year.] (2) Justin *T*homas, a competitor in the US Open, is not an exceptionally talented amateur golfer. [Indeed, he's a former major champion.] (3) Accordingly, Justin Thomas is a professional golfer. Let $x \in C$; (1) $(x)(Px \vee Ax)$; (2) ~At; (3) ∴ Pt. Valid. DDS.

Homework Assignment 13

1. (1) Anything is true of *K*'ung-fu-tzu exactly when it is true of Confucius. (2) So K'ung-fu-tzu is Confucius. (1) (*P*)(*P*k ↔ *P*c); (2) ∴ k = c. Id.
2. (1) If a *m*aximally great being does not exist, then the modal version of the ontological argument is not *s*ound. (2) But if there's *n*o logical contradiction or category mistake in the concept of a maximally great being, then the modal version of the ontological argument is sound. (3) Assuming there's no logical contradiction or category mistake in the concept of a maximally great being, then, a maximally great being exists. (1) ~M → ~S; (2) N → S; (3) ∴ N → M. RHS.
3. (1) *L*ara is a *h*ospice chaplain. (2) So a hospice chaplain exists. (1) Hl; (2) ∴ (∃*x*)H*x*. EG.
4. (1) Every single *p*oint in spacetime is *s*ubject to the gravitational field equations of the universe. (2) No *d*ivine person is subject to the gravitational field equations of the universe. (3) From this it follows that no divine person is a point in spacetime. (1) (*x*)(P*x* → S*x*); (2) (*x*)(D*x* → ~S*x*); (3) ∴ (*x*)(D*x* → ~P*x*). URHS.

Homework Assignment 14

NOTE: My letter choices are italicized. Background information is bracketed.

Argument 1

Whatever is a *b*icycle has *t*wo wheels. [Dwiane really likes riding his bicycle.] Only things used in the Olympics have two wheels. So bicycles are used in the Olympics. And it's a fact that either I *d*on't need to practice the piano or bicycles are used in the Olympics. [I haven't seriously practiced the piano since I was an undergraduate.]

1. (*x*)(B*x* → T*x*)
2. (*x*)(T*x* → O*x*)
3. ∴ (*x*)(B*x* → O*x*) (UHS, 1, 2) Subconclusion
4. ∴ D ∨ (*x*)(B*x* → O*x*) (Add, 3) Conclusion

Argument 2

If Sid Vicious were to have *c*hallenged Vader for the World Title at Starrcade '93 or *w*on the title at the event, then Sid Vicious would have *b*eaten Ric Flair. But Sid Vicious lost to Ric Flair. [I was so cheering for Ric Flair in that match!] So it's false that Sid Vicious challenged Vader for the World Title at Starrcade '93 or won the title at the event. Accordingly, Sid Vicious didn't challenge Vader for the World Title at Starrcade '93 and didn't win the title at the event. So Sid Vicious didn't win the World Title at Starrcade '93. [Ric Flair's World Title victory at Starrcade 93 is arguably the greatest match in Starrcade history.]

1. (C ∨ W) → B
2. ~B
3. ∴ ~(C ∨ W) (MT, 1, 2) Subconclusion
4. ∴ ~C · ~W (DeM, 3) Subconclusion
5. ∴ ~W (Simp, 4) Conclusion

Homework Assignment 15

NOTE: My letter choices are italicized. Background information is bracketed.

Argument 1

I'm sitting in the *d*entist's office precisely when I need to *a*ccompany a family member to the dentist. [I hate the dentist!] Hence I'm sitting in the dentist's office and I need to accompany a family member to the dentist, or I'm not sitting in the dentist's office and I don't need to accompany a family member to the dentist. [I haven't gone to the dentist for myself ever since I was in high school. And I've never had a cavity in the interim. Take that, dentists!] For these reasons, either the *s*ky is blue, or I'm sitting in the dentist's office and I need to accompany a family member to the dentist, or I'm not sitting in the dentist's office and I don't need to accompany a family member to the dentist.

1. D ↔ A
2. ∴ (D · A) ∨ (~D · ~A) (ME, 1) Subconclusion
3. ∴ S ∨ (D · A) ∨ (~D · ~A) (Add, 2) Conclusion

Argument 2

I'm eating a *t*una fish sandwich and drinking a *p*rotein shake only if I'm going to *w*ork out. [Melanie makes the best tuna fish sandwiches. She gets the contents of two whole cans, dried and combined with Miracle Whip, into one sandwich.] And I'm eating a tuna fish sandwich. Hence if I'm eating a tuna fish sandwich, then I'm drinking a protein shake only if I'm going to work out. So assuming I'm drinking a protein shake, I'm going to work out. [But I don't enjoy working out.] It follows that if I'm not going to work out, I'm not drinking a protein shake. [Thinking of the taste of a protein shake makes me nauseated.]

1. $(T \cdot P) \rightarrow W$
2. T
3. $\therefore T \rightarrow (P \rightarrow W)$ (Exp, 1) Subconclusion
4. $\therefore P \rightarrow W$ (MP, 3, 2) Subconclusion
5. $\therefore {\sim}W \rightarrow {\sim}P$ (Cont, 4) Conclusion

Homework Assignment 16

1. Traditional Square of Opposition (Sq)

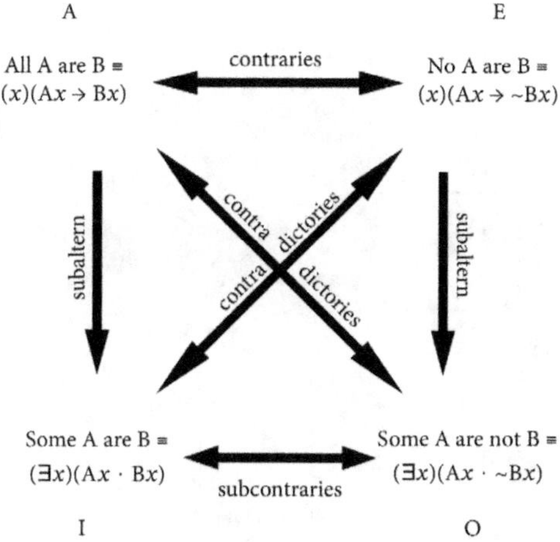

2. *Modus Tollens*
    1. A → B
    2. ~B
    3. ∴ ~A (MT)
3. Hypothetical Syllogism
    1. A → B
    2. B → C
    3. ∴ A → C (HS)
4. Constructive Dilemma
    1. (A → C) · (B → D)
    2. A ∨ B
    3. ∴ C ∨ D (CD)
5. Exportation

    (A · B) → C ≡ A → (B → C) (Ex)

Homework Assignment 17

Proof 1

1. P → (Q → R)
2. P
3. ~R
4. ~S → Q ∴ S
5. Q → R (MP, 1, 2)
6. ~Q (MT, 5, 3)
7. S (MT, 4, 6)

Proof 2

1. k = m
2. ~T → ~*(P)*(*P*k ↔ *P*m) ∴ T
3. *(P)*(*P*k ↔ *P*m) (Id, 1)
4. T (MT, 2, 3)

Proof 3

1. S · (S ∨ T)
2. S → ~Uf ∴ ~Uf
3. S (Simp, 1)
4. ~Uf (MP, 2, 3)

Homework Assignment 18

Proof 1

1. (*P*)(*P*a ↔ *P*b)
2. R ↔ (a ≠ b) ∴ R → S
3. a = b (Id, 1)
4. (R → (a ≠ b)) · ((a ≠ b) → R) (ME, 2)
5. R → (a ≠ b) (Simp, 4)
6. ~R (MT, 5, 3)
7. ~R ∨ S (Add, 6)
8. R → S (MI, 7)

Proof 2

1. ~(∃*x*)(P*x* · Q*x*)
2. Pk
3. R → Qk
4. ~S ↔ R ∴ S
5. (*x*)(P*x* → ~Q*x*) (Sq, 1)
6. ~Qk (UMP, 5, 2)
7. (~S → R) · (R → ~S) (ME, 4)
8. ~S → R (Simp, 7)
9. ~S → Qk (HS, 8, 3)
10. S (MT, 9, 6)

Proof 3

1. ~(x)(Px → ~Qx)
2. (∃x)(Px · Qx) → ((R · (R ∨ S)) ∨ T)
3. ~R
4. ~U → ~T ∴ U
5. (∃x)(Px · Qx) (Sq, 1)
6. (R · (R ∨ S)) ∨ T (MP, 2, 5)
7. R ∨ T (Abs, 6)
8. T (DS, 7, 3)
9. U (MT, 4, 8)

Homework Assignment 19

Proof 1

1. ~S
2. ~T → S ∴ P → (T ∨ (T · U))
    3. P (Assume for CP)
    4. T (MT, 2, 1)
    5. T ∨ (T · U) (Abs, 4)
6. P → T ∨ (T · U) (CP, 3–5)

Proof 2

1. Rd
2. (∃x)Rx → (x)(Sx → Tx) ∴ (x)(Ux · Vx) → ((x)(Sx → Tx) ∨ (∃x)Wx)
    3. (x)(Ux · Vx) (Assume for CP)
    4. (∃x)Rx (EG, 1)
    5. (x)(Sx → Tx) (MP, 2, 4)
    6. (x)(Sx → Tx) ∨ (∃x)Wx (Add, 5)
7. (x)(Ux · Vx) → ((x)(Sx → Tx) ∨ (∃x)Wx) (CP, 3-6)

Homework Assignment 20

Proof 1

1. k = m
2. ~T → ~(*P*)(*P*k ↔ *P*m) ∴ T
    3. ~T (Assume for RAA)
    4. ~(*P*)(*P*k ↔ *P*m) (MP, 2, 3)
    5. k ≠ m (Id, 4)
    6. (k = m) · (k ≠ m) (Conj, 1, 5)
7. T (RAA, 3–6)

Proof 2

1. P ∨ (Q · R)
2. P → ~Sf ∴ ~Sf
    3. Sf (Assume for RAA)
    4. ~P (MT, 2, 3)
    5. P (Abs, 1)
    6. P · ~P (Conj, 5, 4)
7. ~Sf (RAA, 3–6)

Homework Assignment 21

Proof 1

1. (~Pc · Rc) → Qc
2. ~(Rc → Qc)
3. Pc ↔ (S ∨ T) ∴ ~S → T
4. ~Pc → (Rc → Qc) (Ex, 1)
5. Pc (MT, 4, 2)
6. (Pc → (S ∨ T)) · ((S ∨ T) → Pc) (ME, 3)
7. Pc → (S ∨ T) (Simp, 6)
8. S ∨ T (MP, 7, 5)
9. ~S → T (MI, 8)

Proof 2

1. $(P)(Pa \leftrightarrow Pb)$
2. $\sim(U \vee V) \rightarrow (a \neq b)$
3. $(\sim W \rightarrow \sim U) \cdot (V \rightarrow (x)(Rx \rightarrow \sim Sx))$ $\therefore$ $W \vee \sim(\exists x)(Rx \cdot Sx)$
4. $a = b$ (Id, 1)
5. $U \vee V$ (MT, 2, 4)
6. $(U \rightarrow W) \cdot (V \rightarrow (x)(Rx \rightarrow \sim Sx))$ (Cont, 3)
7. $W \vee (x)(Rx \rightarrow \sim Sx)$ (CD, 6, 5)
8. $W \vee \sim(\exists x)(Rx \cdot Sx)$ (Sq, 7)

Homework Assignment 22

1. We abbreviate ears of corn as E, healthy things as H, things that taste bad as TB, and the ear of corn I just picked as e.

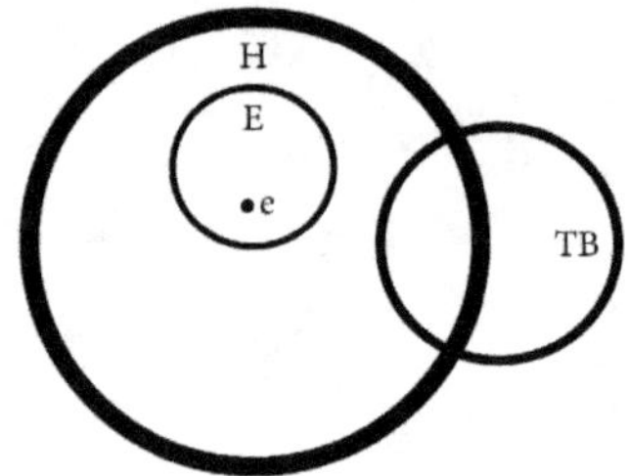

Invalid

2. We abbreviate cirrus clouds as C, white things as W, and barns as B.

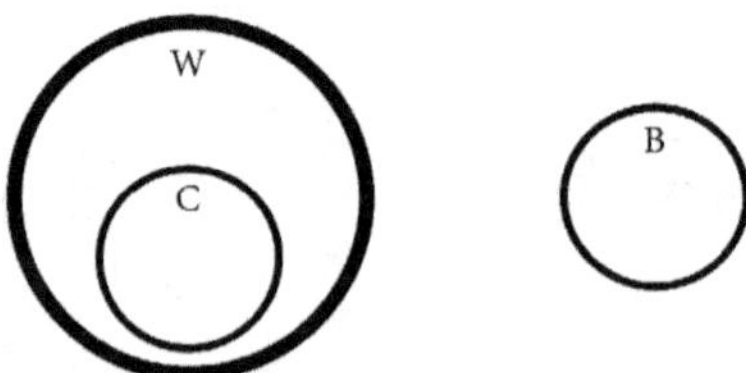

Valid

3. We abbreviate bears as B, mean things as M, and traffic signs as TS.

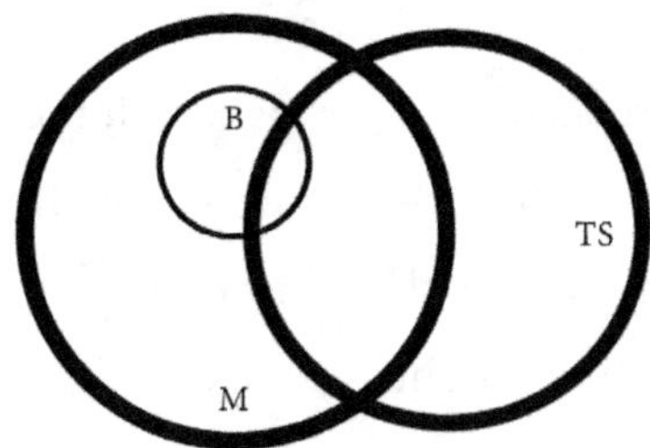

Invalid

Homework Assignment 23

1. *Ad hominem* abusive
2. Counterfeit universal hypothetical syllogism
3. Genetic fallacy
4. Straw man

Homework Assignment 24

1. *Ad ignorantiam*
2. *Ad misericordiam*
3. Confusing correlation with causation
4. *Ad populum*
5. Fallacy of division
6. *Ignorantio elenchi*

Homework Assignment 25

1. Line-drawing fallacy
2. Appeal to guilt
3. Confusing correlation with identity
4. *Post hoc ergo propter hoc*
5. Appeal to tradition

Homework Assignment 26

1. If Kierkegaard developed the concept of the leap of faith, then God is infinite and humans are finite.
2. There are 5,812 ancient Greek manuscripts of the New Testament.
3. If pillows are soft, then Melissa never dated a guy with red hair.
4. Molina finished writing the *Concordia*.
5. If I'm not too tired on Thursday night, then I take out the trash on Friday.

Homework Assignment 27

1. *Sufficient assumption:* Barth or Tillich is my favorite twentieth-century theologian.

   Contradictory: Neither Barth nor Tillich is my favorite twentieth-century theologian.

   Strengthener: My favorite twentieth-century theologian was not born in the United States. (Barth was born in Switzerland; Tillich was born in Germany.)

   Weakener: I have significant theological disagreements with both Barth and Tillich.

2. *Sufficient assumption:* If the president was not impeached in 1998, then the Senate wouldn't have held an impeachment trial in 1999.

   Contradictory: The president was not impeached in 1998 and the Senate held an impeachment trial in 1999.

   Strengthener: No political office holder below the office of the president committed a crime between 1998 and 1999.

   Weakener: Many political office holders below the office of the president committed crimes between 1998 and 1999.

Homework Assignment 28

1. *Destructor:* All trumpet mouthpieces with the capacity to independently buzz notes above high D are impossible for most trumpet players to play.

Necessary assumption: Some trumpet mouthpieces with the capacity to independently buzz notes above high D are possible for most trumpet players to play.

2. *Destructor:* No forty-year-old tradition correlated with success should be continued.

   Necessary assumption: Some forty-year-old traditions correlated with success should be continued.

3. *Destructor:* No wonderful-tasting ice cream is widely produced by ice cream companies.

   Necessary assumption: Some wonderful-tasting ice cream is widely produced by ice cream companies.

Homework Assignment 29

1. *Destructor:* Art can be successfully defined in terms of factors other than beauty.

   Necessary assumption: Art cannot be successfully defined in terms of factors other than beauty.

   Strengthener: No art historian finds persuasive a sociohistorical definition of art that makes no reference to aesthetic qualities.

   Weakener: Some art historians find persuasive a sociohistorical definition of art that makes no reference to aesthetic qualities.

2. Whether objective moral values are grounded in the perfectly good nature of God.

3. Guido understands infallibility to extend only to matters of faith and morals and not to matters of history.

Homework Assignment 30

Solution 1

[1][Many people consider the doctrine of the Trinity a mystery at best or a logical contradiction at worst.] [2][They ask, "How could three be one or one be three?"] [3][Yet contemporary philosophers have developed plausible models of the Trinity.] [4][These models focus on either the unity or the plurality.] [5][But if a model focuses on the unity, it must be careful to avoid positing a single person with multiple aspects; and if a model focuses

on the plurality, it must be careful to avoid positing three gods.] [6][So contemporary models must be careful to avoid either positing a single person with multiple aspects or positing three gods,] [7][notwithstanding the fact that both of these challenges can be met.]

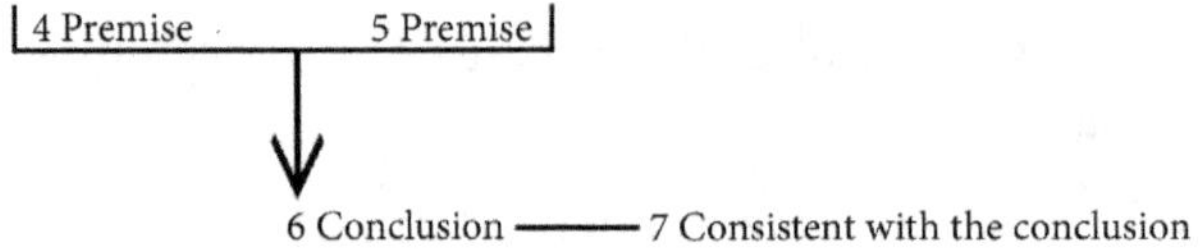

Solution 2

[1][Tomorrow Jill is going to the doctor] [2][because she's worried about her health.] [3][Her family has a history of heart attacks, strokes, and cancer.] [4][But if Jill eats at Pizza Hut tomorrow, she will not go to the doctor tomorrow.] [5][Therefore, Jill won't eat at Pizza Hut tomorrow.] [6][It is the case, then, that Jill won't eat at Pizza Hut tomorrow, and either Jill won't eat at Pizza Hut tomorrow or she'll miss church this Sunday.]

3 Background information

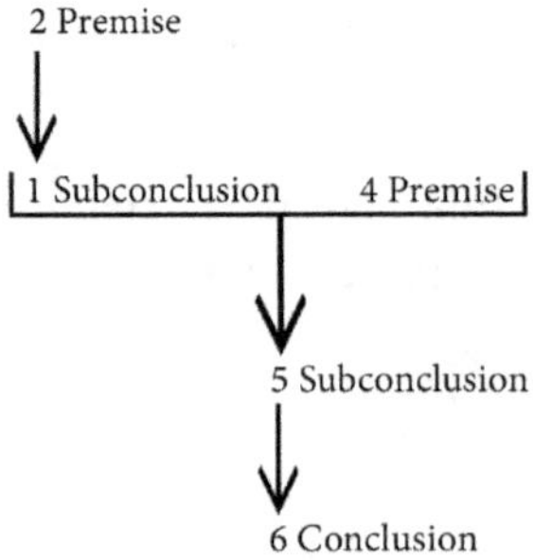

Homework Assignment 31

NOTE: My letter choices are italicized. Here I abbreviate the conclusion as "Conc" and subconclusions as "Sub." You can adopt this practice or state after completing your proof, as we did in the chapter, what is the conclusion and what are subconclusions.

Statement Set 1

Some *d*iet pop is *c*affeinated. If some *g*old rings aren't *b*ooks, then *t*ruth is the same as fact. If all gold rings are books, then no diet pop is caffeinated.

Proof 1

1. $(\exists x)(Dx \cdot Cx)$
2. $(\exists x)(Gx \cdot \sim Bx) \rightarrow T$
3. $(x)(Gx \rightarrow Bx) \rightarrow (x)(Dx \rightarrow \sim Cx)$

1. $\sim(x)(Dx \rightarrow \sim Cx)$ (Sq, 1)	It's false that no diet pop is caffeinated. Sub
5. $\sim(x)(Gx \rightarrow Bx)$ (MT, 3, 4)	It's false that all gold rings are books. Sub
6. $(\exists x)(Gx \cdot \sim Bx)$ (Sq, 5)	Some gold rings aren't books. Sub
7. T (MP, 2, 6)	Truth is the same as fact. Conc

Statement Set 2

My remote control isn't *r*eliable only if I *w*ashed my car. My remote control isn't reliable unless the red pillow is *s*oft, and I washed my car only if *f*ireworks are loud. If *t*hundersnow isn't awesome, then fireworks aren't loud. And the red pillow isn't soft.

Proof 2

1. $\sim R \rightarrow W$
2. $(R \rightarrow S) \cdot (W \rightarrow F)$
3. $\sim T \rightarrow \sim F$
4. $\sim S$

5. $R \vee W$ (MI, 1)	My remote control is reliable or I washed my car. Sub
6. $S \vee F$ (CD, 2, 5)	The red pillow is soft or fireworks are loud. Sub
7. F (DS, 6, 4)	Fireworks are loud. Sub
8. T (MT, 3, 7)	Thundersnow is awesome. Conc

Homework Assignment 32

1. People get haircuts when their hair grows too long.
2. This argument is valid. The proof reads:
    1. $\Box(E \rightarrow N)$ (E ≡ "2 + 2 = 8"; N ≡ "3 + 3 = 9")
    2. $\sim\Box N \quad \therefore \sim\Box E$

3. $\Box E \rightarrow \Box N$ (ML, 1)
4. $\sim\Box E$ (MT, 3, 2)

1. This argument commits the fallacy of confusing the necessity of the disjunction with the necessity of the disjuncts. It is symbolized:

    5. $\Box(T \vee L)$ $\therefore$ $\Box T \vee \Box L$ (T ≡ "Joe is telling the truth"; L ≡ "Joe is lying")

Glossary

ad antiquatatem: Latin for "[appeal] to tradition"; a case of the fallacy of deriving an ought from an is which mistakenly reasons that because something has always been done a certain way, it should keep being done in that way

ad baculum vel metum: Latin for "appeal to force or fear"; an informal logical fallacy which incorrectly concludes from the observation that something bad is going to happen to you if you hold a position that the position is false

ad hominem: Latin for "against the person"; an informal logical fallacy that incorrectly attacks the person(s) holding a position instead of the position itself

ad hominem abusive: An *ad hominem* fallacy that incorrectly concludes from a character defect of a person holding a position that the position is false

ad hominem circumstantial: An *ad hominem* fallacy which incorrectly concludes from the observation that the circumstances of a person who holds a position gives them motive to consciously or unconsciously skew the truth about the position (i.e., the circumstances make the person biased) that the position is false

ad hominem hypocritical: An *ad hominem* fallacy which incorrectly concludes from the observation that a person holding a position is a hypocrite (i.e., not believing part or all of their own position) that the position is false

ad ignorantiam: Latin for "[argument] from ignorance"; the informal logical fallacy that occurs when the absence of evidence for or against something is wrongfully taken as evidence that the thing is respectively false or true

ad misericordiam: Latin for "[appeal] to pity"; the informal logical fallacy claiming that because you feel sorry for a person, you should believe or do something

ad populum: Latin for "[appeal] to the people"; the informal logical fallacy that incorrectly reasons either that if everyone else in question believes something or does something, then you should too or that if you want to be part of or accepted by a group that believes something, the thing in question is true

ad verecundiam: Latin for "[appeal] to illegitimate authority"; the informal logical fallacy that incorrectly reasons that since an authority in an irrelevant field or a biased authority in the relevant field says something, it is true

affirming the consequent: The formal logical fallacy that incorrectly runs (1) $A \rightarrow B$; (2) B; (3) $\therefore$ A

antecedent: Latin for "that which comes before"; the clause that follows "if" (but not the word "if") in a conditional

appeal to guilt: The informal logical fallacy which incorrectly reasons that someone else should believe or do something because "they owe you"

appeal to the past: The informal logical fallacy which occurs when a person incorrectly reasons that because something was true in the past that the thing is still true

arrow: The logical connector $\rightarrow$, which means "if (what's left of the arrow), then (what's right of the arrow)"

background information: Information accompanying an argument that may put the argument in context but is not part of the argument and must be separated from it

bad analogy: The informal logical fallacy which incorrectly reasons that since two things are alike in some respects, they are alike in the relevant respect

bad argument: An argument whose conclusion does not follow highly probably (think ≥ 95 percent) from its premises (i.e., is weak or invalid), which contains at least one false premise, or both; accordingly, the argument is either uncogent or unsound

bidirectional arrow: The logical connector ↔, which means "(what's left of the arrow) if and only if (what's right of the arrow)"

cogent: The property of an argument which is both strong and has all true premises

compound proposition: A proposition that must be written as a sentence including at least one of the logical connectors "and," "or," "not," "if . . . , then . . . ," "iff," or a synonym of any of these

conclusion: The central point of an argument of which the argument is trying to persuade us

conditional (statement): An "if . . . , then . . . " statement

conditional proof (CP): A form of indirect proof that assumes the if-clause (antecedent) we want to prove and, using this assumption and the premise(s), deduces the then-clause (consequent) we want to prove

confusing correlation with causation: The informal logical fallacy which incorrectly reasons that because two things happen together (i.e., they are correlated), one of the two things causes the other thing

confusing correlation with identity: The informal logical fallacy which incorrectly reasons that because two things are correlated, they're really just the same thing

confusing inclusive or for exclusive or: The formal logical fallacy that incorrectly runs (1) A ∨ B; (2) A; (3) ∴ ~B or (1) A ∨ B; (2) B; (3) ∴ ~A; or that lets $x \in D$ and incorrectly runs (1) $(x)(\mathrm{A}x \vee \mathrm{B}x)$; (2) Ac; (3) ∴ ~Bc or $(x)(\mathrm{A}x \vee \mathrm{B}x)$; (2) Bc; (3) ∴ ~Ac

confusing percentages with amounts: The informal logical fallacy which incorrectly draws a conclusion about an amount from a percentage without regard to the number that it's a percentage of

confusing possibility with probability or certainty: The informal logical fallacy which incorrectly reasons that because something is possible, it's probably true or just plain true

confusing the necessity of the consequence with the necessity of the consequent: The formal logical fallacy that incorrectly runs (1) $\Box(A \rightarrow B)$; (2) A; (3) $\therefore \Box B$

confusing the necessity of the disjunction with the necessity of the disjuncts: The formal logical fallacy that incorrectly runs (1) $\Box(A \vee B)$; (2) $\therefore \Box A \vee \Box B$

confusing $\vee$ *for* $\cdot$ *(confusing disjunction for conjunction)*: The formal logical fallacy that incorrectly runs (1) A; (2) $\therefore$ A $\cdot$ B

conjunction: An "and" statement

conjuncts: The simple propositions making up an "and" statement

consequent: Latin for "that which comes afterward"; the clause that follows "then" (but not the word "then") in a conditional

consistent (or compatible) with the conclusion: Any truth that logically can be or is conjoined to a conclusion

constructive dilemma (CD): The valid argument form that runs (1) $(A \rightarrow C) \cdot (B \rightarrow D)$; (2) $A \vee B$; (3) $\therefore C \vee D$

contingent truth: Any truth that is possibly true (i.e., could have been false)

contradictory: A statement that has the opposite truth-value of the original statement under any circumstances

contrapositive: For any $X \rightarrow Y$, the contrapositive (logical equivalent) is $\sim Y \rightarrow \sim X$

contraries: The relationship of two statements such that when one is true, the other is false, but they can both be false

converse: For any $X \rightarrow Y$, the converse is $Y \rightarrow X$

converse error: The formal logical fallacy that incorrectly runs (1) $X \rightarrow Y$; (2) $\therefore Y \rightarrow X$; this confuses a statement for its converse (the two are not logically equivalent)

copula: "Are" or "is" (both forms of the linking verb "to be"), which must be the verb of a properly formed quantified statement

counterfeit universal hypothetical syllogism: A formal logical fallacy in which an argument appears to be a universal hypothetical syllogism but its premises are something other than "all" statements, such as "almost all" statements, "most" statements, "many" statements, etc., or a combination thereof

DeMorgan's Laws (DeM): The logical laws holding that $\sim(A \cdot B) \equiv \sim A \vee \sim B$ and $\sim(A \vee B) \equiv \sim A \cdot \sim B$

denying the antecedent: The formal logical fallacy that incorrectly runs (1) $A \rightarrow B$; (2) $\sim A$; (3) $\therefore \sim B$

deriving an ought from an is: The informal logical fallacy that incorrectly draws a prescriptive conclusion (i.e., a conclusion about what ought to be) from purely descriptive premises (i.e., premises about what actually is the case)

destructor: A proposition that is consistent with the truth of an argument's premises and, if added to the argument, makes the argument's conclusion necessarily false

direct proof: A proof that contains no assumptions (i.e., things we suppose are true without knowing whether or not they are true); accordingly, everything in a direct proof is an inference from a previous step or steps and therefore known to be true

discount: A rhetorical diversion that admits an inconvenient truth alongside a conclusion by minimizing it with a synonym of "and" like "despite" or "nevertheless," thus trying to lead the hearer not to pay attention to it

disjunction: an "or" statement

disjunctive syllogism: the valid argument form that runs (1) $A \vee B$; (2) $\sim A$; (3) $\therefore$ B or (1) $A \vee B$; (2) $\sim B$; (3) $\therefore$ A

disjuncts: The simple propositions making up an "or" statement

domain disjunctive syllogism (DDS): The valid argument form that lets $x \in D$ and runs (1) $(x)(Ax \vee Bx)$; (2) $\sim Ac$; (3) $\therefore$ Bc or (1) $(x)(Ax \vee Bx)$; (2) $\sim Bc$; (3) Ac; the quantified version of disjunctive syllogism

dot: The logical connector $\cdot$, which means "and" and its synonyms

end of the chain: The proposition that only occurs as the consequent of one if-then statement which has a link in the if-clause

equivocation of terms: An informal logical fallacy that incorrectly makes an argument appear valid by meaning one thing by a term in one part of an argument and meaning something else by the term in another part of the argument *existential generalization (EG)*: The valid argument form that runs (1) Ac; (2) ∴ $(\exists x)Ax$

fallacy of composition: The informal logical fallacy which incorrectly reasons that because all the parts of something have a property, the whole thing has that property

fallacy of division: The informal logical fallacy which incorrectly reasons that because a thing has a property, all the parts of the thing have that property

fallacy of subtraction: The formal logical fallacy that incorrectly runs (1) $A \vee B$; (2) ∴ A or (1) $A \vee B$; (2) ∴ B

formal logical fallacy: A fallacy in which something is wrong with an argument's structure, such that the argument is structured so poorly that even if all its premises are true, its conclusion still does not follow

genetic fallacy: An informal logical fallacy that incorrectly concludes that a position is false based on how that position originated

good argument: An argument whose conclusion follows highly probably (think ≥ 95 percent) from the premises (i.e., is strong or valid) and which contains all true premises; accordingly, the argument is either cogent or sound

hypothetical syllogism (HS): The valid argument form that runs (1) $A \rightarrow B$; (2) $B \rightarrow C$; (3) ∴ $A \rightarrow C$

ignorantio elenchi (red herring): An informal logical fallacy which occurs when a position is allegedly refuted with distracting premises that have nothing to do with that position

indirect proof: A proof that contains at least one assumption (i.e., something we suppose is true without knowing whether or not it is true)

informal logical fallacy: A fallacy in which something is wrong with an argument's content, such that the content of one or more of the premises makes it impossible to infer the conclusion from the truth of the premises

invalid: The property of an argument whose conclusion does not follow inescapably from its premises

inverse: For any $X \rightarrow Y$, the inverse is $\sim X \rightarrow \sim Y$

inverse error: The formal logical fallacy that incorrectly runs (1) $X \rightarrow Y$; (2) ∴ $\sim X \rightarrow \sim Y$; this confuses a statement for its inverse (the two are not logically equivalent) *inverse error argument*: The formal logical fallacy that incorrectly runs (1) A → B; (2) C → ~A; (3) ∴ C → ~B

law of absorption (Abs): The logical law holding that A → B ≡ A → (A · B), that A ≡ A · (A ∨ B), and that A ≡ A ∨ (A · B)

law of addition (Add): The valid argument form that runs (1) A; (2) ∴ A ∨ B

law of association (Assoc): The logical law holding that A ∨ (B ∨ C) ≡ (A ∨ B) ∨ C and that A · (B · C) ≡ (A · B) · C

law of commutation (Com): The logical law holding that conjuncts can be interchanged with each other (A · B ≡ B · A) and that disjuncts can be interchanged with each other (A ∨ B ≡ B ∨ A)

law of conjunction (Conj): The valid argument form that runs (1) A; (2) B; (3) ∴ A · B

law of contraposition (Cont): The logical law holding that X → Y ≡ ~Y → ~X

law of distribution (Dist): The logical law holding that A · (B ∨ C) ≡ (A · B) ∨ (A · C) and that A ∨ (B · C) ≡ (A ∨ B) · (A ∨ C)

law of double negation (DN): The logical law holding that two negatives make a positive, such that ~~A ≡ A

law of excluded middle: At any given time and sense, a proposition is either true or false; there is no middle ground between truth and falsity

law of exportation (Ex): The logical law holding that (A · B) → C ≡ A → (B → C)

law of idempotence (Idem): The logical law holding that A ≡ A ∨ A and that A ≡ A · A

law of identity (Id): The logical law holding that $x = x$ and that $(x)(y)((x = y) \equiv (P)(Px \leftrightarrow Py))$

law of material implication (MI): The logical law holding that A → B ≡ ~A ∨ B

law of noncontradiction: A proposition cannot be both true and false at the same time and in the same sense

law of simplification (Simp): The valid argument form that runs (1) A · B; (2) ∴ A or (1) A · B; (2) ∴ B

line-drawing fallacy: The informal logical fallacy which incorrectly reasons for some position A that since we cannot stipulate exactly when A stops being true and ~A starts being true, there's no actual distinction between A and ~A

link in the chain: A proposition that occurs as the consequent of one if-then statement and the antecedent of another if-then statement

material equivalence (ME): The logical law holding that $A \leftrightarrow B \equiv (A \rightarrow B) \cdot (B \rightarrow A)$ and that $A \leftrightarrow B \equiv (A \cdot B) \vee (\sim A \cdot \sim B)$

modal logic (ML): The branch of logic concerning what is necessary, possible, and contingent

modus ponens (MP): Latin for "the way of affirming"; the valid argument form that runs (1) $A \rightarrow B$; (2) A; (3) $\therefore$ B

modus tollens (MT): Latin for "the way of denying"; the valid argument form that runs (1) $A \rightarrow B$; (2) ~B; (3) $\therefore$ ~A

necessary assumption: An assumption which makes the conclusion of an invalid argument more probably true and whose contradictory makes the conclusion impossible

necessary condition: A prerequisite for something to happen stating what must be true for the thing to happen; however, it does not guarantee that the thing happens

necessary truth: A truth that could not be false under any circumstances; "necessarily" is denoted by $\Box$

negating a conditional (NC): The logical law holding that $\sim(A \rightarrow B) \equiv A \cdot \sim B$

particular affirmative statement: A "some" statement, such that "Some A are B" $\equiv (\exists x)(Ax \cdot Bx)$

particular negative statement: A "some . . . not" statement, such that "Some A are not B" $\equiv (\exists x)(Ax \cdot \sim Bx)$

petitio principii: Latin for "begging the question"; the informal logical fallacy which occurs when a conclusion is allegedly—but not actually—proven by sneaking the conclusion into at least one of the premises

point of contention: In a dispute, the place where both people have a belief and where those two beliefs contradict each other; also known as the point at issue

population: A whole group

possible truth: Something that is true under some circumstances and false under other circumstances; "possibly" is denoted by ◊

post hoc ergo propter hoc: Latin for "after this; therefore, because of this"; the informal logical fallacy which incorrectly reasons that because thing 2 happened after thing 1, thing 1 caused thing 2; also known as the false cause fallacy

premise: A step in an argument furnishing evidence for the argument's conclusion

principle: A rule that logically links the facts of a case to the resolution of the case and generalizes this linkage so that it applies to any other case like the present case

proof: A logical demonstration that an argument is valid

proposition: The content of a declarative sentence

reasoning about a population from an unrepresentative sample: The informal logical fallacy which occurs when someone draws a conclusion about a whole group (population) from a subset of that group (sample) that is either too small, too biased, or improperly studied; also known as hasty generalization

reductio ad absurdum (RAA): Latin for "reducing to absurdity"; a strategy where you prove the conclusion of an argument is true by proving that the negation of the conclusion, combined with some of the premises, leads to a contradiction; also known as proof by contradiction

relativist fallacy: The informal logical fallacy which incorrectly reasons that since many people disagree over whether A or ~A is true, neither of them is objectively true, such that the truth-value of each is subjective

representative sample: A sample that sufficiently mirrors the population

reverse hypothetical syllogism (RHS): The valid argument form that runs (1) A → B; (2) C → ~B; (3) ∴ C → ~A

sample: A subset of a whole group

simple proposition: A proposition that can be written as a sentence not including any of the logical connectors "and," "or," "not," "if . . . , then . . . ," "iff," "therefore," or a synonym of any of these

sound: The property of an argument which is both valid and contains all true premises

start of the chain: The proposition that only occurs as the antecedent of one if-then statement which has a link in the then-clause

straw man: An informal logical fallacy that refutes a caricature of a position instead of refuting the position itself

strong: The property of an argument structured in such a way that the conclusion follows highly probably but not inescapably from the premises

subconclusion: A statement that at least one other statement supports and that supports at least one other statement

subcontraries: The relationship of two statements such that when one is false, the other is true, but they can both be true

sufficient assumption: The premise missing from an invalid argument that, if added to the argument, makes the argument valid

sufficient condition: Enough for something to happen, guaranteeing that the thing happens

therefore: The logical symbol ∴, which means "therefore" and its synonyms

tilde: The logical connector ~, which means "not" and its synonyms

traditional square of opposition (Sq): The logical law expressed in the following image:

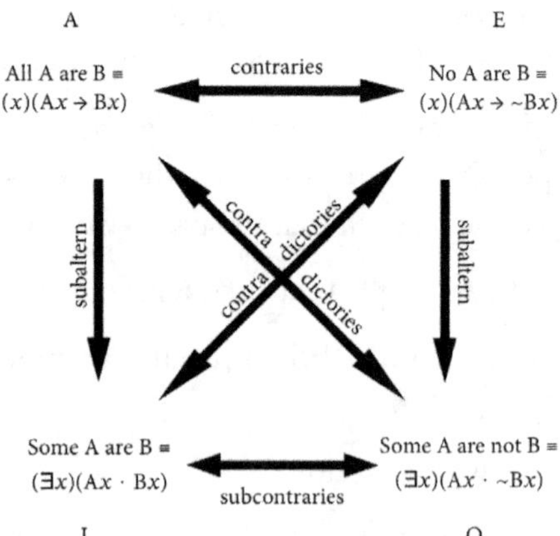

uncogent: The property of an argument which is either weak, has at least one false premise, or both

universal affirmative statement: An "all" statement, such that "All A are B" $\equiv (x)(Ax \rightarrow Bx)$

universal affirming the consequent: The formal logical fallacy that incorrectly runs (1) $(x)(Ax \rightarrow Bx)$; (2) Bc; (3) $\therefore$ Ac; the quantified version of affirming the consequent

universal converse error: The formal logical fallacy that incorrectly runs (1) $(x)(Ax \rightarrow Bx)$; (2) $\therefore$ $(x)(Bx \rightarrow Ax)$; the quantified version of the converse error

universal denying the antecedent: The formal logical fallacy that incorrectly runs (1) $(x)(Ax \rightarrow Bx)$; (2) ~Ac; (3) $\therefore$ ~Bc; the quantified version of denying the antecedent

universal hypothetical syllogism (UHS): The valid argument form that runs (1) $(x)(Ax \rightarrow Bx)$; (2) $(x)(Bx \rightarrow Cx)$; (3) $\therefore$ $(x)(Ax \rightarrow Cx)$; the quantified version of hypothetical syllogism

universal inverse error: The formal logical fallacy that incorrectly runs (1) $(x)(Ax \rightarrow Bx)$; (2) $\therefore$ $(x)(\sim Ax \rightarrow \sim Bx)$; the quantified version of the inverse error

universal modus ponens (UMP): The valid argument form that runs (1) $(x)(Ax \rightarrow Bx)$; (2) Ac; (3) $\therefore$ Bc; the quantified version of *modus ponens*

universal modus tollens (UMT): The valid argument form that runs (1) $(x)(Ax \rightarrow Bx)$; (2) ~Bc; (3) $\therefore$ ~Ac; the quantified version of *modus tollens*

universal negative statement: A "no" statement, such that "No A are B" $\equiv$ $(x)(Ax \rightarrow \sim Bx)$

universal inverse error argument: The formal logical fallacy that incorrectly runs (1) $(x)(Ax \rightarrow Bx)$; (2) $(x)(Cx \rightarrow \sim Ax)$; (3) $\therefore$ $(x)(Cx \rightarrow \sim Bx)$; the quantified version of the inverse error argument

universal reverse hypothetical syllogism (URHS): The valid argument form that runs (1) $(x)(Ax \rightarrow Bx)$; (2) $(x)(Cx \rightarrow \sim Bx)$; (3) $\therefore$ $(x)(Cx \rightarrow \sim Ax)$; the quantified version of reverse hypothetical syllogism

unrepresentative sample: A sample that does not sufficiently mirror the population

unsound: The property of an argument which is either invalid, contains at least one false premise, or both

vacuously true: A statement which is true simply as a matter of definition and communicates no actual content, such as any if-then statement with a false antecedent

valid: The property of an argument whose conclusion follows inescapably from its premises

vee: The logical connector ∨, which means "or" and its synonyms

weak: The property of an argument structured in such a way that the conclusion does not follow highly probably from the premises

Bibliography

Crossan, John Dominic. *The Historical Jesus: The Life of a Mediterranean Jewish Peasant.* San Francisco: HarperSanFrancisco, 1991.

Descartes, René. *Meditations on First Philosophy.* Translated by Donald A. Cress. 3rd ed. Indianapolis: Hackett, 1993.

Epp, Susanna S. *Discrete Mathematics with Applications.* 2nd ed. Boston: PWS, 1995.

Epstein, Richard L., and Michael Rooney. *Critical Thinking.* Illustrated by Alex Raffi. 5th ed. Socorro, NM: Advanced Reasoning Forum, 2017.

Kneale, William, and Martha Kneale. *The Development of Logic.* Oxford: Clarendon, 1962.

Leibniz, Gottfried Wilhelm. *Discourse on Metaphysics, Correspondence with Arnauld, and Monadology.* Translated by George Montgomery. Chicago: Open Court, 1902.

MacGregor, Kirk R. *Paul Tillich and Religious Socialism: Towards a Kingdom of Peace and Justice.* Lanham, MD: Lexington, 2021.

Moreland, J. P. *Scaling the Secular City: A Defense of Christianity.* Grand Rapids: Baker, 1987.

Moreland, J. P., and William Lane Craig. *Philosophical Foundations for a Christian Worldview.* 2nd ed. Downers Grove, IL: IVP Academic, 2017.

Otto, Rudolf. *The Idea of the Holy: An Inquiry into the Non-Rational Factor in the Idea of the Divine and Its Relation to the Rational.* Trans. John W. Harvey. 2nd ed. Oxford: Oxford University Press, 1950.

Rickabaugh, Brandon, and J. P. Moreland. *The Substance of Consciousness: A Comprehensive Defense of Contemporary Substance Dualism.* Hoboken, NJ: Wiley-Blackwell, 2023.

Rodriguez-Pereyra, Gonzalo. *Two Arguments for the Identity of Indiscernibles.* Oxford: Oxford University Press, 2022.

Seuren, Pieter A. M. "Saving the Square of Opposition." *History and Philosophy of Logic* 42 (2021) 72–96.

Index

www.ingramcontent.com/pod-product-compliance
Lightning Source LLC
LaVergne TN
LVHW050614100826
845148LV00011B/1585

* 9 7 9 8 3 8 5 2 6 3 4 5 5 *